Axel Madsen is a Los Angeles-based writer who has lived and worked on four continents. As he explains in the introduction to *Private Power*, he approached the subject 'not as an economist or other specialist but as an inquiring journalist with a writer's licence to talk to anyone and to travel anywhere'.

He is the author of ten books.

Axel Madsen

PRIVATE POWER
Multinational Corporations for the
Survival of our Planet

First published in Great Britain in ABACUS, 1981
by Sphere Books Ltd
30–32 Gray's Inn Road, London WC1X 8JL

Copyright © 1980 by Axel Madsen

Printed and bound in Great Britain by
Cox & Wyman Ltd, Reading

Contents

'I am a brigand: I live by robbing the rich.'
'I am a gentleman: I live by robbing the poor.
Shake hands.'

Bernard Shaw, *Man and Superman*

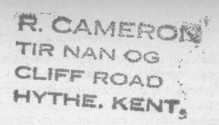

Introduction

All power is private. Power means authority, power to decide, to say yes or no. Decisions are made by people, whether they sit in the Kremlin or midtown Manhattan. When we read planning, our inner eye begins to imagine the faces of the planners. Power is fascinating, but as any screenwriter knows, power has to be attached to somebody.

Our everyday lives and mental landscapes are filled with *its* —governments, OPEC, political parties, multinational corporations, the Pentagon. A government is the ultimate incarnation of power. Whether monolithic or pluralistic, it recognizes no law superior to the one it chooses to write. It holds sway over all and everything within the realm. It is almighty. The United Nations is not the supreme world order; it is an association of sovereign states.

But power is fleeting. Governments are voted out of office; dictators die. We may be at the tail end of the century that cut up all landmass except Antarctica into nation-states—at last count 152 flags flutter in alphabetic order in front of the UN, and seven more are waiting to be hoisted—but we're also living at the dawn of interdependence and global concerns. By force of habit and familiarity of politics, we tend to look for national solutions to energy, overpopulation, and development. But our aspirations, both latent and official, are changing. We begin to realize that threats to peace and internal order may have little to do with any nuclear standoff, that the new menaces are economic, biological, and environmental. Runaway population growth can destroy a country's ecosystem and disrupt its social structure more ruthlessly than a foreign adversary; encroaching desert may pose a greater danger than invading armies. Economic isolation can leave a country backward and uninspired.

9

Twice in this century, Europeans ravaged their societies and threw away their economic supremacy in thoughtless obedience to nationalistic doctrines. Now, they elect members to the Europarliament. East-West relations tend to run in cycles—détente, entente, cold war, and back again—but political hostilities and confrontations don't prevent Soviet leaders from seeking credits and trade. Business, on the other hand, has always been relatively free of ideology ("Merchants," Thomas Jefferson once observed, "have no country. The mere spot they stand on does not constitute so strong an attachment as that for which they draw their gain").

Is our evolution ultimately divergent or convergent? Will we fission into ever slimmer ethnic particles or melt into a common destiny? Nationalism, as Bismarck said, sorted out the tribes, and wars of conquest seem archaic. The only armed struggle left is indeed tribal, fought by people who feel frustrated in their aspirations—Kurds, Basques, Eritreans, Palestinians. It is not only Croatians in Yugoslavia or Jews and Ukrainians in the Soviet Union, but Corsicans in France, Scots in Britain, and Quebecers in Canada who, if threatened in their peoplehood and sense of survival, are ready for martyrdom. Tribalism is ancient and profound and not easily dealt with in a dispassionate manner.

Yet no nation is an island. For better and for worse, we are very much locked into the dynamics of a global economy. And here, governments have a habit of turning away from problems when those problems become most serious and of dissipating their energies on quarrels among themselves. What international order exists is built on consent, not sovereignty, which ultimately rests on the legitimate use of force. If most nations print their own money—and not all 159 are actually capable of doing that—governments are unable to find cures for such modern plagues as inflation and even of understanding it. Nor can they find new energy. For that they rely on a handful of private companies. Inflationary fevers here send temperatures up there. No one is immune. Marxist theorists may label inflation "a defect of the capitalist system," but global energy and commodity price hikes seep relentlessly into the supposedly closed-circuit Communist economy of Eastern Europe, causing Moscow to increase the "friendship price" of oil and natural gas it supplies Poland, Czechoslovakia, Hungary, and other Comecon members and exposing rubles, zlotys, and forints for what they are—money worthless to anyone but the countries of origin. Everywhere each new wave of inflation seems to erode the authority of national policies.

Inflation, energy, and money are largely beyond the control of even the richest of nation-states. Bankers have become supervisors of shaky economics, telling countries how to write their tax laws, when to reschedule their debt. Nation-states gave up holding their currencies in any fixed relationship with each other in 1971, and since then the flow of money across borders and continents has become too large for governments to match with any confidence.

And so much the better. What is dynamic and forward-looking is invented, blueprinted, tooled up, and put into production by individuals, by private power, not by governments. There is nothing new or very startling in this assertion. What is new is our sometimes reluctant perception of our interdependence, our growing realization that we may not have time to muddle through with governments that cannot adapt. Cities, armies, books, hospitals, democracy, libraries, courts of justice, republicanism, diplomatic relations, and hierarchies were all in place before Christ. International trade was invented by the Phoenicians over 3,000 years ago. Yet multinational corporations are revolutionary new powers. They are world citizens and as such a counterforce to the extremes of nationalism. "Inevitably, there will be more public involvement in corporations," Roy C. Amara, president of the Institute for the Future, told this author in 1978, "but you can already envision a time when allegiance to the company may be more important than to the state. Because corporate markets are global, this switched allegiance could be the beginning of the evolution of a true worldwide mentality."

The strongest defense of global enterprise is that it stands in stunning contrast to government power. The fastest economic growth is in countries where governments stay out of technology's way, and, in contrast, progress lags wherever it is subject to bureaucracy. National governments are inadequate when it comes to dealing with the planet's necessities, and we may legitimately wonder whether the importance of nation-states isn't greatly exaggerated and whether politicians deserve star status. When compared to the abysmal inefficiency of our political systems, concepts, and leadership, C. Northcote Parkinson has said, business is a shining example: "In human as well as international relations, it is the highminded and intolerant people who do the damage. People in business know it is folly to quarrel with your customer, or even your rivals." [1]

If no one quite knows how to get from here to there, from the bickering 159-nation Babel to unity of purpose, multinational companies are showing one way. They deal here and now with the complexities of coordinating activities in many countries, of making products that are globally interchangeable, of managements made up of people with different passports, and of personnel demanding opportunities and responsibilities regardless of geographic location. Polyglot banks recycle the world's wealth and tend to its financial requirements with stateless money markets that are dynamic and complicated but largely outside government controls. And the leading edge of technology belongs to these private powers, not to governments. Oil-exporting countries nationalize their fields, set up state-owned companies, and crowd Exxon, Shell, Mobil, Texaco, BP, Chevron, and Gulf Oil in the turbulent, expensive, and increasingly politicized oil market, but it is still the Seven Sisters who *find* the precious stuff. Most important, the corporate mammoths are agents of change. They can change themselves, "roll over," and become something else. Overcoming entropy—the running down of a product or a process—is one of the essential characteristics of global enterprise. Until the energy crisis, the Seven Sisters were basically in one business, but they are fast transforming themselves. Siemens and Hitachi are evolving from heavy machinery to microprocessing. The pharmaceutical and chemical giants are cross-fertilizing into biology—altered molecular research, recombinant DNA, Interferon—and IBM and ITT are engaging in a corporate star war over satellite transmission of information. With Daimler-Benz and Volkswagen being the notable exceptions, the carmakers may be the first multinational casualties of entropy since their future largely depends on radical changes in the role of the car itself.

This book is about this power to change and about the globalism that is already here. The book explores how the multinational giants have come to be where they are. There is no natural affinity among capitalist growth, political freedom, and social justice, but neither is there any natural attraction between democracy and poverty, underdevelopment and respect for in-

[1] C. Northcote Parkinson, "European House of Lords Could Provide Multinational Companies Voice," in *International Herald Tribune*, September 30, 1975.

dividual rights. This book is not about morality or about history as catechism, but about a world view that governments don't like to hear about because they cannot share it and don't want to understand it. It is about the growing conflict between nationalism and economics. It is about multinational enterprise as bogeyman and scapegoat for third world despair, and about multinational enterprise as torchbearer of a rational future.

To write this book I have approached the subject not as an economist or other specialist but as an inquiring journalist with a writer's license to talk to anyone and to travel everywhere. My fascination with corporate power has been with me since the late 1960s when I worked briefly for Twentieth Century-Fox in Hollywood and first encountered the endemic problem of keeping essentially creative executives happy in essentially administrative roles. Show biz may not seem an obvious vantage point for observing corporate power. Yet to deal in intangibles, if not hot air, is perhaps a training ground as good as any.

For the present volume I have gathered data since 1973 and interviewed scores of business and government leaders, economists, and specialists on four continents.

This book is an inquiry into the minds of people who are asked to tap financial and human resources on a world scale. It is the story of the contradictions and inner logic of global business and of an onrushing world order that will require emotional acceptance of coexistence on one planet. With flexibility as its only ideology, private enterprise has muddled and improvised its way to being a formidable part of the equation of planetary survival. If this book ultimately comes down on the side of global enterprise, it is not because the author is beholden to any chamber of commerce grant or corporate PR handout but because his inquiry leads him, and perhaps his readers, to the conclusion that when it comes to managing our biosphere as an integrated unit, there is precious little else. Change is coming faster than governments and institutions can adapt to, but we are all learning that, in a small world, actions taken by others can have rapid and serious effects on us. The closer we look, the more advanced global enterprise seems to be. And the most advanced aspect of multinational enterprise is not its size: it is its world view.

1

Power Beyond Flag and Country

In studying the structure of scientific revolutions, Thomas Kuhn told us that when knowledge and experience outgrow existing theory, we need new theories better to understand the new knowledge and experience. Ours is an age of loss of faith, an age that has outgrown one theory but has not yet discovered the new theory that will allow us to move forward. We're stuck with the mythology of the nation-state.

When the oceans, which still belong to everybody, are threatened with pollution or overfishing, we send delegates to an international conference, usually in Geneva. There, around a conference table, we sit behind national nameplates and little flags and, with goodwill and patience, try to solve the problem. We know of no other way. We can imagine the world's fishermen, say, occupying the seats around the conference table to sort out their own affairs, but any solution arrived at would have to be sanctioned by their respective governments. It is fine for the United Auto Workers to bargain for both American and Canadian workers so long as whatever the union agrees on doesn't conflict with either country's laws; government has the last word, even if the agreement is ratified by each and every member and is of no concern to anyone but auto workers. No two foreigners on earth can legally agree to anything if what they agree to runs counter to either's national law. We have no mechanism for fishermen *qua* fishermen solving fishermen's problems, even on the high seas.

We smile at the idea of the Olympic Games with discus throwers whose names begin with A competing against discus throwers whose names begin with B and so on down the alphabet, regardless of nationality. We do have an International Court in the Hague and a substantial body of "international law," but a child born 10,000 meters above the Pacific is not stateless; as a last resort, he gets the nationality of the plane's registration. The court in the Hague is really nothing more than an arbitration board and international law nothing more than a series of civilized practices. The principle of sovereignty is absolute, and nowhere on the horizon do we see the sort of original political thinking in foreign affairs that earlier centuries contributed to the theory of government.

Yet we feel we are at the end of an age of innocence, the end of the "grand causes." The last ideology to stir Western youth was Maoism, but it died with the pragmatism with which the Chinese leadership settled Mao Zedong's succession. Ardor, fervor, and zeal seem to be emotions as much out of style as the notion that the state should incorporate all our dreams and is entitled to interfere everywhere, pursue every social injustice, and champion every issue. The concept of the state as divine guide is on the decline, even in the Soviet Union. Since World War II, the British people have discovered that even mild socialism can lead to lower standards of living. Successive Venezuelan presidents have learned that, despite the abundance of oil, they received a "mortgaged" country from their predecessors. The Portuguese have realized that a drift to the left may be halted, but not the drift into bankruptcy, and the Burmese that twenty years of nonalignment and self-reliance have left Burma one of the most isolated and backward nations in Asia. French economists have seen proof that their government is not only incapable of fighting inflation but may not really understand the phenomenon at all, and in the bumbling drama of the energy crisis Americans have heard their politicians blame each other for a crisis they denied existed. The frequent get-togethers of Western heads of state come off as genteel exercises in goodwill and not as meetings where the root causes of international problems are solved. All the summit talks, secret negotiations, open conferences, and joint resolutions leave the impression of confusion, inertia, and déja vu. The leaders may sense a profound popular wish for an overall solution, and they may realize the need for a synergetic approach, but each is a prisoner of his own constituent traditions and points of view. Each is at the top of the nation-state pyramid, each standing isolated like the giant Easter Island figures, mute and frozen in history, each perhaps aware that pyramids are obsolete but unable to imagine a different world.

Ideologies profess to be global in their humanism, yet Western liberalism, with its idea of optimum freedom for the individual, is synonymous with the pursuit of self-interest. Marxism professes to combat private exploitation of social labor while harboring deep mistrust of the individual. Even proponents of "alternatives," such as ecologists, who see us all as definitely facing a common destiny have an excessive sense of grievance against society.

Governments seem to be both suffocatingly powerful and giants with feet of clay. Octavio Paz, a committed leftist, has said that "the state's reality is so enormous that it seems unreal; it is everywhere yet it has no face." Nevertheless, South American governments are continually driven in the vicious circle of military oppressive, military populist, and civilian populist—the last two of which become so inflationary, radical, and corrupt that they spark coups by military oppressives and start the vicious circle again. Brazil's military men have usually ignored the social cost and the objections of the politicians they despise. Few people are willing to give Brazil's authoritarian soldiers any credit for the country's undoubted, if shaky, economic achievements.

Ninety percent of the one hundred fifty-two members of the UN are dictatorships, meaning that their economies are, at best, in the hands of technocrats. But thirty years of "planned economy" brought Argentina from opulence to near ruin. And, with the exception of Scandinavia, socialism has nowhere found a way of reconciling public ownership of capital and means of production with high standards of living. Nowhere has regulation of industry protected the consumer from high costs or promoted healthy and innovative enterprise. Social programs enacted for the noblest of motives have a tendency to fail to achieve their intended objectives, whether they be welfare, job creation, health, urban renewal, or saving the family farm. In the United States, three successive Presidents have tried to implement energy plans, and three different Congresses have refused to pass the laws needed to deal with the country's economic future. Many Congressmen have lost confidence in their own ability—indeed, in the ability of government—to resolve complex questions. To increasing numbers of Americans, jingoism seems beside the point; the country's energy needs assume such a degree of worldwide don't-rock-the-boat interdependence that closed-border self-sufficiency—e.g., nationalism—appears preposterous.

Most of us tend to look first to our government to solve almost any problem; most of us still see patriotism and economics as complementary. "Modern politics claim allegiance to what, in

one sense, are the two contrary ideas of citizenship and eco-
nomism," Raymond Aron has written.[1] When it suits their purposes, leaders don't mind admitting that we are all in it together.
To chastise the Organization of Petroleum Exporting Countries
(OPEC) before one of the cartel's price hikes, former Treasury
Secretary W. Michael Blumenthal could say in 1979, "we are
part of the same world; unemployment, recession, inflation hurts
them as much as us. There is no place to hide or isolate your-
self," and President Valéry Giscard d'Estaing that "no country
can win on its own and all can lose." What no Western governments said that year was that they all counted on OPEC to *raise*
its prices so as to force Western industries and consumers to
conserve energy, a move critical to cooling their inflation-heated
economies. Recession and fear of popular anger make every
modern government act instinctively, resulting in a kind of
myopia in decision making and an inability to see down the
road. In turn, governments are often perceived as no longer in-
fluencing events, of being only clumsy and complex, unrespon-
sive and accountable to no one.

And this is not only a phenomenon of the tired West. Even if
the prophetic and utopian bent of Marxism continues to hold
sway over many minds, no one looks to the Soviet Union for
inspiration. To third world revolutionaries, Moscow is, at best,
an arms provider. No ardent young revolutionary wants to go
live there, and the dream of worldwide revolution is absurd, unless backward Russia is prepared to become a vast quasi-colonial
territory to be exploited by ruthless, subtle, sophisticated, and
efficient Marxist Americans, Japanese, Chinese, and West Europeans. As seen in sociology and in the arts, the trend in Soviet
life is a tentative withdrawal into private worlds that some Russians believe is eroding social conscience and ideological commitment. "At a time when no one in the west (fools and fanatics
excepted) has a very clear idea of where we are going," Edward
Crankshaw says, "it is important to understand that there is an
even greater lack of direction, though for different reasons, on
the other side of the hill. And there is more hope for us because
we are not permanently blinded by dogma, only crippled by
prejudice, ignorance and inertia." [2] With the possible exception

[1] Raymond Aron, *In Defense of Decadent Europe* (South Bend: Regnery/
Gateway, 1979), p. 321.
[2] Edward Crankshaw, "Consensus in Russia," *The New York Times Magazine*, November 30, 1975, p. 15.

of Islamic new-old fundamentalism, the sense of historical will, of manifest destiny, is disappearing everywhere.

Ideology as doctrine, myth, symbol, and prejudice of social movement is looking increasingly irrelevant, both on the world scale and in partisan politics. Common ideology doesn't prevent the Soviet Union and China from being at each other's throat or China from feeling a need "to teach Vietnam a lesson." Totally opposite ideologies don't prevent Zambia and Zimbabwe from sharing electric power from the jointly owned Kariba Dam on the Zambesi River or Zambia from exporting its copper by rail across South Africa. Whatever doctrinaire politics and rhetoric underpin political parties, the edifice tends to crumble as soon as each party assumes power and faces reality. Obviously, there are fundamental differences in party approaches to public spending and social programs, in perceptions and goals, but these divisions seem more pointed within each party than between them. The fact that every British government since 1959 has come to power opposed to an official income policy and that every government has adapted one strongly suggests, in the words of *The London Times*, that governments have no real choice.[3]

Modern nations live on an abstraction of their political institutions because governments come to power on razor-thin majorities and because the guilt of colonialism allows any speck of island and former administrative enclave to constitute a nation. "We are now accepting the caricature of democracy with those one or two percent election majorities . . . forgetting that when the ballot box was invented two hundred years ago, the Third Estate was, when opposed to nobility and clergy, a crushing majority," the late André Malraux said in 1975. "We have kept the words, but with a one percent majority, governments don't govern; they make deals."[4] New countries enter modern history before they have the expertise even to print their own money or passports. The worst atomization has happened in the former British and Portuguese empires, with such Caribbean and African countries as Dominica (population 80,000) and São Tomé and Príncipe (83,000), and such Oceanic creations as the constitutional monarchy of Tuvalu, a country of 9.5 square miles and 8,000 inhabitants, and the republic of Nauru (8 square miles and 7,000 citizens). London's De La Rue Co. engraves the faces of new

[3] *The New York Times,* October 3, 1976, p. D1.
[4] Axel Madsen, *Malraux* (New York: William Morrow & Co., 1976), p. 358.

leaders and the vignettes of battle scenes for the banknotes and a good portion of the passports of one hundred countries. In his novels V. S. Naipaul chronicles the darker visions of new countries where impressive buildings go up for no clear purpose, local toughs are bundled into the army, and presidents for life rule by rhetoric, guile, sorcery, and often a strong helping of terror.

The world of the 1980s and 1990s, former U. S. Secretary of State Cyrus Vance said shortly before Afghanistan chilled détente to cryonic temperatures, cannot be organized on the basis of a Pax Americana or a Pax Sovietica, but only as a "global community." "There can be no illusions that the United States is omnipotent," he said. The U. S. will have to work closely with other countries toward "goals we share but cannot achieve separately." [5]

But working together is exceedingly difficult, not to say antithetical, to nation-states, each of which feels itself endowed by a divine or historic mission. No collective action beyond the passing of carefully worded resolutions was indicated when Iranian students seized the U.S. embassy in Tehran. Plenty of sympathy for the United States was voiced, even praise for President Jimmy Carter's "restraint," but no practical common policies developed to deal with diplomatic anarchy. A few years earlier it was skyjacking and terrorists finding sanctuaries in other lands. Everybody agreed to condemn it, but Arab states were unwilling to turn away Palestinians seeking sanctuary; Americans and Swedes couldn't bring themselves to turn East Europeans and Soviet hijackers back to the regimes they fled; and the Bonn government rejected the exchange of Yugoslav terrorists for the West German terrorists it sought from Belgrade. All governments recognize the danger of anarchy but cannot combine in a common front against it. There is perhaps nothing wrong with this—each feels itself fully justified by its own ideals. We must simply recognize this approach as one of the limits of government. There are a number of things that governments do more or less successfully —such as collecting taxes—and there are things they are not equipped to do. To promote the ideals of a fused humanity is one of the latter.

One thing they will all do anything to acquire is growth. They will even bargain away a chip of their sovereignty to achieve the bounties of technology. When things go wrong and polyglot

[5] Cyrus R. Vance, speech in Chicago, May 3, 1979, from Leonard Silk, "New U.S. View of the World," *The New York Times*, May 4, 1979, p. D2.

banks and other countries will no longer extend them credit, they will swallow their pride and let bankers and the International Monetary Fund (IMF) dictate budgets and economic convalescence. The closer a country is to bankruptcy, the harsher the IMF medicine—cut spending, governments are told, including subsidies for basics; devalue the currency to make exports attractive; hold down wages to stem runaway inflation. The social costs can be harrowing. Eight years of leftist military rule saw Peru's inflation soar (the price of bread jumped 1,000 percent in three years), its foreign debt become the biggest of any developing country, and its population growth spurt ahead of its output of goods and services. The austerity imposed by the IMF to forestall total collapse slashed the real buying power of workers by half, causing the death of some 500,000 infants as per capita calorie and protein intake plummeted below the UN Food and Agriculture Organization (FAO) minimums. It is not only the economic basket cases that have had the IMF and international banks impose controls in return for further credit. Great Britain has been through the wringer; South Africa and Italy, too. In 1980, it was ex-miracle worker Brazil's turn.

What nation-states have in common is the power to marshal and manipulate behavior through incentives and to disguise coercion in the form of economic penalty and reward. All states levy taxes and print money, but they also hand out subsidies and guarantee loans. Governments sell goods and services, along with patronage and the spoils of a future they believe is theirs. They also train workers and employ a significant percentage of the work force. Some people complain governments try to do too much, but most say they do too little. The utterly dismal theorem, as *The New York Times*'s Leonard Silk has often said, is that corporations and individuals cannot be trusted to pursue their self-interest without doing irreparable damage to society, but governments cannot be trusted to pursue the public interest without doing irreparable damage to individuals and corporations, and hence to society.

All economies are mixed. In the United States, government has been "big" since President Franklin D. Roosevelt, and if not always the servant and booster of business, it has often been its best customer. But a government's complexity, its diversity and size, are no guarantee that it is loved or trusted. Like generals who are always ready to fight the last war, governments often seem to be fighting last year's battles and not to recognize tomorrow's adversary. No U. S. administration has explained how a handful of oil-exporting countries got to hold power over America beyond Russian dreams. At the height of the 1979 energy blame passing and finger pointing in Washington, *The New York Times* said it was unfortunate that the energy crisis coincided with a crisis in political authority, without wondering if there was a possible cause and effect.

In sheer pain, those at the bottom suffer most. By Gross National Product (GNP), that standard measure of relative wealth, two-thirds of mankind are poor. The rich third controls more than two-thirds of the planet's wealth and possesses 95 percent of its existing science and technology. To put it crudely, what the poor want is what the rich got. In the acrobatic human mind, it is possible to wish for something, indeed strive for it, while at the same time to resent it. The fact that young Asians and Africans may despise their commodity-laden, blue-jeaned Western contemporaries is no reason for their not emulating, when possible, both style and wealth. The corridors of the UN and its agencies echo with this resentment and the undeniable fact that the richest 10 percent of humanity produces half the $6.7 trillion that make up the yearly Gross World Product.

The sense of despondency and mood of impotence are not confined to the slowdown and confusion in the economics of the industrialized countries. Developing countries squabble among themselves, with the newly developing nations such as Brazil and South Korea lobbying for wide-open world trade and the least developed countries—uncharitably referred to as "the basket cases" and sometimes more politely as the fourth world—demanding radical measures to redistribute the planet's resources. Sometimes the poorest get lectured by the Communist bloc for "passivity and lack of militancy" in their failure to distinguish between the inequities of capitalism and the benefits of alignment with the Soviet Union. Sometimes even a Marxist like Sgigeto Tsuru can recognize that socialism may not be for the poorest of the poor since it loads the greatest administrative burden on the countries least able to bear it.

Multinational corporations suffer none of these ills. Most of them have been around a long time, have survived world wars and countless revolutions. They have seen kings and sheiks come and go, new countries invented and old ones decline, while they themselves have grown confident and become indispensable and uniquely international entities far removed from the jealousies, divergent interests, mutual suspicions, and ill-concealed fears of the nation-states. If the world economy can be characterized by slow growth, chronic underemployment, large trade deficits, and pronounced instability, the "transnationals," as UN bureaucrats like to call them, give every appearance of permanence and stability. If they aren't totally citizens of the world yet, they earn profits, build factories, and sell products in a bewildering number of places. Their home countries are not the only ones whose interests they take into account.

Multinationals once stood for polyglot American firms—when not for U. S. imperialism—and if anything has changed in the last decade, it is the internationalization of the multinationals. German, French, Dutch, Swiss, and British companies that formerly concentrated on export are now serious players in the multinational game, while Japanese, Brazilian, Korean, and Singaporean enterprises are getting réady in the wings. The top companies among the global firms are expanding faster than most countries can increase their GNP. Ironically, the multinationals' driving force and success are what a nation-state's are not—apolitical. They try to have no territorial definition.

The very size and power of the biggest industrial companies has created an almost pathological love-hate relationship. People see them as some sort of vague threat, even as their achievements mark the triumph of technology over want and disorder. Their unique position, long-term profits, and longer views of the future command our attention, but not our affection. They are resented for the control they exercise, for their ability to influence or circumvent local aspirations. The greater their resources, the more we are inclined to suspect their methods, if not their very existence. After ten years of convulsive upheavals in energy, no one —not even OPEC—has any precise idea of what the Seven Sisters' profits actually are in the Middle East.

The resentment, say the executives of multinational enterprises, is unfortunate and largely in the eyes of the beholder. To corporate leaders, popular irritation and anger are a matter of perception, not a fatal flaw in their technology or productivity. And big business is learning to interact with political and social forms that have little to do with the dictates of the marketplace. The trend is both toward "going native" and—out of the public eye—toward free-floating statelessness, toward belonging to no country, existing in a self-defined no-man's-land between the fixed areas of government and national business, being needed by governments more than these giants need governments.

A quarter of the earth's commerce is intracorporate trade. Despite the continental size of the American home market, U. S. companies have gone abroad in search of greater opportunities and greater profits. The U. S. Department of Commerce estimates that with $200 billion in overseas equity, American corporations may control assets of close to half a trillion dollars; the International Chamber of Commerce, headquartered in Paris, estimates that U.S. multinationals churn out one-third of the Gross World Product. Yet U. S.-based multinationals are by no means the most polyglot of them all. Information processors like IBM and NCR may derive over half their revenues from outside the United States and Exxon 73 percent, but NV Philips (Norelco in the United States) makes 90 percent of its profits outside Holland and British Petroleum (BP) 81 percent outside Britain. Hoffman-LaRoche does only 3 percent of its business in Switzerland. Some multinationals are world-famous and powerful—Shell, for example, is in 120 countries; some are obscure and powerful —Akzo NV controls nearly 2 percent of total world production of chemicals and 7 percent of the planet's chemical fibers.

Trade is, by essence, extracommunal. Its long and colorful history, beginning with primitive barter, is intimately associated with the growth of civilization, with the shaping of economic ideas at critical periods when new means of communications and transport brought about a widening of markets. Expansion is irresistible, and if you are making a smart vacuum cleaner there's no logical reason to stop selling it at the border. The term multinational has been painstakingly defined by various authorities in various ways, but the basic idea is simple: a multinational corporation is a firm which owns income-generating assets in more than one country. To qualify for the label, however, most authorities agree that a company should operate in six or more countries and that its business should be important enough to influence its overall politics and actions. In practice, multinationals whose annual foreign sales are less than a billion dollars can be ignored. To be multinational is to be big.

The key is globalism, that is, having significant assets in many parts of the world. Ford Motor Co. and General Motors gross far less than 50 percent of their business outside the United States, but they build cars in a dozen countries. Boeing, Lockheed, and McDonnell Douglas, on the other hand, are not yet true multinationals; they just export a lot of planes they make in Seattle and southern California—although they, too, are ready to bargain away subcontracts to foreign makers of components in exchange for firm commitments.

The impact of Exxon, Shell, Unilever, Volkswagen, and Hitachi is formidable. They have created their own free-floating money market—the most important innovation of advanced capitalism. The Euromarket, or xenodollars (to use the newest "newspeak" to describe stateless money) is estimated to be approaching a trillion dollars.*

The real breakthrough, however, has been in accounting. Since the giant corporations operate in many different countries, they have opportunities for making money on money by shifting profits —and losses—from countries with high taxes to those with low tax rates. They can borrow where interest is low and use the money where rates are high; their worldwide operations give them invaluable intelligence on the strengths and weaknesses of national currencies, information not available to national governments. This stateless banking system is tied together by a computer link that allows banks to buy and sell deposits in a unified global money market and to make loans anywhere and anytime. Instead of being forced to deal within the confines of a single nation, the polyglot banks are free to tap the far deeper liquidity of not only New York and London, but also Bahrain, Frankfurt, Hongkong, Singapore, Nassau, and Panama. Ironically, the borrowers are not only multinationals, who sometimes bypass the banks altogether and set up their own foreign-exchange dealing rooms: they are also governments.

What is easily forgotten in headier geopolitical debates is the fact that the big companies are very good at what they are doing. Svenska Kullagerfabriken (SKF) does make the world's best ball bearings and Daimler-Benz some of the best automobiles. Loewenbrau has been brewing beer since the Middle Ages. Singer has been making sewing machines for over a century, and it would probably take that long in research to match the scientific knowhow of the big Swiss pharmaceuticals like Ciba-Geigy or Hoffman-LaRoche. Since the mid-1960s, European governments have put $1.4 billion into the computer industry and lost most of it without making a serious dent in IBM. Thoughtful Brazilians fear that their government's decision to go for a national solution to mini-

* In 1979, *The Economist* estimated the total deposits in the international banking system to exceed $800 billion.

computers is doomed, because deliberate go-it-alone is suicidal in a field where dramatic changes happen very quickly.

National profiles are hard to distinguish in many cases because multinationals shy away from being identified with any one country; most are proud of the fact that their subsidiaries are considered indigenous everywhere. How many Americans know that Pullman no longer makes railway passenger cars in America, but automobiles in the Soviet Union? Hoechst is also Wyandotte in the United States, and Unilever is Wisk Liquid Laundry Detergent, Imperial Margarine, Dove Soap, and Aim and Close-up Toothpastes. Standard Oil Company of Ohio is a BP subsidiary. Liquid Air is a division of L'Air Liquide of France. Gimbels and the Saks Fifth Avenue stores are subsidiaries of BAT Industries (formerly British American Tobacco), Moore Business Forms is owned by Moore Corporation of Canada, and A & P by the Tengelmann Group of Germany. Allied Chemical belongs to Solvay & Cie of Belgium and Fed Mart to Germany's Mann Gmbh. The Valium we pop are really Swiss, the Baskin-Robbins ice cream British, and Timex belongs to two obscure Norwegians. The engine in your Chrysler Omni is made by Volkswagen and the whole of your Dodge Colt by Mitsubishi. But why continue? The point is not that foreigners control such American-as-apple-pie nameplates as Brylcreem and Pepsodent, Libby's string beans, and Bantam Books, but that Bayer means aspirin in a hundred countries. The trend is toward increasingly global structures and decision making, and toward allocating corporate resources on a world scale. Cost, not ideology, is the driving force.

The early multinational company was headed by home country managements and "natives" further down the totem pole. Today's global corporation is a horizontal enterprise: "In our top management anybody of any nationality can reach any position in the company if he is recognized as able to do the job," says Nestlé's Pierre Liotard Vogt. IBM's twenty-six research laboratories in the United States and Europe are meshed independently of sales divisions in the same countries. Shell and Unilever each have two parent companies—one Dutch and one British—that run subsidiaries in one hundred twenty and seventy countries respectively. Business leaders have always had a bad press; they are portrayed as slow-witted Babbitts or magnificent Citizen Kane scoundrels. Politicians can be fast-track stars with instinct and stamina. But the men who put together incongruous conglomerates, leaping from one financial ledge to the next, keeping the act together, are portrayed as conventional men with little flair who rate "hard work" rather than exceptional intelligence or creativity as their key to success.

Technology is what separates the rich from the poor. Leaders of the most radical—and desperate—nations not only want advanced technology; they want it for free, claiming it is not only the industrialized world's moral duty but in its own best interest to hand it over. Almost 20 percent of humanity lives in the first world, but as population grows in the third world while leveling off in industrial nations, the proportion living in the rich world is forecast to plummet to a mere 4 percent by 2050. Unless the poor get richer, twenty-four out of every twenty-five of us will be living in poverty.

The quickest way to technology, capital, and productivity for a poor country is through local subsidiaries of global corpora-tions. Investments in Research and Development are made by the technically advanced nations; $97 out of every $100 spent on Research and Development (R and D) is invested by advanced nations. Seven out of eight scientists and engineers work in rich countries. The stakes are enormous. American technology brings in $4 billion in profits from overseas sales of high-technology goods and services. The transfer of know-how is one of the fastest growing items in world trade. It was worth $2.7 billion in 1965 and more than $11 billion ten years later. Ninety percent of it, however, takes place within the first world and over half of *that* within multinational corporations. Parent companies invent or design new processes and sell them to their affiliates for a lump sum or on a royalty basis. To get a piece of the action, the less developed nations banded together in 1974 as the Group of 77— since swollen to 120—and maneuvered the UN into setting up the Conference on Science and Technology for Development. Of late, however, they have moderated the rhetoric that only a few years ago branded the multinationals as the handmaidens of neocolonial exploitation and oppression. "Most developing coun-tries now feel they would like to have foreign enterprise coming to their shores," says N. T. Wang, director of informational analysis of the UN Center of Transnational Corporations. "The more these countries develop, the more they realize they cannot be totally unaware of the rest of the world." Post-Maoist China quickly looked around and saw who was developing and who wasn't. Less than three years after Mao's death, the Seven Sisters were drilling under contract to Peking.

Direct foreign investment by multinationals outside their home bases averages $25 billion a year, which, very roughly, is 2 percent of total investment throughout the world. Tiny, on the face of it, this private investment is concentrated in manufacturing and services, and it is done by a couple of dozen private firms. A hundred years ago, today's rich countries invested about 12 percent of their GNP. In the 1980s, developing countries are expected to manage a higher investment ratio than Europe and North America in the last quarter of the nineteenth century. This rise in investment is the reason optimists believe most poor countries are set on a fairly steep growth curve.

Armchair liberals in affluent countries may blame industrialization for a variety of social ills and sins, but emerging countries have little sense of ecological guilt and few environmental scruples. Development—that is, industrialization—is the only hope of overcoming poverty, misery, and despair. Production of almost *anything* adds to GNP, increases employment, and stimulates the economy. Global corporations pay taxes in third world countries. They cheat less when compared to local interests, the latter often clutching to privilege, and multinationals are not only accused of taking advantage of cheap labor, but also of paying too high wages. International companies upgrade the levels of education through employee training and, in countries much given to one-party and one-man rule, tend to break down frontiers and to promote new ideas. They bring a measure of prosperity and in general are a force on the side of peace. Compared with life in a police state, corporate rule is relatively benign.

The countries that are developing the fastest are, by and large, those which follow a capitalist mode and which, if they don't exactly love the multinationals, at least respect their rights. More and more, the advisers to developing governments have attended the same U. S. business schools as the executives of global corporations. Demands that companies become social entrepreneurs and that they commit themselves to attacking social ills are increasingly confined to the UN where the developing bloc has an automatic majority. In the real world, most leaders know that to get anywhere, they must come to terms with costs, not ideology. "We have to accept that the profit motive is the basis for personal and corporate initiative," says Hongkong's Chamber of Commerce president J. D. McGregor. "If companies cannot make profits here, they won't stay."

The people in charge of global corporations have no inherent reason for preferring production in one geographical location to another. Unrestricted trade would flow to the best market by the shortest route if it wasn't for nation-states, which, for economic purposes, are often too small. Governments eager to improve their trade balances wield an array of carrots and sticks to get subsidiaries of foreign companies to produce more locally and, in true beggar-thy-neighbor fashion, to force them to export as much as possible to other countries. When countries are big enough to have multinationals of their own, their leaders become positively cagey. Giscard d'Estaing may charge that by undercutting the prices and productivity of French steel mills, Nippon Steel is, in effect, exporting Japanese unemployment, but the French President is sure not to mention Saint-Gobain-Pont-à-Mousson or Michelin in the same breath. The Giscard d'Estaing Administration recognizes the need to underpin France's direct export effort by establishing a strong industrial presence abroad (Britain and West Germany both invest twice as much abroad as France), but it is afraid of its powerful leftist unions, which claim exporting investments means exporting jobs. Saint-Gobain and Michelin have argued that they owe their survival in France to their success abroad, but the unions won't listen.

The basic aim of the multinationals is to maximize worldwide profits, without regard to source of product. General Electric's International Sales Group operates as an in-house trading company with the objective of promoting exports from *any* GE plant. GE do Brasil sells refrigerators in the Middle East and locomotives to Mozambique, but parts of the refrigerators and locomotives are made in GE factories in the United States and Europe. If Brazilian government planners manage to pistol-whip GE into making the entire refrigerators and locomotives in Brazil, the U. S. balance of trade and European treasuries will suffer, not GE's.

To see business and government as enemies, opposite and antagonistic powers, is naive. In most countries, business and national governments entertain the coziest of relationships. The men who run government and the men who run corporations often come from the same *"grandes écoles,"* pass through the same revolving doors of government and business. They share common assumptions, perceptions, and prejudices, thrive on reciprocal favors. They are men of substance, interested in the preservation of wealth and power. In the less developed world, where people tend to survive by accurately sensing the limits of each other's distress and where so much is uncertain and therefore negotiable, leaders of industry and government are the only elite there is, men whose concern for one another makes an instinct for self-survival.

Corporate presidents are also chosen for their political acumen, their sense of direction and drift of society; most businessmen will either not understand or evade such questions as whether a company can or should have loyalties besides those to its shareholders or whether it should be responsible to anyone, ultimately. A Dutch multinational is likely to have a Dutch chairman of the board and a Swedish firm a Swede, but even if the biggest of the globals must have headquarters *somewhere* and therefore possess a nominal nationality, it really has no geographical center. This is especially apparent in troubled times, leading to armed conflict, and in wartime. As late as mid-1941, Louis B. Mayer told Metro-Goldwyn-Mayer film directors to go easy on anti-Nazi propaganda because the United States was technically at war with no one, and MGM had theaters in Germany, too. Once Pearl Harbor had forced the United States into the war, Exxon and Texaco were roundly castigated for exchanging vital information with I. G. Farben and for dodging a British naval embargo to deliver Colombian oil to Hamburg. Multinational corporations tend to see war as a transitory phenomenon and business as permanent. When it suits a national government, a country can deliberately leave part of its foreign policy to private enterprise. For a quarter century after the creation of Israel, the U.S. State Department delegated its Arab policy to American oil companies because it suited Washington to separate its own pro-Israeli foreign policy from the geopolitics of oil. After the disastrous Anglo-French Suez invasion of 1956, Shell was able to do business in Cairo while British diplomats were still *non grata*; more than twenty years later, U. S. companies were doing an increasing amount of business with the Iraqis, although Washington had no diplomatic relations with Baghdad. There are Hilton, Sheraton, and Ramada hotels both in Jerusalem and Riyadh, and General Tire and Rubber makes tires in both Morocco and Israel.

The concept of national power is fixed, often massive, cumbersome; the idea of business is dynamic, innovative. A global view encourages a corporation to treat governments cavalierly—it deals with so many. In general, the bigger and more global a firm, the less visible its profile. The movement of funds, sophisticated investment strategies, allocation of export markets to subsidiaries, and the way decisions are made on where to locate new plants are never discussed in public, and only with governments under the severest of pressures. Like the rest of us, corporations are law-abiding to a fault. If the law regulating a sphere of business is vague, companies will do precisely as much as their lawyers think they can get away with. There is nothing immoral about this. If a law doesn't exist, it doesn't exist. But what complicates things is that multinationals work in what has been called "the business in-between," where it is hard to know where one country's legal powers end and another country's jurisdiction begins. Raymond Vernon, the director of Harvard's Center for International Affairs and the principal American guru on multinationalism, calls this in-between gap between nation-states and global business an "asymmetry" that can only be tolerated up to a point. The sovereignty of the state requires that it be responsible for all that occurs within its borders, while the principle of commerce ideally requires a free flow of capital, goods, and labor as if there were no borders. The United States seeks to maintain its military superiority on the basis of its sophisticated weaponry, and the Pentagon now and then objects to the sale of an advanced computer to the Soviet Union on the grounds that it is suitable for nuclear weapons calculations, missile tracking, and many other military applications. But almost all computer technology has wide varieties of civilian functions and industrial Research and Development, and IBM, Control Data, Siemens, Philips, Mitsubishi, Honeywell, and Olivetti have transferred to the Soviet Union almost all basic systems. The big question is whether enough people can recognize the benefits of a merging humanity or whether our concealed fears, egotism, and ethnic differences keep us apart, each tribe holding onto a promise and a vision of a separate future. The giants usually have better intelligence on political changes than big-power spy organizations. Mack Trucks, Turner Constructions International, and Morrison-Knudsen Co. smelled trouble in Iran two years before the Central Intelligence Agency gave the Carter Administration the first hint of the Shah's impending overthrow. Field representatives know how to get good local partners, how to spread the risk, and how to be needed. Mack Trucks managed to get out of Iran relatively cleanly, while Morrison-Knudsen, Fluor, and Bechtel spread their heavy construction business over several continents in dozens of countries, thereby insulating themselves against losing the company shirt. "Yes, the multinationals are ahead of us in information," says Fred Kayser of the U. S. Bureau of International Commerce. "They often know more about a country's inner struggles and politics sooner than we (the government) do. They often prefer to deal on their own and don't go to American embassies for help." At the collapse of the Shah, *The New York Times* quoted a construction contractor as saying embassy officials are "extremely poor" and that they "just don't put in properly qualified people." [6]

Governments are resentful of the globals' ability to allocate markets, of faraway corporate headquarters dictating which subsidiary can export what to whom. They also dislike subsidiaries being forced to import components that could be purchased locally and, in reverse, take offense when local affiliates accede to the wishes, laws, and policies of another country. Outgrowing their national bases, corporations are not within the political framework but tend to overshadow it. By 1985, some 300 firms are expected to produce more than half the world's goods and services, and, says John Kenneth Galbraith, "those who would break up the large corporations within national boundaries are at war with history and circumstance." [7]

Yet the attempts—and the futility—continue. In the United States, federal trustbusters prepare monster cases that, in the words of antitrust lawyer Paul Warnke, are "basically untryable." In 1973, the Federal Trade Commission charged eight of the largest oil companies with conspiring to destroy competition and with conspiring to cheat the public out of billions of dollars by price fixing. Seven years later, the companies were still in court, fighting those charges. The legal assumption behind the Justice Department's attempt to break up International Business Machines is that it can prove IBM's "intent" to monopolize its market. Thousands of exhibits, years of hearings, transcripts as thick as telephone books—counsel for IBM predicts the deposition of fifty million documents—and staggering court costs will do doubt result in a legal stalemate, as even the Supreme Court probably lacks the self-confidence to restructure American industry through innovative interpretations of antitrust laws.

Because of the less than wholesome history of nineteenth century capitalism, fear of monopolies has remained a peculiarly

[6] Robert C. Toth, "U.S. Is Fearing Losing Lead in Technology," *The New York Times*, January 14, 1979, p. D4.

[7] John Kenneth Galbraith, *The Age of Uncertainty* (Boston: Houghton Mifflin, 1977), p. 277.

American phenomenon. In most other advanced and developing countries, the symbiosis between government and private enterprise is taken for granted, when it isn't actively promoted. Governments force companies to gang together, actively twisting arms and jawboning to make them share trade knowledge or to avoid competition in certain markets. Governments create state corporations and legislate monopolies for them. Foreigners coming to work in the American climate of government-enterprise antagonism are baffled. Coen Solleveld, the chairman of Philips' Polygram record division, shakes his head over the securities and antitrust regulations governing American business. "In Europe at least I feel free to talk to a competitor," said Solleveld, after moving the division headquarters to New York from Baarn in the Netherlands. "Here you're already in jail if you're seen together."

Something about business raises people's hackles, and the multinationals *are* big. Before the oil shock of 1973, the Western world was used to an apparently endless abundance of natural resources and an unlimited freedom to waste them. When the crunch came, Big Oil was the ready-made scapegoat, and politicians everywhere capitalized on the antiestablishment mood. In Washington, they jumped in with charges of conspiracy and cover-up and searched for evidence of collusion and price fixing in the great American tradition. There is political mileage in this, and essentially emotional reactions allow politicians to escape responsibility for their grandstanding. Senator Henry Jackson called the seven oil company executives to appear before his permanent subcommittee on investigations, telling them their function would be to advise the Senators on energy problems, and then proceeded to flay them. "The American people want to know if there is an oil shortage," he began.

Politics always trail behind economics, which may explain why the consensus that should govern economics always seems to be absent. After a few years in office, most governments have little economic credibility to draw on. Pursuing now the spending policies of the traditional liberal agenda, now the restrictive diets of monetarism, they rarely achieve the objectives of either. Historians and economists are of little help. Nobody has explained why people become entrepreneurial and why they cease to be. Defenders of socialism claim England's decline didn't start with Labor's ascent to power after World War II but began much earlier, in the 1880s. Yet they don't explain *why* Britain declined. Political parties are collections of contradictions. They all want to reduce taxes, to spend much more on what people want, and to balance the budget—and none of them like to specify what programs they would cut to achieve that balance, while collecting less in taxes and spending more.

To be multinational practically means to be on or near the leading edge of innovation. The corporations' greatest fear is entropy, and no sharp line can be drawn between their obsession with growth and with warding off the process of decline. Nothing similar inhibits governments and, in the largest sense, social organizations. Cities, factories, books, schools, hospitals, democracy, strikes, and state-supported education were all invented in antiquity; trade unions, cabinets with prime ministers, unemployment insurance, prisons, and kindergartens before 1800. Our social institutions and systems are so ossified and monopolistic that they have difficulty in adapting to new circumstances. Countries pride themselves on how little they have changed their social heritage; some, like Iran, cheerfully try to march backwards a millennium. Our present systems of law, education, welfare, and municipal government can be traced back four or five thousand years. Changes have modified these structures but not created new systems. Present governments are almost overwhelmed by the sheer demand to provide services and cannot be expected to invent new methods. As futurist D. Stuart Conger of Saskatchewan's NewStart program puts it, Ford Motor Co. devoted huge amounts of technical and consumer research to design the Edsel, but the car was not popular, and Ford was able to discontinue it: "If the Edsel had been developed by a government agency, it would still be in production and would be given to underdeveloped countries as foreign aid or as a bonus for buying our wheat." [8]

We have a vested interest in the way things are, and we are apprehensive about implications of any tampering with society. Our approach to unemployment is still largely to blame the unemployed for being without jobs. No one has come up with new ways of settling strikes. Hoechst, Ciba-Geigy, Hoffmann-La Roche, and Merck—the Big Four in pharmaceuticals—spend $1 billion

---

[8] D. Stuart Conger, "Social Inventions," *1999—The World of Tomorrow* (Washington, D.C.: World Future Society, 1978), p. 143.

a year in Research and Development, or just under 4 percent of their total sales. If the U. S. government were to spend 4 percent of its total revenues in the same fashion, it would have $18 billion a year, not to spend on education, health, income security, and administration of justice, but on new ways of teaching and of alleviating poverty and reducing crime.

We can all see we need new ideas. We can also feel, some of the time, that we are perhaps at the end of an era, that high noon has maybe come and gone for governments in their present form as supreme arbiters. Futurists have come to the startling conclusion that almost anything can be done in twenty years. Only four years were needed to unleash the awesome power of the atom and only eight years to put man on the moon. Armed with powerful ideas, the people of the poorest nations might become the richest in less than a generation. "With the right ideas," says Edward Cornish of the World Future Society, "the people of the world might soon throw war, poverty, famine and disease into the ashcan of history." [9]

Transnational power may seem vaguely threatening as we wind down the predatory empire-building phase of history. But as planetary survival becomes the central moral issue and people show a deep wish for a rational approach to the uses of finite resources, global corporations appear more benevolent, if not outright wholesome. They, at least, have a first foot in the supranational tomorrow, while many governments don't have the talent, perspective, and foresight to understand the nature of the challenges of the approaching century.

Yet the nation-state is the only legitimate process we have for groping for solutions to nearly all our problems. Politics and squabbles among our own kind have a familiarity that is absent from the blanket rationality of centralized private power structures. Within the next twenty years, however, the Hudson Institute's Herman Kahn expects to see a "unified but multipolar, partially competitive, mostly global and technological economy," while Germany's elder Socialist statesman Willy Brandt thinks tomorrow's leaders "will be those who respond to the global needs of humanity with relevant and realistic ideas and can put those ideas into practice."

[9] Edward Cornish, "Toward a Philosophy of Futurism," *1999—The World of Tomorrow* (Washington, D.C.: World Future Society, 1978), p. 158.

Rich and Poor—Who's Who

The World Bank divides us all into five categories:

LOW-INCOME COUNTRIES. Those where income per capita is less than $150 a year. The "basket cases" are: Afghanistan, Bangladesh, Benin, Bhutan, Botswana, Burundi, Cape Verde, Central African Republic, Chad, Comoros, Ethiopia, Gambia, Guinea, Haiti, Laos, Lesotho, Malawi, Maldives, Mali, Nepal, Niger, Rwanda, Samoa, Somalia, Sudan, Tanzania, Uganda, Upper Volta, Yemen, Southern Yemen.

MIDDLE-INCOME COUNTRIES. Nations with per capita annual income above $250 but still broadly recognized as Less Developed Countries (LDCs). They include five southern European countries—Greece, Portugal, Spain, Turkey, Yugoslavia.

OIL SURPLUS EXPORTERS. The 6 *nouveaux riches*: Kuwait, Libya, Oman, Qatar, United Arab Emirates, and Saudi Arabia which have a "structural" (virtually permanent) balance-of-payment excess.

CENTRALLY PLANNNED ECONOMIES. The Communist bloc, sometimes called the second world: USSR, Eastern Europe, China, Vietnam, North Korea, Cuba.

INDUSTRIALIZED WORLD. North America, Western Europe, Japan, Australia, South Africa.

A newer classification adds two acronyms:

OPEC. The Organization of Petroleum Exporting Countries. Besides the 6 *nouveaux riches*, the category includes the so-called "high absorbing" oil exporters, countries which can spend all the money they make: Algeria, Ecuador, Gabon, Indonesia, Iran, Iraq, Nigeria, Venezuela.

NICs. Newly Industrialized Countries which have a growing industrial base heavily geared to exports. Five are the Mediterranean countries of the middle-income category; 4 are Asian: Hongkong, Taiwan, Singapore, South Korea, and 2 are Latin American: Brazil, Mexico.

Source: World Bank, UN Committee for Development & Planning.

2

By Any Other Name

John D. Rockefeller was a little ahead of his time—and of the federal government. Imposing control on the early wildcat chaos and building a continental-sized oil company was something the late nineteenth century government didn't understand yet. "The world after 1865," wrote Henry Adams, "became a bankers' world." The American continent offered more natural resources than any country except Russia, and for the man of ability and energy, as the saying went, the rewards for exploiting them were staggering. Andrew Carnegie's annual income was over $12.5 million; his total fortune reached $1 billion (in 1919 dollars); the check he received for the sale of his share of U.S. Steel Corp. totaled more than the entire value of the United States a hundred years earlier. Rockefeller amassed slightly more than $500 million. The Guggenheim interests took $2 million from the Montana copper ranges. William Vanderbilt II inherited $100 million and added $90 million to it in six years. John Pierpont Morgan's fortune equaled Carnegie's.

To Rockefeller—and his fellow millionaires—the trustbusters of the Sherman Act were economic simpletons living in the past. Multinational managers don't have the wealth of the oil, steel, bank, and railroad barons of capitalism's gilded age, but they share their impatience with government. Today's governments, they feel, are also living in the past and trying to prevent companies from achieving their logical reach.

To "roll over" from function to function and to go multinational are vital steps that modern giant corporations must be able to make if they are to prevent their own entropy. In this struggle to ward off the process of decline and chaos, companies see governments as their unwitting enemies, but when multinational managers talk about this they put it in different, more readily understood terms of nationalism—"we" and "them." When Rawleigh Warner, Jr., wants to say he wishes Washington would streamline its ground rules and get off business' back, the Mobil Oil Corp. chairman puts it in a frame of reference Americans are familiar with. When the United States was said to have "world power" in the 1960s, this didn't just mean military prowess, but diplomacy, fiscal stability, scientific advancement, production of capital goods, and international trade, Warner says. For more than forty years, the United States was the world's undisputed leading exporter of high-technology goods, but, he adds, the margin began to narrow in 1970, and the present conditions are not likely to reverse themselves.

"There are three principal reasons for the downturn. First, few American companies have aggressively sought to create foreign markets for their goods or have felt the need to do so. In 1977, only one percent of the companies in the United States accounted for 95 percent of the exports. Second, some countries have raised tariff and nontariff barriers against imports from the U. S. But the most compelling reason for the decline is the fact that the U. S. government has put obstacles in the way of international trade and has also fostered an inconsistent, stop-and-go policy that has crippled the efforts of American companies. This lack of direction has been compounded by the failure of America's leadership to understand the revolution in international trade in the last 30 years." [1]

Put in global newspeak, Warner is saying that governments are a hindrance to economic progress. If America has regressed in recent years, the reasons are three, he observes: one, not enough U. S.-based corporations went global (but in 1977 the multinationals accounted for a staggering 95 percent of all American exports), and two and three, nation-states complicate corporate strategies and stand in the way of another economic leap forward.

We are not used to seeing our problems in global terms, nor are our leaders used to addressing us in anything but a tribal "we" and "they" dichotomy. The plight of the starving Cambodian refugees and that of thousands fleeing Vietnam can focus world concern, but we tend to confront it in political or national terms. Yet economics—not arms—are what motivate contemporary migrations. Wetbacks wading across the Rio Grande into Texas, planes loaded with Korean construction workers arriving in Saudi Arabia, West Germany's famously efficient car plants manned by

---

[1] Rawleigh Warner, Jr., "First Word," *Omni*, December 1979, p. 6.

Yugoslavs and Turks; all are part of the twenty million or so migrant workers. This migration from one country to another has become a central characteristic of the global economic system.

"International enterprise," former Secretary of State George Ball says, "is the biggest challenge facing the nation-state since the beginning of the decline of the Catholic Church in the 15th century." Private enterprise has indeed become one of the prodigies of the world, but it isn't much loved.

"It's appalling," Pitney Bowes chairman Fred T. Allen said in 1975 (when the Gulf Oil and Lockheed Corp. scandals led over eighty American companies to admit to questionable overseas payoffs), "we who have devoted our lives to the growth of large corporations are thought of collectively as little more than manicured hoodlums." Rockefeller's monopoly, his destruction of rivals and corruption of politicians cast a long shadow. The government broke his Standard Oil into thirty companies in 1911, but Big Business' all-too-frequent disregard for the public interests has continued to fuel popular resentment and suspicion. There is no natural affinity among corporate growth, political freedom, and social justice. Successive generations—and their elected officials—have often felt themselves to be consenting adults in their own corruption.

Firms own each other in a bewildering maze of interests and cross-purposes and are linked by interlocking directorships and financial institutions. A return on capital is the businessman's credo, and when it comes to the larger issues and perspectives, corporate leaders think pretty much alike. Growth rewards those individuals who bring it about. Expansion means more subordinates, more responsibility, more prestige, and more pay, and those on top tend naturally to believe in the preservation of wealth and power. The big corporations they run don't compete with each other in any classic sense. Size has given industrial leaders control of prices, which in turn has allowed them to escape much of the tyranny of the marketplace. "Capitalism is the extraordinary belief that the nastiest of men for the nastiest of motives will somehow work for the benefit of us all," said John Maynard Keynes. Nearly one hundred years of antitrust laws—the Sherman Act was passed in 1890—have not checked the great modern concentration. And antitrust legislation, it must be remembered, is a particularly American phenomenon. In the rest of the nonsocialist world, big corporations are not regarded as Frankenstein monsters but as indispensable parts of national economics, as steady contributors to the balance of payments, to the national progress and pride. Governments are busy shoring them up, finding finances and markets for them, investing in them, and, all too often, subsidizing them when they can no longer compete. State interventionism is the rule, not the exception, even if state capitalism is often little more than subsidized full employment and a smoke screen over long-term economic problems that don't get solved.

"Sixty firms control the capitalist system," *Der Spiegel* headlined a three-part inquiry into global enterprise in 1974. By 1985, the Organization for Economic Cooperation and Development (OECD) estimates, some 300 companies will produce more than half the world's goods and services, but already in 1967, *Fortune* magazine could say that the inner core of capitalism consisted of 60 enterprises, controlled by less than 1,000 individuals. Our mental image of big business is one of companies making overpublicized products—IBM means computers, and Shell means oil. But Mobil Oil makes paperboard packaging in Mexico, Venezuela, and Colombia and owns condominiums in Hongkong. Corning Glass makes blood analyzers in Hungary; Tenneco is in chemicals in 17 countries and retails farm equipment in 140 countries. Guinness means beer around the world, but it also means plastics in California and Singapore. Technology—and tastes—change. A company may start life producing movies (Rank) and develop to concentrate on photocopiers. There is evidence that the big oil conglomerates are no longer as interested in finding oil as in developing minerals: in 1978, Exxon bought copper mines from the Chilean government, and two years later it joined Arco, BP, Philips, Getty, and Gulf in pushing for legislation to open Alaska for hard-rock mining. Conglomerates like to call themselves something else—multiform industrials, diversified groups, a family of companies. A government will never admit that its own massive intervention in the marketplace is often inept and inefficient, or that the resulting distortions and higher prices often tend to swamp the benefits of its own remedies, even when the promises are fulfilled. But if globals can argue that they often don't know where one national jurisdiction begins and another ends, governments often feel they are dealing with slippery entities. After the oil tanker *Amoco Cadiz* ran aground on the French Channel coast in 1978, the French government had the hardest time untangling ownership, let alone responsibility. "How can International Amoco, an American company, freely register ships in Liberia, maintain headquarters in Bermuda and offices in Chicago and hire Italian seamen when Washington is the world's toughest government on ocean pollution?" *Le Monde* asked in a front-page editorial when it became clear that the *Amoco Cadiz* had caused the then world's greatest oil spill.[2]

Nationalization, the radical purging of foreign devils, is usually the easiest part. Oil flows, and it is impractical, if not downright impossible, to imagine that you can nationalize a section of a garden hose. The Saudis learned that after they nationalized the Arabian American Oil Co. (Aramco) in 1975. The "downstream" skills and marketing clout of Standard Oil of California, Exxon, Texaco, and Mobil were not included in the price, and with the remarkable Arab ability to hold several contradictory positions at the same time, the Saudi government never got around to approving the final takeover of Aramco. The four American "Sisters" still own 40 percent of Aramco, although they maintain their accounts as if the Riyadh government had taken over the company. Oil producers need the close-knit group of oil companies to maintain the stability of their cartel.

But governments keep on nationalizing, even if they rarely learn anything in the process. It has never occurred to any government that the state of the art of strategic planning in top multinational corporations may be years, if not decades, ahead of national planning everywhere. Governments suffer from the absence of an overall sense of direction, well-defined goals and objectives, strategies for achieving such goals, and a process for answering difficult "what if" questions. IBM, Shell, Hitachi, and Nestlé, on the other hand, know exactly what their objectives are and the strategies needed for achieving such goals, and they keep in the corporate vault a slew of scenarios for all possible and impossible contingencies.

Paradoxes abound. After a century of growth unprecedented in history, human wants and needs seem again to exceed the means of satisfying them. Hard times have a way of humbling us all, nationalists included. Two devaluations in two months in 1976 saw the Mexican peso drop more than 50 percent against the U. S. dollar. Mexico's problem was basically that it had lived beyond its means. To finance its balance-of-payment deficit, the government borrowed abroad until worried businessmen began moving out of the peso. The capital flight led to the first devaluation, and because neither business nor the general public believed in the government's ability to handle the economy, the flight triggered the second devaluation. To make sure foreign investments were of "significant benefit" to Canadians, the Ottawa government created a foreign investment review agency in 1973. Those were the palmy days of strong economic growth, and Ontario, the most heavily industrial province, imposed a 20 percent tax on commercial, industrial, and residential land sales to foreigners (read: Americans). Three years later, when the world economy began to wobble, Ontario repealed the tax; five years later, when recession was upon the advanced countries and Canada's unemployment shot up while its real growth plummeted, Ottawa was no longer opposed to job-creating investments by foreigners. In the early 1970s, Guyana nationalized virtually every foreign investment of consequence, from the sugar and retailing business of Booker McConnell Limited (Great Britain) to the bauxite mining of Alcan (Canada) and Reynolds Metals (United States). By 1977, when the country's socialist government was having painful second thoughts, it was surprised to find out that the multinationals weren't rushing back in. "Governments like Guyana's," said *Forbes* magazine in reporting the country's new demand for capital from the foreign investors it had just dispossessed, "are slowly learning that while big foreign companies no longer have gunboats at their disposal, they still have something which is, in the long run, far more powerful—capital." [3] Economic adversity doesn't just humiliate small states. Richard Nixon's trade and currency measures of 1971 revealed, albeit only in hindsight, that the American giant had feet of clay and that world money was built on sand.

Governments throughout the West have virtually abandoned the theories of John Maynard Keynes, who believed governments could and should spend their way back to prosperity by pumping new money into the economy, in favor of the austere monetarist ideas of Nobel laureate Milton Friedman and the new conservative economists. Big government is killing the golden goose, the new economists are saying, and the recipe for curing inflation and restoring growth is for governments to print less money and stop protecting inefficient industries against stronger competitors. Martin Feldstein, the superstar of neoconservative economics, says the American economy is overstimulated, overregulated and overtaxed (Friedman calls Hongkong's economy the world's freest today).

[3] *Forbes*, June 15, 1977, p. 65.

Together with Arthur B. Laffer, Robert Lucas, and Rudolph Penner, Friedman and Feldstein say vigor won't be restored merely by licking inflation: governments must stop growing and their tax systems must be rewritten so as to give a big push to investment. For nearly fifty years Keynesian, or "demandside," economists have dreamed they could usher industrial countries into a Promised Land of full employment and stable prices by clever manipulation of demands for goods and services and of national budgets. Now, they are yielding in influence to the new "supplyside" economists, who say the only way out of the late-twentieth-century blues is to encourage people to save and to make it attractive for corporations to invest in better factories and machinery. Feldstein feels the basic solution for a lagging economy is to increase the amount of money that business has available for investment.

The idea of enacting laws that favor the rich and powerful, as capital-formation tax laws inevitably do, is a difficult one for people in older democracies where governments' responsibilities are thought to include the duty to diminish social inequities. Yet the most astonishing modern example of fast and uninflationary growth—Japan—has worked because government outlays (and thus taxes) have been low, because trade unions have been weak, and—the Keynesian joker in the cards perhaps—because successive administrations in Tokyo haven't been afraid of applying very harsh medicine when the economy appeared to be overheating. The reason governments have difficulty keeping the new monetarist faith is that it takes years before a tight-money policy begins to yield dividends, investments pick up, and business confidence is restored. In the meantime, high interest rates risk hurting economic activity and provoke nasty unemployment. The supplyside path to virtue is a risky one for politicians facing elections every four years. C. Douglas Vaugham of London's City University Business School has calculated that four years of stringent and concerted monetary discipline by western countries will result in a two percent drop in inflation at the cost of five percent less growth. And, he said, "is it not likely that democracies experiencing virtually stagnant output year after year will flinch from continuing a monetary squeeze of this intensity when faced with prospective elections?"

Giant multinational corporations are not democracies and their bosses don't have to get themselves re-elected, even though they do have to be successful. The executive turnover is not great, but even more remarkable is the staying power of the corporations themselves. Through thick and thin of Keynesian and Friedmanian economics, the companies remain. International Telephone and Telegraph (ITT) is a sixty-year veteran of corporate investing in Latin America, for example, and although ITT has been pilloried as the ultimate evil of private power and although it has been scarred by bitter expropriations, it is still very much there. In Mexico, it anticipated rising pressures for "Mexicanization" by selling 40 percent of its Industrial de Telecomunicacion (Indetel) subsidiary to local private investors and to the government, its chief customer, and, six years later, by selling another 11 percent and becoming a minority partner. The strategy helped boost sales and earnings ninefold and enabled Indetel to overtake the Mexican subsidiary of Sweden's L. M. Ericsson, which formerly dominated the market. Exxon's Venezuelan operations were nationalized on New Year's Day 1976, but Exxon stayed on in a new role as technology supplier and marketer of Venezuelan oil, collecting annual fees of nearly $100 million for supplying know-how to Petroven, the state oil company. Exxon is furnishing up to 80,000 man-hours a year of technical and management consultation. Beyond that, Petroven can call in another 150 Exxon employees on a full-time basis. The package includes teachers, training courses, manuals, and computer programs. The sale of technology itself has become big business.

Multinational executives are seeing one Latin American country after another pull back from radicalism. "The balance between risk and reward is delicate," says Shell's senior managing director, C. C. Pocock, "and there is a tendency for multinationals to change their role from direct investment toward the providing of services for money." On the other hand, he adds, the multinationals are being discreetly wooed by those countries which feel a need for development. "They know in their hearts there is a close relationship between those countries which have lagged in economic development and those which are hostile to foreign investment."

What developing countries would like to get is managerial expertise, capital markets, and research facilities that come along with multinational headquarters. What they are likely to get, with their unskilled labor force and uncluttered land, are chemical plants, oil refineries, and sprawling, messy, labor-intensive industries. As pollution and environmental restrictions become more stringent in advanced countries, the multinationals are likely to tempt developing regions with smelly eyesores. (Multinationals in primary resources have no choice, of course, but to go where the oil, copper, manganese, nickel, and potash are, however messy such mining can be.)

Numbers count—both ways. Of the Newly Industrialized Countries (the NICs), Brazil has more bargaining power with the multinationals than most because it has a big and fast-growing domestic market. With a GNP exceeding $100 billion, Brazil is sizable enough to enable manufacturers to achieve significant economies of scale. Roughly 40 percent of total foreign investments in the developing countries is concentrated in the NICs. "If you take out of the eighty-eight less developed countries the ten where nearly 80 percent of our business is," says G. A. Costanzo, vice chairman of Citicorp, "Mexico, Brazil, Argentina, Colombia, maybe Peru, Korea, Taiwan, Hongkong, the Philippines and Indonesia—if you take these ten countries, their relative share is increasing. Their growth rates are a lot better than Europe's. You're going to see very high growth rates in Latin America and Southeast Asia in the next twenty-five years—8 and 10 percent a year—far exceeding the 3 to 4 percent in the U. S. and Europe."

But if governments seem befuddled, clumsy, and downright ignorant in allocating resources and setting targets, giant corporations aren't immune to stupidity, elephantism, and geriatric woes. Former presidential candidate John Connally says, "There's an amazing amount of mediocrity among even the top, top businessmen. I know, I've seen them. Ninety percent are mediocre, pompous, narrow, stupid Neanderthals." [4]

American corporations tend to employ chief executives for short periods of time and to judge them by how much money they earn while in office. This makes American business shortsighted and incapable of looking twenty years into the future. Everything is short-term. Unlike Japanese corporations, for example, American companies tend to finance investments from their own savings. If tomorrow's investments have to be financed out of today's profits, firms are apt to slight current activities that would contribute to future profits. Borrowing from outside sources plays a much larger role in investment among true multinational corporations. Many of them have been in their various markets for fifty, sixty years and have all intentions of being there in the next century as well.

Futurists aren't too sure how the global corporations will look

[4] Steven Brill, "Connally—Coming on Tough," *The New York Times Magazine*, November 18, 1979, p. 37.

fifty years from now. If adaptability is the key word, there are both encouraging and disturbing signs. Paul Strassmann, vice president of the Informational Product Group at Xerox Corp., thinks that the first world is riding toward the end of the industrial society, that the society to follow will not necessarily be a corporate state, and that not all business will be conducted by behemoth corporations working on a worldwide scale. Clusters of small "cottage" industries will· act·as "feeders" to the corporate giants, supplying them with parts, capital equipment, and support services, but only the giants will be able to afford the cost of innovation—a trend that some believe will inevitably slow the pace at which discoveries are made and put to work in the future.

Many giants are already short on planning and creativity and long on executive perks and cronyism. Planning is often more form than substance, with endless committee meetings and few decisions. The emphasis is too often on loyalty and avoidance of error, rather than on innovation. Former General Motors group vice president John Z. DeLorean has portrayed the automobile giant as riddled with fawning, indecisive executives and explained GM's leadership as having more to do with its tremendous economic power than with management competence.[5] Anthony Sampson has described Royal Dutch/Shell executives as enclosed in their world of private dining rooms, planes, and chauffeurs, maintaining a lofty and skeptical attitude toward governments and vainly trying to educate politicians in the eternal verities of oil.[6]

"Multinational bashing," as *The Economist* of London eloquently named the pillorying that imperiled the global corporations' prospects, tarnished their image, and dismayed their leaders, reached its height in the mid-1970s, when multinationalism stood for every possible sin from tax evasion to the killing of African babies or the overthrow of Latin American presidents. A whole body of literature appeared, much of it a beguiling mixture of insight and fantasy. In *Sovereignty at Bay*, Harvard Professor Raymond Vernon sounded the central theme, which critics have embellished since, when he argued that the size, financial strength, superior technology, and organization of vast international enterprises set them beyond the control of governments and in effect made "sovereign states feel naked." The gloom of the decade's end

[5] J. Patrick Wright, *On a Clear Day You Can See General Motors* (Grosse Pointe, Mich.: Wright Enterprises, 1979).

[6] Anthony Sampson, *The Seven Sisters* (New York: Viking Press, 1975), p. 14.

turned debate upside down. Government constraints, coupled with antibusiness prejudice, led some business philosophers to conclude that the advanced industrial countries cannot possibly survive as planetary leaders. "The question is," Herbert Gerjouy of the Future Group said, "will America be a Holland or a Turkey? Will we gracefully find a place for ourselves as the Netherlands did, or will we look to past glories and blame the rest of the world, as Turkey has?"[7] "What happened to the Idea of Progress?" *The New York Times* asked in its end-of-decade editorial pages.[8]

But a new industrial revolution, powered by such microcircuitry as the silicon chip that can contain the equivalent of 68,000 transistor switches that enable computers to think, is expected to carry Western economies to new heights. Consumerism, environmentalism, antitrust and government regulation are supposed to remain in place, while high technology pulls us to the shores beyond soaring energy prices, accelerating inflation, higher unemployment, declining productivity, and sluggish growth. As if on cue, business has started to show a new cohesiveness, even new assertiveness in a quiet but dramatic change in the flow of power and influence in many government centers. There may be a worrisome decline in government outlays for Research and Development, a falloff in university research and in the proportion of public spending, but the United States, Western Europe, and Japan still lead in innovative technology. IBM, Siemens, Hitachi tool up to give us computers packing "up to seven times more bang for a buck."

The end-of-decade decline was blamed on everything from the lowering of science education to corporate addiction to short-term profits at the expense of long-range research, but such argument presumed companies to be narrowly national; that, in effect, the decline of the United States must mean the decline of IBM. The decline of Great Britain has not meant the regression of BP but its diversification, and all signs point to communications becoming the biggest and most far-reaching industry in the early decade of the twenty-first century. "In the next ten years, we will improve the computing power and make it easier to program giant number-crunchers to understand English," says Lewis Branscomb, IBM's chief scientist. "It will make computers more friendly, supportive, and informative." Information means power.

[7] *Business Week, 50th Anniversary Issue,* September 3, 1979, p. 198.
[8] *The New York Times,* December 30, 1979.

"With our computers, our firm has access to more information more quickly than people working in Congress," says Thomas Hale Boggs, Jr., one of Washington's most effective and sought-after corporate lawyers.

The economic situation of the early 1980s cannot be regarded in conventional business-cycle terms. The world is undergoing an historic adjustment to the end of cheap energy, and if global corporations are neither languishing nor growing smaller, they are adjusting, concentrating investments on fewer and narrower markets, looking to increased research to spur growth, and, in some instances, spending more time weighing alternatives to scarcer venture capital. "The nature of the game is to take calculated risks," says E. I. Du Pont de Nemours chairman Irving S. Shapiro, predicting that the trend toward specialization and more research will be the tune of the remainder of the century. Global firms have growth that is less visible now than in the 1960s and 1970s, and a realistic view of their future is that they will do well in a service-based economy in which nationalism is not the yardstick of leadership and eminence.

3

Who Are They?

Exxon and General Motors are the world's biggest commercial enterprises. One year Exxon heads *Fortune*'s list of the top 500 American corporations, another year GM is Number 1; but Exxon earns 74 percent of its money outside the United States, GM barely 22 percent. The big Japanese automakers export in greater quantity than Volkswagen, but Volkswagen *makes* cars in half a dozen countries. Its Brazilian assets alone are $1.5 billion, and just over half the market and a quarter of the cars that Brazil exports are VWs. Japan's big electronics firms have begun a massive shift to overseas production, but only Hitachi is big enough to be big—that is, to have annual revenues over $10 billion—and international enough to be a multinational—that is, deriving at least 51 percent of its earnings outside its national home base.

Eighteen corporations belong to this exclusive club.

At the rear of the $10 billion-plus phalanx are two German chemical giants, BASF and Bayer: Badische Anilin & Soda Fabrik with $10.7 billion in 1978 revenues (51 percent earned outside the Federal Republic), Bayer AG with $11.3 billion (70 percent foreign-earned). Neither company can be said to be diversified, although Bayer has 312 foreign subsidiaries, ranging from Agfa-Gavaert in Belgium to Sumitomo Bayer Urethane in Japan. "We have to build only in chemistry and we have to make chemicals that are difficult to make," says Bayer chairman Herbert Grüne-wald, who has developed a unique management system to control the far-flung empire. No board member is supposed to be away from headquarters in Leverkusen, near Düsseldorf, the first week of each month. The week starts Friday, so that board members can study reports over the weekend and spend the next four days in division and policy conferences.

Both companies are heavily committed to the scientific race in plastics. The chains of molecules used in plastics are so complicated and contorted that bonding two different polymer chains is a hard task. Finding polymers that do link up and, at the same time, produce a material with superior qualities is a hit-and-miss affair, and company researchers sift through thousands of combinations to come up with something useful. To try and figure out what has happened chemically so that promising laboratory results can be refined into a production process is exhausting, but one new development is a polyurethane tire made by Bayer that may go on cars in 1985. A BASF breakthrough is in glass-reinforced polyurethane allowing corner panels on cars that yield and then bounce back into shape after bumps. GM uses this to feature "friendly fenders" on some 1981 models.

Both Bayer and BASF have billion-dollar investments in the United States—BASF as Wyandotte and Dow Badishe, Bayer as Mobay Chemical, Cutter Laboratories, and Miles Laboratories. North America is the only place Bayer can't operate under its own name. Founded by Friederich Bayer in 1863, the company became an enemy alien in 1917. Its assets and trademarks were confiscated and then transferred to Sterling Drug Corp. which still makes and sells the famous aspirin.

When *The New York Times Magazine* did a cover story on the multinationals in 1973, its cover illustration was a singularly unappetizing rendition of a Nestlé chocolate bar pouring melted brown goo over the planet.[1] Nestlé Alimentana SA had its origin in Henri Nestlé's 1865 discovery of condensed milk, and if its name doesn't evoke the image of many-tentacled power like ITT, the company nevertheless owns a mind-boggling array of subsidiaries. Its employees nickname themselves "Roman legions" because they practically swear allegiance to Nestlé, and the company in turn promises almost Japanese-style lifelong employment. With a combination of tight financial controls and loose operating rules, top management in Vevey, on Lake Geneva east of Lausanne, directs the company's activities in one hundred countries. Most of its array of products are made in the countries where they are consumed, and over the decades, Nestlé has scored successes in the marketplace more consistently than most.

Europe is the most important region for Nestlé, followed by

[1] Harvey D. Shapiro, "The Multinationals—Giants Beyond Flag and Country," *The New York Times Magazine*, March 18, 1973, p. 20.

the Americas, Asia, the Pacific, and Africa. The range of products made in 303 Nestlé factories across the continents covers all sectors of modern foods, with emphasis on processed dairy products. Nestlé has grown with recent trends in convenience foods, especially in Europe, with self-service cafeterias in plants, hospitals, and schools. Its progression in sales, which makes it a third larger than Procter & Gamble and double the size of General Foods, the two biggest American food processors, has come from such wholly owned subsidiaries as Libby, McNeill & Libby and the Stouffer Corporation in the United States, Ursina-Franck in Germany and France, and Blaue Quellen, Germany's second largest mineral water producer. Over half of Nestlé's profits are in processed dairy foods. Twenty percent comes from the famous Nescafé (of which there are forty varieties to cater to national tastes), freeze-dried soups, spices, and frozen convenience foods, and only less than 10 percent from those gooey chocolate bars the *New York Times* illustrator liked so much.

With revenues of $11.3 billion, Nestlé is the world's sixteenth largest company. To keep its reputation, it has always been very particular about quality, in the areas of both raw materials and control over manufacturing, and any new product that any of the one hundred "administrative centers" may develop and want to launch must be quality approved in Vevey. If a new product is approved, headquarters will offer it to the ninety-nine others. "If we believe that this is a very interesting new product and some subsidiaries tell me they are not interested, we may urge initial trials," says Liotard Vogt. "By no means would we ever force any company to launch a new product if its managers didn't think it was acceptable." If a manager wants to introduce a new line and it is okayed in Vevey, he must finance it out of his local budget, but he won't be penalized for losing money on it for a while. Nestlé cadres are trained to think long-term.

The criteria for becoming one of the one hundred managers is not being a "native" in a given market, but understanding and knowing that market. In the developing world, however, Nestlé has avoided the fallout from the worst multinational bashing by offering host countries the opportunity to put capital into the subsidiary and by quickly moving local people into key positions, so that the only *expatriates,* as Africans like to call foreign resident technicians and cadres, are very technical people. This concession to prickly "thirdworldhood" was not popular in Vevey when Liotard Vogt introduced it. "It is not what I wish," he smiles, "but it is the best thing to do because, if we don't, it might turn out one day to be much worse." [2]

Making cars is the world's biggest manufacturing business, creating huge employers. Two million people work for the top two dozen carmakers; an estimated three million more make other automotive components; and a further thirty million depend on motor vehicles for their livelihood. The motor industry is itself a major customer of many other industries, purchasing steel, glass, and rubber, machine tools and electrical goods. All told, there are 280 million cars in the world and a further 70 million trucks, buses, and vans. But with the exception of the Newly Industrialized Countries (NICs) in Latin America and Asia, the auto industry is maturing—forty million new cars every year merely replace existing ones or are second cars. While Detroit is busy "reinventing the car" (two seaters with loads of incredible electronics) for the 1990s, developing countries have no intention of allowing American, European, and Japanese auto giants a free rein to exploit their growing home markets. In fact, most developing countries want to build their own motor industries. Making cars and trucks not only creates a lot of jobs and saves foreign exchange, it provides a solid base for building up the pyramid of modern manufacturing skills.

Daimler-Benz makes Mercedes-Benzes, but it is also the world's biggest truck producer. At home, Daimler is strapped with the world's most expensive labor force, and under Dr. Joachim Zahn's enduring presidency, the big Stuttgart firm has both ruthlessly automated and moved abroad. It makes cars and trucks in Argentina, Brazil, India, Iran, Spain, South Africa, and Turkey and is building an assembly plant in Virginia to assemble up to 6,000 trucks a year from parts shipped in from its Brazilian works. Experts give Daimler the best chance of any multinational truckmaker to crack the tough U. S. truck market.

Zahn is a conciliator, a man quickly in charge of most conversations in half a dozen languages. As Daimler-Benz emerged from the ruins of World War II, three groups owned 80 percent of the company—Friedrich Flick, one of the titans of German steel; Deutsche Bank; and the Quandt group, the other big German family holding company—but none had controlling interest. The balance of power required Zahn's diplomatic skill, but the fact

[2] Interview with *Harvard Business Review*, November–December 1976, p. 39.

that he had only three bases to touch for stockholder support gave him and his eight-man "cabinet" the ability to act very quickly on crucial questions. In 1974, the Quandt group sold most of its shares to Kuwaiti interests. A year later, the Flick group sold nearly three-quarters of its block to Deutsche Bank to finance its heavy investments in the United States, where it bought into W. R. Grace & Co. and U. S. Filter Corp. (Deutsche Bank took over Houston's tallest building, One Shell Plaza; and its biggest, Pennzoil Place; and at one point nearly bought Manhattan's World Trade Center). Deutsche Bank spun off the shares it bought from Friedrich Flick, Germany's richest man, into a holding company whose shares were sold to the public, but the pattern of a few large stockholders has remained.

Zahn and his chief executives rule as an effective organ of collective decision making. Zahn likes *manöverkritik*, sessions when he and his aides fight battles over again to see what went right and what didn't. He expects his executives to tell him where he erred, and, if need be, he will step on their toes until they do. "When I want to put forward my own opinion in a meeting, I am wise enough to do it in the form of a question," he says. When he has a problem, he likes to skip several rungs and talk to the person most directly involved, a practice that causes a certain amount of fluttering in executive dovecotes.

You may have to wait for a year or two to buy your $22,000 Mercedes, but Zahn will not increase production. He has always overruled the pleas of his marketing people to expand production on a crash basis, and, in a now famous lecture at Kiel University in 1967, he explained why. He had noticed that as the market matured, yearly sales tended to fluctuate widely around a slowly growing long-term trend. His idea of keeping production in step with the long-range trend, rather than responding to peaks in demands, paid off handsomely in the 1974–75 car slump when Daimler-Benz was able to live off its order book and avoid layoffs. Profits dipped only slightly, while other carmakers slid deeply into the red. Zahn has remained a contrarian in truck expansion and in suggesting that Daimler-Benz go much more heavily into the U. S. market and diversify down toward the cheap pickup market, but he hates to be called overcautious. With the Austrian specialist manufacturer Steyr-Daimler-Puch, Zahn has pushed into the four-wheel-drive market, and he realizes Daimler-Benz may have to pool research and development with others in the future. The American challenge to Europe's car manufacturers is not only GM's and Ford's "world cars," but their world components. To survive, the smaller Europeans— and that includes Renault and Fiat, as well as Daimler-Benz— will have to accept that they can no longer afford to do everything themselves. Zahn worries about an upcoming free-for-all in the European truck market and about severe regulatory standards in many places, but he recognizes that carmakers must learn how to make vehicles that run on even less fuel and do so more quietly without polluting cities and countryside.

While rising fuel prices depressed sales for much of the world's auto industry in 1980, Daimler-Benz's sales kept rising; despite Arab boycotts and the fact that Kuwait owns a 14 percent share, the Stuttgart carmaker sold 1,100 buses to Israel. Even in Iran, its truck assembly plant was working at 75 percent of capacity a year after the Islamic Revolution. "We see ourselves in an extremely stable position," Gehard Prinz said in 1980 when he took over as chairman from Zahn. "The average order backlog for our cars is at least two years, and even our order inflow is in line with increased production."

Choosing a successor to Zahn is known to have involved a company battle, and the details of the selection of Prinz, the former head of purchasing, remain shrouded. The decision to build a "smaller" (instead of a "small") Mercedes in 1983, however, was understood to have something to do with Prinz's choice. "We're going to stick to our original concept, although we will place a higher priority on the question of fuel consumption than we did earlier," Prinz said in his first news conference as chairman. "It's going to be a Mercedes." Further down the road, Prinz is expected to introduce a hydrogen-powered car. Prototypes have been built, and Daimler-Benz is known to be experimenting with new turbine technology and cylinder cutoffs that permit one cylinder to be turned off at times to save fuel.

Hitachi, the "General Electric of Japan," is Number 14 and aspires to be the world's next IBM. Hitachi is reported to be Japan's best-run and hardest-running company. It spends more than any other Japanese firm on research and boasts of a R and D department with 500 Ph.D.s, who have provided it with more than 30,000 patents and with the best-engineered products in its fields. Hitachi began as a motor repair shop in 1910, serving a copper mine in the hills above the fishing village of Hitachi, 110 kilometers north of Tokyo. After building five-horsepower electric motors, the company expanded into manufacture of heavy electrical engineering, metalworks, turbines, copper cables, and rolling stock. In 1924, it built Japan's first electric locomotive and two years later entered the export market with a shipment of electric fans to America. Today, it makes more than 40,000 products and has 151 offices in 39 countries. It assembles TV sets in Taiwan and builds integrated circuits in Compton, California.

President Hirokichi Yoshiyama has been with the company since 1935 and, like many Hitachi officials, studied electrical engineering at Tokyo University. He rules the company from one of downtown Tokyo's older office buildings and is variously described as shy and stubborn. The shift away from heavy electric and transportation equipment was started under Yoshiyama's predecessor, but the thrust into computers is all his. Until 1976, Hitachi used RCA's patents under license. Today, Hitachi's semiconductor division employs 10,000, and Hitachi is the most popular firm among graduating university students; graduates flock there for jobs. Backed by $2 billion in government subsidies, Hitachi, along with Nippon Electric Co. (NEC) and Fujitsu, will soon challenge IBM directly and even hopes to leapfrog IBM's next generation of hardware. William Givens, president of Twain Associates, a consulting firm specializing in U. S.-Japan trade and investment, thinks the future of Hitachi, NEC, and Fujitsu is the central issue of our times. "If they can achieve their goals with computers," says Givens, "it could ensure their general economic dominance well into the twenty-first century."

Hitachi's metal-oxide silicons (one of the basic integrated circuit designs), its bipolar large-scale integration (which puts 100 or more transistors on a single chip), and other sophisticated semiconductor products are turned out by 2,000 workers in Musashi near Tokyo. The atmosphere is twenty-first century, with workers wearing white gloves, caps, booties, and surgical masks; before entering production areas, they are "washed down" by ten-second air showers to prevent impurities in the chips. In 1980, Hitachi opens a plant near Dallas where it will assemble advanced memories.

But Yoshiyama is a prudent man. If computers, semiconductors, telephone exchanges, and research and medical instruments account for a fifth of Hitachi's total sales, another fifth is made in nuclear, hydroelectric, and thermal power plants; a third fifth in heavy industrial equipment; a fourth fifth in television, stereo, and other consumer electronics; and the final fifth in rolled copper, special steels, wires, and cables. U. S. Justice Department trustbusters scuttled a joint venture with GE to build TV sets, and Hitachi Cable Ltd. has been indicted in Los Angeles on charges of fraud, bribery, and racketeering offenses in connection with efforts to secure an $8.9 million telephone cable contract from Anchorage Telephone Co. In 1979, Hitachi Sales Corp. was under investigation by the U. S. Attorney's office in New York for alleged payoffs to a Teamsters Union local. *Forbes* quoted a Hitachi spokesman as saying the Teamsters came to Hitachi, asking the company to buy tickets to some event and to take out ads in one of the union publications. "We did it because we thought it was the custom in America, but in any case, it was a small amount." [3]

Volkswagen is the world's thirteenth largest corporation and the most international carmaker, if by international we mean making cars in the largest number of countries and earning the highest percentage points (59 percent) of its revenues outside its home base. GM, Ford, Toyota, Nissan Motor, and Peugeot-Citroën make more cars than VW, but Toni Schmucker, who came in as chief executive at the darkest hour in 1975, is a global strategist. North America produces Volkswagens for its own market; the Brazilian and Nigerian subsidiaries supply much of South America and the third world; Mexico supplements Brazil in Latin America and builds special types of vehicles for more sophisticated markets; and the plant in Wolfsburg, West Germany, builds cars for Europe and parts of the Middle East only. The Beetle is now manufactured only in Brazil, Mexico, and Nigeria. Under Schmucker, VW also assembles Porsche 924s in its Audi plants, supplies automatic transmissions for Fiat, builds diesel engines for Volvo and gasoline motors for the Chrysler Horizon and Omni. It also imports to Wolfsburg major components, including engines, from its Latin American factories to offset the high cost of making cars in West Germany.

It wasn't like that the gray February morning Schmucker took over. VW was on the ropes, with a loss of $313 million on worldwide sales of $6.6 billion. Rudolf Leiding had already moved Volkswagen away from the ubiquitous Beetle that the world had grown tired of, but Leiding lacked the diplomatic touch to handle

[3] Norman Pearlstine, "That Old Nobushi Spirit," *Forbes,* July 23, 1979, p. 48.

the ten labor representatives on the twenty-man supervisory board. Both the Bonn government and the state government in Lower Saxony, which together control 40 percent of Volkswagen's stock, were headed by Social Democrats, and when Leiding appealed for wage restraints over the heads of the union by sending a personal letter to the home of each employee, a majority of the supervisory board decided he had to go.

Enter Schmucker, one of the few top German executives who was once a car-factory worker (at Ford's Cologne plant). His actual arrival in Wolfsburg caused something of a stir because he came alone—"without anybody, without wife, secretary, or dog"—moved into a guest house instead of the VW president's villa and commuted on weekends to home and wife in Essen. Diplomacy or not, his first task was to trim the swollen work force by 25,000, an unprecedented step for VW and an immediate test of Schmucker's ability to deal with the unions. After agonizing negotiations and sweetening the deal with $6,000 for each worker who quit, he got his way. He was also able to carry through the decision to set up a production plant in the United States, a move blocked by the unions when Leiding ran VW.

"There will be no alternative to the automobile as the individual means of transportation in the 1990s," says the bullish Schmucker, who plans to pump some $6 billion into production and plants by 1982 in Wolfsburg, the United States, Brazil, and Mexico. To be ready for the next decade, Schmucker and his design chief Ernst Fiala are hard at work on the wilder shores of automotive research, including electric drives and more exotic fuels, and plan to move the company "upmarket"—as late as 1972, half the cars sold worldwide were Beetles—with Audis, Passats (Dasher in America), Polos, Derbys, and Golfs/Rabbits. The new models have so many elements in common ("building blocks," in automotive jargon) that production costs can be held down even at a time when wages in West Germany are the world's highest.

Schmucker enjoys the satisfaction of having turned a unique company around. "What can there be for me after Volkswagen?" he asked in 1979. Everybody in Wolfsburg would be happy if he'd bring his wife up from Essen and move into the chief executive's villa.

If the frontiers between industries are blurring in the electronics and computer age, Siemens AG is, like GE, Westinghouse, Hitachi, and Mitsubishi (Japan's largest corporation), its own multicompany. The Munich juggernaut, with annual revenues of $14.5 billion, is Germany's leading technology firm. And down the road, says president Bernard Plettner, technology will converge "with everybody coming up with parts of the overall solution and then do some trading." It will happen in digital telecommunications; it might happen in computers, in process control on more than a few parts at a time. Plettner intends to pay the price in R and D for a ticket to these races.

Siemens dates back to 1847 and Werner von Siemens, who invented the forerunner of today's teleprinter and made a fortune stringing telegraph lines across Europe. Later, he pioneered the dynamo principle in electric power generation. The company largely shuns consumer markets, but it is the world's third largest supplier of telecommunications (after Western Electric and ITT). In nuclear generating equipment, Siemens made the breeder reactor breakthrough that landed it a contract to supply Brazil with four nuclear power plants (and drew the Carter Administration's wrath). Siemens ignored the criticism. The company is the world's largest supplier of X-ray equipment. It sells body and brain scanners, and since the 1970s has been determined to stay in the computer race, a field not for the fainthearted as the dropping out of GE and RCA proves. Siemens decided to hang in there because it felt frustrated by its lack of participation in the newest electronic and data-processing fields. "We were brilliant in X-ray but not in information technique," says Friedrich Kuhrt of the Siemens computer division, telling how the British conglomerate EMI introduced a brain and body scanner in 1972 that nearly knocked Siemens out of the market. "It was very hard for us to master the electronics of a scanner, but we did it. We had to develop our own microprocessor technology, not as a matter of cost, but because it's impossible to develop process control without a very intimate knowledge of microprocessing." The chip is important in telecommunications, too, and, like other telephone makers, Siemens thinks another great leap is on the horizon. The newest telephone exchanges convert signals into digital impulses, and the industry expects to develop microelectronic components that will convert the voice signals in the handset itself, resulting in huge cost reductions. Siemens' components group chief Friedrich Baur thinks that by 1985 chips will be so "intelligent" that there won't be much business left in telephones and, indeed, in computers. "If half a computer system is made of things on a chip, you have to be careful you're not just a software house with a bit of cabinet design," says Baur.

But it is along the southern edge of San Francisco Bay that the ideas powering the chip revolution are concentrated. The area is known as Silicon Valley, and it is here that computer whizzes in their twenties become partners of ITT only two years after starting out in the family garage, and former IBM analysts talk of taking away $500 million of IBM's business. Plettner and Baur know that the small and nimble California companies are very different in style and spirit from their own slow and careful product development. To keep up with the Bay area, Plettner has bought into Fuji Electric, which owns part of Fujitsu, and has licensing agreements with one of the Silicon Valley stars, Advanced Micro Devices (AMD). With Fujitsu, Siemens has a joint venture next to AMD, General Numeric Corp.

Fritz-Rudolf Guntsch, head of the electronics industry department of the Technology Ministry in Bonn, thinks Siemens missed out in two areas. In fiberglass cables, the Ministry has had to push the Munich giant to crank up an R and D program, and Guntsch feels the company could have done better in lasers. "Siemens will have to struggle very hard to be first in some areas —and then just as hard to be second in some other areas," says Guntsch.

NV Philips Gloeilampenfabrieken—to use the full Dutch name —employs 97,000 in Holland and another 275,000 in 60 other countries. Philips likes to think of itself not so much as a corporation as a federation, and most of the 275,000 people it employs outside the Netherlands are "natives." The company has fewer than 700 Dutch and non-Dutch expatriates running its operations in the 50 countries where it has manufacturing activities. Its annual sales are $15 billion, 90 percent of it derived from outside the Netherlands.

Philips is Philips everywhere except in the United States where, because of Phillips Petroleum, the corporate name is North American Philips, or Norelco. Philips is an electronic and electrical manufacturing enterprise of dizzying scope and ramifications. It makes lighting equipment, home appliances, TV and stereo equipment, telecommunications and defense systems, data processing, X-ray and medical equipment, pharmaceutical and chemical products, music cassettes and records (Magnavox is a Philips subsidiary). With Siemens, it is the fifty-fifty owner of Polygram, the first billion-dollar record and music company that few people have ever heard of, but one for which performers such as the Bee Gees, Eric Clapton, Donna Summer, and Robin Williams cut their records. In Hollywood, Polygram bankrolls movies for Casablanca Record & Film Works to the tune of $100 million, but its main area of interests remains records with such labels as Deutsche Grammaphon, Mercury, MGM, Verve, and, its newest acquisition, Decca. It has controlling interests in Robert Stigwood (who delighted Philips by grossing over $100 million apiece on *Saturday Night Fever* and *Grease* in the United States and Canada alone). In Europe, Polygram has 26 percent of the music market, in Japan 14 percent, and worldwide a fifth of the market. Rock stars like to sign with Polygram because it is a global company and because it isn't afraid of spending money to make money.

Polygram is run from New York by Coen Solleveld, a veteran Philips executive. Like the heads of other divisions, the mustachioed Solleveld needs an OK from Eindhoven—Philips' home base—for major outlays, but he works on a five-year plan and finds American executives' preoccupation with short-term planning and profits all wrong. "I wouldn't relish that," he says. "After all, you are not in business for this year or next year. You are in business for eternity." In order to be in business in the next century Philips is, with Siemens, the only European company seriously in the semiconductor race. By 1986, European governments plan to have spent about half a billion dollars to try and keep up with the United States and Japan, but that amount seems to be chickenfeed. Philips is behind Texas Instruments and ahead of Siemens in European market share, but worldwide both Philips and Siemens are behind IBM, Texas Instruments, NEC, and Hitachi.

But, like Nestlé, Philips is polyglot. To emphasize the world citizenship, president H. A. C. van Riemsdijk doesn't meet his division managers in Eindhoven, a drab company town of 181,000 in the southern Netherlands, but in Ouchy, near Lausanne in Switzerland. The conscious decentralization also means that product divisions deal directly with sales departments in the sixty countries. A board of management keeps this work under review so that engineering, quality control, and marketing can be kept to the same standards. Heads of national subsidiaries concerned with a particular line of products meet from time to time. There are scheduled company flights, and a fleet of planes stands by in Eindhoven to facilitate this travel.

* * *

With $18 billion in sales—51 percent of it in foreign revenues —Gulf Oil is the smallest of the storied Seven Sisters, a company belonging to the second tier, with Standard Oil of Indiana, Italy's Ente Nazionale d'idrocarburi (ENI), and Compagnie Française des Pétroles (CEP). The Pittsburgh company, which is 20 percent owned by the conservative Mellon family, is recovering from its political scandals and lack of direction of the mid-1970s and, under the leadership of lifelong oilman Jerry McAfee, is concentrating on "things we know best." Gulf lost its first-class status in 1975 when Kuwait took over its concessions and cut the company's daily supply by 500,000 barrels; it has since tried to recoup by concentrating on new energy. Gulf is spending $200 million a year on explorations inside the United States. It is heavily into North Sea oil but is not exploring offshore for China or the Soviet Union. It pumps 20 percent of its total production out of American wells, 19 percent out of Iranian, and 27 percent out of the Kuwaiti fields it no longer owns. It knows that oil will not last forever, and, like some of the bigger Sisters, it has diversified into alternative energy, keeping its interests focused on coal and uranium in North America.

Anthony Lucas, a former Austrian officer, was the first engineer to drill for oil in Texas. He hit pay dirt in 1901 at Spindletop, near Beaumont, on the Gulf coast. To finance his venture, he went to two prominent Pittsburgh prospectors who raised a $300,000 loan from Thomas Mellon & Sons. Largely because Tom's son Andrew saw possibilities in oil, in aluminum, and in other fields, the Mellons are now worth $5 billion, far more than the Fords and the Rockefellers. Andrew Mellon himself became, under Harding and Coolidge, Secretary of the Treasury and lived to be pilloried under Franklin Roosevelt as "a malefactor of great wealth." The Spindletop gusher lasted less than two years before running dry, but by 1906, Gulf found huge new reserves in Tulsa, Oklahoma, and by 1913, the company was a formidable rival of the trustbusted Standard companies.

In 1974, Senator Frank Church's subcommittee on multinational corporations revealed that Gulf had bribed government officials in South Korea and Bolivia to the tune of $4 million; the following year, the Securities and Exchange Commission established that Gulf had spent $5 million to buy influence among Washington lawmakers (its naive but disarming defense was that it thought everybody else did it, too). The company was not accustomed to such public agonies. Bob Dorsey was forced to resign as chairman, and when McAfee took over, heads rolled. In recent years, the affable McAfee, who, unlike Dorsey, doesn't mind riding in elevators with employees, has succeeded in lowering Gulf's profile and managed to pull the company back toward hushed respectability.

Unilever is Europe's biggest company. The British-Dutch household products giant has worldwide sales of over $20 billion; that is, more than Procter & Gamble, Colgate-Palmolive, Bristol Myers, American Home Products, and Norton Simon combined. With production facilities in 49 countries and a worldwide work force of 338,000, Unilever is ruled from a handsome office tower fronting Rotterdam's Jacobplein *and* from a crescent-shaped granite command post at the foot of the Embankment in London. In North America, where the corporate entity is Lever Brothers Co., things are run from a gleaming, green glass tower on New York's Park Avenue.

Everywhere, Unilever projects a down-home image. To the American housewife, Unilever is Lipton Tea, Wisk Liquid Detergent, Imperial Margarine, Dove Soap, All Detergent, Lux Dishwashing Liquid, and Aim and Close-up Toothpaste. Its management, however, is not encouraged to grow too local roots. "One cannot run a multinational corporation with managers all of whose experience has been in a single country," says chairman Sir David Orr. If anyone asks him if it isn't true that polyglot companies are largely beyond the control of any single government, Orr smiles and says that's, of course, true, "but only because we come under the control of *all* the governments of the countries in which we operate for everything over which those governments exercise jurisdiction. Our problem is to ensure that any given action is only controlled by one government; and quite often, especially in tax matters, we fail."

In the early 1970s, Africa was Unilever's great hope, but partial nationalization in Nigeria and Zaire has hurt. Unilever's earnings in Cameroon, Congo, Gabon, Ivory Coast, Kenya, Malawi, Nigeria, Sierra Leone, South Africa, Tanzania, Uganda, Zaire, Zambia, and Zimbabwe were twice the North American returns on investment (15 percent vs. 7.4 percent). Orr doesn't buy the oft-repeated third world accusation that international corporations prevent the growth of local enterprises by aggressive and unfair competition. If anything, he says, enterprises in India, Nigeria, and Spain have grown by copying Unilever's products and marketing methods. "We sometimes think *their* methods of competition are aggressive and unfair," he says. To the charge that technology is imported and imposed by the parent company, thereby depriving developing countries from developing research, Sir David says Unilever subsidiaries of any size do their own research. The company prefers 100 percent ownership of its daughter companies—in North and Central America, Pakistan, Chile, and Kenya it has managed to do just that—for reasons that have nothing to do with capitalist imperialism. Says Orr, "We prefer 100 percent ownership because it makes for a more effective conduct of the business as a whole. With local equity holdings, there is always a risk of conflict of interests."

After years of benevolent neglect of Lever Brothers, Thomas J. Lipton Inc., and National Starch and Chemical Corp., Unilever is paying special attention to the less than earth-shattering performance of its American subsidiaries. Most innovations in household products come from the United States, but Lever Brothers is only a tenth the size of Procter & Gamble, and its management has a hard time deciding whether to tackle P & G head-on or to try a flanking attack from protected niches in related fields. On sales of $8.2 billion (27 percent foreign), P & G nets $512 million, just a shade less than what Unilever earns on three times the volume. And while Unilever's cash reserve of $600 million may look big in London and Rotterdam, it doesn't in Cincinnati, where P & G is headquartered and keeps $800 million in cash on hand. Lever Brothers' brands are aging—Aim and Close-up were introduced in the 1960s—and to remain competitive it needs to introduce at least one new product every year. Unilever has three-fourths of its capital invested in Europe, but European profits have also been undermined by price wars and eroding earnings.

International Telephone and Telegraph Corp. is the world's eighth largest corporation and the creation of one man. The storied company is a multifaceted conglomerate put together by the controversial Harold Sydney Geneen, a fusion of 250 subsidiaries with annual sales of $20 billion, 200,000 shareholders, over 400,000 employees, and operations in 90 countries. ITT is Wonder Bread and Sheraton Hotels, Hartford Insurance and Avis Rent-a-Car, Bobbs-Merrill Publishing and Burpee Lawn and Garden Products, even if the vast telecommunications and electronics business is the centerpiece.

Rotten telephone systems—or no phone systems at all—have long been the lot of most third world countries, but governments in places like Cairo, Ryadh, Tehran, Lagos, and Al Kuwait are ordering sophisticated new systems, loosing a frenetic scramble among ITT, Siemens, Philips, NEC, and Ericsson. ITT's hardware is considered world-class—in fact, Siemens decided not to take on ITT's advanced digital switching systems in West Germany in 1979. The stakes are nearly $75 billion over the next decade. Nearly a third of the world's phones are in the United States—ninety-five for every one hundred households—and most other advanced countries are also near saturation. "Which explains the ferocity of the competition for third world systems," says ITT's senior vice president Frank Barnes. "We all want this business. Every time a contract comes up for bid, it's like a bunch of hunting dogs after a rabbit."

Many would say that to call Geneen a hunting dog would be too kind. The bubbling conglomerateur—who, with his slicked-back hair and steel-rimmed glasses, looks like an elder version of former World Bank president Robert McNamara—has been called an ogre in a business suit, the greatest corporate manager, an unimaginative numbers grubber, and a great leader. During his heyday, his identity merged with that of ITT. He had no hobbies or interests outside of business; he traveled only on ITT business on ITT jets and was reputed to work nineteen hours a day. Throughout the conglomerate, a constant flow of detail moved upward to Geneen, enabling him, it was said, to develop countermeasures to problems that hadn't happened yet. His monthly meetings around a huge horseshoe table in the ITT skyscraper in New York were legendary. Around the table sat the ITT managers, like diplomats, and in the middle was Geneen, watching the expressions on the faces of the men reeling off their figures. Geneen sometimes kept his executives meeting for up to ten days a month.

ITT was founded in 1920 by Sosthenes Behn, who was born of French and Danish parents in the Virgin Islands and educated in Paris. Starting out as a sugar broker, he got into telecommunications almost by accident when he and his brother Hernand bought a small, foundering telephone company in Puerto Rico. The brothers soon acquired another phone system in Cuba, moved on into Spain and bought the international holdings of Western Electric. By the mid-1920's, the fledgling empire was known as IT & T, a name chosen to echo, and possibly to be confused with, the mighty American Telephone and Telegraph (AT & T). When Hernand died in 1933, Sosthenes became the undisputed master. Geneen took over in 1959, two years after Behn's death, and liked to call himself as much a man of his time as Behn had been of his. If conglomerating and fusing the complex personalities and conflicting drives of a huge business bureaucracy were the marks of the go-go 1960s and early 1970s, Geneen was of his times. The ITT he bent to his will and complex personality was the closest thing to a sovereign state. Typically, he could say in 1977 that the U. S. economy was so big and so diverse that there was very little any government in Washington could do about it. In 1978, he formally gave up the chief executive's chair to Lyman Hamilton, Jr., and, officially at least, all the powers that went with it. But Hamilton, a World Bank alumnus, lasted less than a year before he was ousted and replaced by a "Geneen man," Rand V. Araskog.

Araskog began by dismantling part of the "Geneen Machine," as ITT was tagged during Geneen's eighteen years as chief executive. He sold off many Geneen acquisitions in Europe, shifted power from 320 Park Avenue to the operating divisions, defanged much of the fabled Geneen reporting and auditing systems, and cut $6 million in executive salaries. He reduced layers of scrutiny from teams of corporate officers above business managers. "Unnecessary layers confuse, cause more reporting and more errors," Araskog said. Grandson of Swedish immigrants, Araskog calls himself a disciplined, straight-talking, uncomplicated man and his job "the biggest meat-grinder job in corporate management." The length of his term as ITT's leader is expected to be determined by the results of his redefinition of power within the conglomerate and the limits of Geneen's methods.

Geneen was in charge during the most tumultuous years, which began with an antitrust action against ITT ordering the corporation to divest itself of several companies if it were to retain Hartford Fire Insurance Co. Geneen had barely finished assuring uneasy stockholders that the divestitures had actually resulted in profits when publication of a secret memo, allegedly written by ITT lobbyist Dita Beard, aroused speculation concerning the relationship between the favorable antitrust settlement and financial support of the Republican national convention by Sheraton Hotels. While the matter was under investigation, ITT was accused of initiating and underwriting the cost of CIA intervention in Chile, where its interests appeared threatened.

Geneen first sought the CIA's collaboration to prevent Salvador Allende from becoming president and then to subvert his government, once he had been elected. This, said Senator Church at the multinational subcommittee hearings, raised the issue of global corporations "becoming a Fifth Column in international politics, using their home governments to destroy foreign regimes not to their liking." * The Allende affair gave multinationals their blackest eye and provoked a worldwide revulsion against supranational corporate autocracy. Leftists marched in the streets of Rome, Paris, and Stockholm, and "multinational" became a curse in a hundred languages. The United Nations and its agencies began drafting codes of conduct for transnational business, the U. S. Senate formed its subcommittee, and hundreds of articles and books were published on the evils of the corporate global reach. Somewhat timidly, the International Chamber of Commerce pointed out that a code on corporate behavior should perhaps also spell out the responsibilities of governments. The Charter of Economic Rights and Duties of States, which the UN General Assembly adopted, 120 to 6, in 1975, didn't establish a supranational counterforce but promoted the most craven nationalism. Article two said that if a country expropriates a foreign-owned company, any disagreements about compensation shall be settled "under the domestic law of the nationalizing country." Neither this charter nor the OECD voluntary code of the same year made any mention of reciprocity of government responsibilities, and both were silent on the behavior of state capitalism and government-owned enterprises.

ITT—and Geneen—survived all this untamed. Emerging nations need telephone systems as part of their industrialization, and ITT has figured that on the average, worldwide, every 1,000 phones require an investment of about $1.5 million. Countries that have oil money can handle virtually any costs, and countries that haven't beat a path to the World Bank and foreign governments for capital. They all realize, says Patrick Barrett, vice president of Bell Canada International, that "business just doesn't want to invest in a country without a good phone system. Where phones are, more people will come." ITT has the top expertise. Nigeria spent more than a billion of its oil dollars buying just

---

* Congressional testimony disclosed ITT stood ready to underwrite with cash any efforts the CIA might be considering to prevent the election of Salvador Allende in 1970.

about every kind of equipment, from microwave and super-sophisticated switching systems to earth stations and touch-tone instruments, and then didn't know what it wanted to do with it. Northern Telecommunications of Montreal was involved and then gave up; ITT straightened things out.

The World's seventh largest corporation is also better known by its three initials than its full name. International Business Machines is the world's most resourceful and creative big company. It is the kind of company that always has the competition jumping just to keep up. As computer technology continues to revolutionize society and, in the process, revolutionize itself, IBM can crowd its mainframe competitors on several fronts—data security, mass storage systems, nonimpact printers—while continuing to spend over $1 billion a year on research. IBM is the kind of company that can raise $1 billion in two weeks on the open market. It is a company envied by competitors and coveted by governments, a company that plays a vital role in the world economy. IBM employs 155,000 in the United States (1,600 at its headquarters in Armonk, New York) and 120,000 in the rest of the world in a unique tower of Babel mix (only 575 Americans are posted overseas). Its annual revenues are $21 billion (53 percent foreign-earned), and it is only in one business—the manufacture, marketing, and servicing of data-processing systems and office products.

Ironically, IBM almost missed the boat in one development in its field. It fumbled in its copier confrontation with Xerox and Eastman Kodak (two quasi-multinationals, with 48 and 39 percent foreign earnings respectively). It faces continued challenge in high-potency scientific computers. The leviathan Exxon has entered the fray of business machines through its Vydec subsidiary, and some of IBM's old-line rivals in large mainframes—Control Data, NCR, Honeywell, and Burroughs—show few signs of fading away. Business is at an organizational watershed with respect to information systems and resource management; American companies alone are spending nearly $100 billion a year buying information resources from such major manufacturers as IBM, AT & T, Xerox, and thousands of smaller computer, communications, and office systems suppliers. And it's just the beginning. The ability to tap virtually limitless information instantly will be the key to the way corporations are run fifty years from now—and who will run them. Tomorrow's chief executive will be the person who has the creativity and intelligence to manipulate that information.

Governments don't mess with IBM. If they try, IBM pulls out —as it did in 1978 when both India and Brazil wanted a "national" solution to computers. IBM doesn't do joint ventures, as makers of soap, cars, chemicals, and breakfast cereals do. IBM doesn't have to buy off revolutionaries or bankroll the overthrow of governments. When they have grasped what the three initials stand for, Marxists and fascists alike stand back in awe.

At the same time, IBM is acutely aware of what it means to be an exemplary corporate citizen. No whiff of scandal swirls around the computer giant. The resentment is both deeper and more devious. IBM means high technology, and the jealousies and grievances are the complaints of the also-rans and left-behinds, complaints that tend to provoke irritation and impatience in self-assured, creative, and innovative people.

Frank T. Carey, a balding native of Gooding, Idaho, makes over $900,000 a year as IBM's chairman. He is notoriously tight-lipped about the company's internal programs and expenditures, but the organization of the corporate pyramid is no secret. IBM has made a conscious effort to develop international management by offering international careers to outstanding personnel of any nationality. The president of IBM World Trade Corp., responsible for IBM's business outside the United States, is Jacques Maisonrouge, and his staff is made up of people of twenty-two nationalities. IBM's labor relations run the gamut from no unions at all in the United States to one-third employee representation on the board of IBM Germany. Within national constraints, the same personnel policies apply to all employees throughout the world, including merit pay, job evaluation, and counseling. IBM pays slightly higher than prevailing wages everywhere, and tens of thousands of non-Americans own its shares, which are quoted on twelve stock exchanges outside the United States. With the exception of GM, no company spends more on R and D than IBM. The efforts are carried out in thirty laboratories—twenty-one in the United States, nine in Europe and Asia—each with a defined mission and each tied in with the others through computer-based communications. All branches, depots, distribution centers, and headquarters are interlaced and IBM has bought satellite space to handle the flow. "Almost all the data bases—the files and accumulation of knowledge—the company needs to run are on there," says Tom Crotty of Gartner Group Inc., a company which provides research and is possibly the most acute and well-informed among the mini intelligence agencies and other "IBM watchers" that have sprung up.[4] The labs need an advanced industrial environment, where a critical mass of scientists and highly skilled manpower is readily available, and are generally located near universities and thriving scientific communities. In the past few years, IBM scientists have learned to use electron beams, controlled by a computer, to etch the complicated circuitry onto matchhead-sized chips of silicon much more accurately and efficiently than was previously possible, and they are working to improve computers by reducing their interior temperature to absolute zero (minus 273° centigrade). (In extreme cold, materials lose much of their electrical resistance and become "superconductors"; IBM scientists think a superconductor computer immersed in liquid helium cooled to near absolute zero would work twenty times faster than today's models on the same amount of energy.) One plant makes a special product for the entire European market, and this item is not produced in any other European plant. This "product by plant" policy turns IBM operations into export earners for countries in which it has manufacturing plants.

To be in the computer game at all takes frightful amounts of money—as Hitachi, Siemens, Philips, and the others can testify. To be Number 1 requires still bigger cash hoards. In 1976, IBM's cash position towered at $6.5 billion (more than the foreign exchange reserves of Sweden or Canada), but three years later it had to borrow $1 billion, after nailing down a $1.5 billion line of credit with its banks. Capacity expansions are needed with every leap forward to meet the overwhelming demand for new products, including the 4300 series of mainframe processors—computer jargon for central processing units in equipment systems—in 1979 and the H series of computers of 1980. IBM is believed to have put $4 billion into capital spending in 1978 alone, mainly to finance automated manufacturing to defend its markets in mainframe computers against growing Japanese competition. The heavy outlays came at a time when IBM's customers made an unexpected but massive shift from buying to leasing of computers, as industry waited for the new series before committing money to new systems.

[4] Harold Seneker, "IBM: The Empire Strikes Back," *Forbes*, June 23, 1980, p. 42.

High tech electronics have a way of making things converge. Satellites bounce telephone calls from continent to continent, from coast to coast, but they also transmit video images and, perhaps most important, data between computers. AT & T has three satellites hanging 36,000 kilometers above the equator, transmitting long-distance telephone, video, and TV images; in 1978, they were joined by two rival satellites, owned by Satellite Business Systems, a company 40 percent owned by IBM. This kind of corporate *Star Wars* is a conflict neither company particularly wants and one that was unthinkable twenty years ago, when AT & T and IBM were partners in a separate-but-equal relationship and their engineers met informally to make sure their hardware was technically compatible. The stakes are high for both. Telecommunications and data computing are growing at about 12 percent a year and the struggle for the business communications market involves at least $4 billion in revenues annually, the largest part of each former industry's expected new yearly growth. Telecommunications are state monopolies in most countries, but the monopoly is being undermined by the mind-boggling array of superintelligent machines that can "talk" to each other via network that transmits and processes any kind of information, whether voice, video, facsimile or computer data. IBM—and Hitachi, Siemens, Philips, and a few lesser mammoths —are now part of the world's nervous system and, as such, largely beyond the competence of national governments. As if to confirm this, the Carter Administration lowered the bar between the telephone business and the data-processing industry in 1980, authorizing perhaps the most sweeping deregulation of American business to date. The full implication is not expected to be clear for years, but for starters, AT & T was allowed to enter the computer and data-processing fields, offering everything from complete computer systems and data links between them to such unlikely consumer applications as home computers, remote-reading utility meters, and computerized home heat and light control. In turn, IBM and Xerox were given freer access to areas of high-speed data transmission.

The frontiers of technology make for ever newer star wars. In the home video entertainment market, IBM is a partner with Philips and Hollywood's MCA Inc. for the exploitation of laser-based videodisks, which have the capacity for storing billions of bits of computer information. The partnership may branch into the consumer field. The Philips-MCA system is slugging it out with RCA Corp.'s SelectaVision videodisk system, and both are fighting videotape recorders, manufactured by Matsushita Electric and Sony Corp. Like the movies before the 35mm, four-sprocket-per-frame standardization of 1889, the video world is a disconcerting, if joyous, confusion. A Philips-MCA videodisk cannot snap into a SelectaVision player and vice versa, and neither disk can be played on a tape deck. The billion-dollar shakeout is still to come.

Oil is the most dazzling game on earth. Here are the world's largest, wealthiest companies matching wits with lumbering bureaucracies and astute statesmen. Here developing nations become Croesus-rich overnight. Here mesmerized millions place their bets on a future of energy and hope for the best. Here the rules and the game itself are so complex and fast-changing that practically no one understands them.

With revenues of $24 billion (60 percent of it foreign), Standard Oil of California is the world's sixth largest corporation. Socal, or Chevron, in the shorthand of the industry, gets 66 percent of its oil from Saudi Arabia, 13 percent from Indonesia, 12 percent from the United States, and 3 percent from Canada. Like the other members of the sorority, it has its conservative feet firmly on the ground; its chairman believes the world can't wait for the politicians, that it must rely on proven policies to encourage energy production. "The choice before us is clear," says H. J. Haynes. "There must be more realistic economic incentives, more realistic energy prices, and government must eliminate the unreasonable environmental barriers that inhibit oil and gas production, and coal and nuclear development. The rest of the world is unable to understand why America hesitates, why our nation seems to be gripped by a form of political paralysis when it comes to effective energy decisions."

Despite its name, Socal was only part of Rockefeller's Standard Trust for eleven short years (1895–1906). Besides its early discovery of oil under Los Angeles, its claim to fame and fortune was to buy a wily New Zealander's option on a concession in the British protectorate of Bahrain for $50,000 ("our billion-dollar error," was Exxon's later response, since Frank Holmes offered the option to Exxon first). Pumping oil out of Bahrain in 1931 allowed Socal to be the first to make a deal with King Ibn Sáud, ironically because the staid San Francisco company knew little about Mideast intrigue and had not been a party to earlier attempts at conning concessions out of Arabs. Chevron began drilling in Saudi Arabia in 1933. The prospectors had a rugged frontier existence, living in tents and huts, relying on a logistical line halfway around the world to San Francisco, and coping with desert sand, burning heat, and loneliness. Chevron found a partner in Texaco, another innocent in the Middle East, and oil flowed in 1939, a year when the United States still had no diplomatic representation in Saudi Arabia and the oilmen did the negotiating with canny King Sáud themselves. In 1944, California Arabian Standard Oil changed its name to Arabian American Oil Co. Three years later, Exxon and Mobil joined the partnership when it became clear Chevron and Texaco lacked both the capital and the markets to absorb more than a fraction of the oil the Saudis were ambitious to put on the market.

From the start, Aramco was a political creature as much as an economic one. Washington recognized the strategic importance of the Middle East and never hesitated to use Aramco to advance its political interests, and the four partners never hesitated to use the U. S. government to advance their commercial interests. The overriding concern for both was elemental—protect the concession and use the riches to advance the American position in that volatile region. Since direct subsidies of the Saudi princes would have involved political problems, Washington resorted again and again to subterfuge, but by the time the Saudi Council of Ministers formally and finally approved the takeover of Aramco in 1976, the fiction that Chevron, Texaco, Exxon, and Mobil controlled the company had been dispelled by the 1973 Arab oil embargo. King Faisal had no sooner gone on the radio to announce his intention of reducing oil production by 10 percent than Aramco chairman Frank Jungers ordered production cut back. Two days later, when Aramco was ordered to supply oil to the Arab war effort in the Yom Kippur conflict, Jungers felt he "had no alternative but to comply." Noncompliance with the boycott, Sheik Zaki Yamani observed when it was all over, would have meant nationalization "at gunpoint."

BP, the world's fifth largest company, had its origins in British imperialism. With total revenues of over $40 billion (81 percent earned outside the United Kingdom), BP has worked hard since the mid-1970s to reduce its dependence on the Middle East and achieve a greater access to the American retail market. It owns 54 percent of the rich Prudhoe Bay fields on Alaska's North

Slope, holds controlling interests in Standard Oil of Ohio, and pumps half a million barrels a day from the North Sea.

According to legend, William Knox d'Arcy staked two brothers with the Australian equivalent of one hundred dollars to allow them to prospect for gold. The year was 1882—the year Rockefeller formed his Standard Trust to bring all his smaller companies under one management—and d'Arcy's prospectors immediately made the biggest gold strike in Australia's history. D'Arcy, a stocky little adventurer, retired to London with a considerable fortune, bought a mansion in Grosvenor Square, and was promptly overcome by boredom.

Oil was a topic at the business lunches and club dinners d'Arcy attended—as were the fabulous amounts of money Rockefeller was making on the stuff. There were those who said oil had already peaked, since Thomas Edison's electric light bulb was making kerosene lamps obsolete, and there were those who thought that, with the invention of the internal combustion engine, petroleum had a future. Among the latter was Sir John Fisher, a Royal Navy officer who complained that one-fourth of the fleet was always in port for recoaling. "If the fleet burned oil," he insisted, "we could refuel at sea from floating tankers. This would increase the use of our ships by 25 percent." For strategic reasons, the Admiralty was not impressed. The British Isles had large coal reserves, but no oil fields. It would be unthinkable to convert warships to oil until the country controlled its own oil reserves.

By 1897, when Rudolf Diesel invented the engine named after him, it was clear that the horseless carriage would soon consume more petroleum than kerosene lamps ever did. Small ships were beginning to use the new gasoline engines, and the Kaiser's navy showed great interest in changing its coal-burning battleships to oil burners. The German interest stirred Sir John Fisher again—and stirred the financial circles d'Arcy frequented. Oil had been discovered in the British Empire—in Burma, and Burmah Oil was already a very profitable company—and Marcel Samuel's Shell Transport and Trading Co. was involved in a syndicate selling Russian oil from the Ural-Caspian fields to the Far East. D'Arcy wasn't averse to the idea of becoming a British Rockefeller. At his leisure, he had studied the American oil empire (presently lobbying Parliament to keep Samuel's oil ships out of the Suez Canal with dark hints of disaster if a tanker blew up in transit) and come to the conclusion that you either drilled in places where oil seeped to the surface, like in the first Pennsylvania fields, or you relied on geology.

In 1901, when Jacques de Moran, a celebrated French archaeologist, said he had stepped into pools of tar and pitch while searching for early ruins in the Zagros Mountains in Persia, d'Arcy jumped. He assembled a group of associates, including de Morgan, a British nobleman who had contact with high-placed customs officials in Persia, and an Armenian and sent the trio to Tehran to negotiate with the Grand Vizier. De Morgan suggested they drill either on the Turkish-Persian border in the northwest territory or in the southwestern corner near the present Iraqi border. The Czar didn't like oil to be discovered too close to his Caspian Sea fields, but de Morgan, the nobleman, and the Armenian took advantage of the absence of the only Russian in their embassy who could read Farsi to get a concession twice the size of Texas for 40,000 pounds and 16 percent of the net profits, if they actually found oil.

As any dimestore novel about oil would have it, d'Arcy nearly went broke over the next ten years. Eventually he had to have Burmah Oil come in with extra capital, but oil was struck on May 26, 1908—when the Royal Navy was finally beginning to convert to oil, and a lush procurement contract went to Burmah. Still, d'Arcy's troubles weren't over. In 1909, he and Burmah Oil formed the Anglo-Persian Oil Company to build the 150-mile pipeline that would bring the oil down from the mountain and the refinery to treat it at the port of Abadan. The pipeline and refinery construction was just as tortuous as the original drilling, and neither was finished when Winston Churchill, a budding Liberal politician of thirty-seven, was appointed First Lord of the Admiralty. Fisher urged him to contract for oil with Shell, but Churchill eyed with increasing interest the new Anglo-Persian company and its vast concession. The Abadan refinery went onstream in 1913, and in July 1914, Churchill told Parliament in a celebrated address that the government should buy 51 percent of the company so as to make the Navy "the independent owner and producer of its own supplies of liquid fuel." Fisher, who believed government ownership was socialism, bitterly denounced Churchill, but the day after World War I broke out, the House of Commons quickly voted the $70 million appropriation for the stock purchase.

The Persian oil was a great bargain. In fact, after the war, the weak and corrupt Qajar government in Tehran learned it had been cheated out of millions by the company's secret agreement to sell oil to the Royal Navy below world prices, in return for British military backup should Persia try to cancel the concession or demand higher royalties.

Anglo-Persian became, in turn, Anglo-Iranian and British Petroleum and held onto its Iranian monopoly until 1951, when the Iranians first tried to nationalize their oil. BP was forced to invite Exxon, Mobil, Socal, Gulf plus Shell, and Compagnie Française des Pétroles to join the exploration (and to face Shah Muhammad Riza Pahlavi's anger; when he found out, he began rationing Iranian output).

BP was never just a procurement agency for the Royal Navy, and if Iran was the crown jewel for sixty-seven years, the company also had oil fields in Iraq, Kuwait, and the emirates. Until the Shah's overthrow in 1978, BP got 39 percent of its crude from Iran, 13 percent from Nigeria, and 12 percent from both Kuwait and the North Sea. It owns 52 percent of Standard Oil of Ohio, bought the European petrochemical facilities of Union Carbide and Monsanto, and has taken over the downstream oil and gas operations of Veba AG in Germany. Its arm's-length relationship with the British government, which now controls only 48 percent of its stock, is elaborate and, says Anthony Sampson in *The Seven Sisters*, based on self-deception. On several occasions, government officials have thought of BP as a Frankenstein monster. The company doesn't take advice from the Foreign Office, and the Treasury Department accountants have never really managed to extract the truth about British Pete's sources of profit. Chairman Eric Drake talks with tolerant amusement about various cabinets' attempts at understanding oil. He can always get to see the Prime Minister and, somewhat condescendingly, hopes Americans will one day realize that the conflict between Washington and the Sisters is wasteful, that all consumers now have the same interest. In 1979, Iran's Revolutionary Council cut BP's umbilical cord to the fields d'Arcy and his roustabouts discovered seventy-one years earlier and forced the company to scramble for alternate, and costly, supplies in Saudi Arabia, Kuwait, and Nigeria to meet its refining operations. The shift has altered BP's historic profile as a major seller of crude to a more integrated posture and forced it into downstream operations, where traditionally it has had little expertise.

Texaco, as well, is an oil giant trying to adapt to dramatically changing times. With revenues of nearly $40 billion (66 percent foreign-earned), Texaco is the world's fourth largest company. It gets 58 percent of its crude from Saudi Arabia, 17 percent from domestic wells, and 11 percent from Indonesia; in this mix lies the trouble that gangling, deceptively amiable Maurice G. (Butch) Granville is trying to correct. Under the long and autocratic rule of Augustus Calvin Long, Texaco developed a style and a strategy that made it one of the wonders of the industry, but Gus Long and the wonder are both gone, as is his vast globe-girdling assumption that there would always be an unending supply of oil.

Texaco always took pride in being the meanest of the big boys. It never pretended it was a benevolent institution for world peace, and it always drove a hard bargain. Its parsimony is legendary. Its middle management people worked harder and longer and were paid less than their counterparts in other companies. Texaco pinched pennies and squeezed dollars, negotiating tough terms with its suppliers and its partners alike. It may have lavished millions on its new executive office building in Westchester County outside New York City (where it was a tenant in the Chrysler building for over half a century), but it neglected to tell its employees that in moving to the suburbs they would be working forty-five minutes longer each day for the same pay. Former Texaco men lovingly exchange stories about the pennypinching. In Libya, it is said, when Texaco cabled Colonel Muammar Qaddafi a new price agreement, executives cabled by cheap night-letter rate.

During the 1950s and 1960s, Gus Long spread the red star the length and breadth of the new interstate system—Texaco was the first to have service stations in all fifty states and to hang on stubbornly to a nationwide system in the post-1973 retrenchment. It acquired Deutsche Erdol, the biggest German oil company, in 1966, and Caltex's European marketing operations—until it was refining 700,000 barrels a day (b/d) of its Saudi crude in Europe. However, Texaco made only half-hearted efforts upstream to diversify away from the Middle East. Its attempts in the North Sea were (until recently) unsuccessful, its efforts in Nigeria and Angola disappointing, and its hopes in the Amazon basin of Colombia, Ecuador, and Peru overoptimistic. In the 1960s, its biggest new source of supply was Libya, where it broke rank with the Sisters in 1970 and agreed to Qaddafi's demand for higher prices. At home, meanwhile, Texaco production peaked out in 1971. It poured half a billion dollars into offshore Texas alone, but it had no real stake in the one big discovery the United States produced in the 1960s—the North Slope ("Gus Long says there's no oil in Alaska," was a company dictum long before Exxon brought in its discovery at Prudhoe Bay). Long always explained Texaco's success in terms of its balance—the company consumed about as much oil as its refineries produced and refined about as much crude as its wells turned out. It neither bought large amounts of high-priced U. S. crude, as Mobil did, nor generally cut prices to move into a glutted world market, as Gulf and Chevron did. Like BP, Texaco was behind the times when OPEC happened, and what mattered was no longer what production profit would support what market loss, but how much profit could be made refining and marketing oil that no longer had any profit whatsoever.

Texaco had its origins in the famous Spindletop gusher in 1901. The Texas Company survived the exhaustion of Spindletop when it found more oil in nearby Sour Lake and over the next seventy years always managed to find new oil in the United States. It is still at it. Since 1970, Texaco has bought $1 billion in federal leases, and it has 6.9 million acres of land not yet fully evaluated. In Canada, it has prime positions in the booming West Pembina and Elmsworth areas of Alberta. In the North Sea, its wholly owned Tartan field, developed at a cost of $450 million, yields 87,000 b/d. Granville has worked out participation agreements with Angola, Ecuador, and Nigeria and service contracts with Venezuela and Saudi Arabia. "I guess we're in the process now of trying to really, fully understand where we stand on refining and marketing profitability," he says. In the past, improving profits all too often meant cutting costs, doing without rather than investing for higher returns, and Texaco notoriously did without the staff work—the planning, the forecasts, the full paraphernalia of modern management methods and controls that other big corporations find essential. Texaco is wary of diversification out of oil but has nonetheless acquired the basic know-how and reserve position in uranium, oil shale, coal, and tar sands. "We've invested over $10 billion in the last seven years," says Granville, "and those investments were made because we expect to make a profit on them. We had to spend a lot of money to stay where we are, but there was also a lot of investment made to improve our position."

* * *

Mobil, like Socal, another offspring of the Rockefeller empire, is an oil giant poor in oil but rich in business savvy. It is also the supreme diversifier, the owner of Montgomery Ward and Container Corp. of America and fast moving into chemicals. Mobil Oil gets 20 percent of its income from businesses other than oil and gas. Its annual revenues are over $40 billion, and 59 percent of it comes from outside the United States. It has much less crude than the other giants; its crude-poor position dates back to its origins. Mobil began in 1866 as Vacuum Oil Co., a sophisticated refiner of lubricants (it's still strong in lubricants and in 1976 introduced Mobil 1, a synthetic engine oil; sales of this pioneering product have by far exceeded expectations). In 1878, Rockefeller bought the controlling interest in Vacuum and three years later folded the company into his Standard Trust. At the same time, he set up Standard Oil Co. of New York (known by its telegraphic address Socony) as the trust's administrative, refining, and marketing arm in the northeastern United States. When the Supreme Court broke up the trust in 1911, Socony and Vacuum were two of the thirty companies spun off, and both quickly started to grow on their own. Vacuum continued to expand in refining, and Socony integrated backward into production. In 1931, the two merged with the blessings of a federal court.

Rawleigh Warner has been chairman and chief executive officer since 1969. Instead of working his way up through the grimy refining end of the business, he climbed to the top on the financial ladder. On the move into nonoil, Warner says he and his staff didn't see the writing on the wall of government intervention in *consuming* countries but did foresee the greater involvement of governments in producing areas way before 1970. The industry rates Mobil, along with Exxon, Shell, and BP, as the most technically sophisticated of the Sisters, but Mobil has never had the success that should go with such expertise. Typically, it "found" more oil in 1974 by negotiating with its Aramco partners than most drillers come across in a lifetime. With some big dollars and the stroke of a pen, it increased its Saudi share from 10 to 15 percent. Today, it gets 56 percent of its crude from Saudi Arabia and 15 percent from the United States.

Mobil is something of a maverick in public relations. Where Texaco is downright secretive and the other majors less than open-mouthed, Mobil deploys every weapon in the PR armory; it is famous for its "issue" and "advocacy" advertising. Few companies can rival Mobil in the artfulness and sophistication with which it presses its opinion on the public, whether it is endorsing oil price controls, resisting Congressional proposals to end vertical acquisitions, or championing the case for mass transit. With strong advocacy goes bristling resistance whenever Mobil sees alleged unfairness on the part of the media. Most corporations prefer to minimize controversy if at all possible, but Mobil has been in a variety of rows—complaining loudly about inaccuracies and distortions on TV newscasts, feuding with the networks about their unwillingness to run TV commercials on "controversial" topics, and lamenting the poor press coverage the oil industry receives when a favorable newsbreak does occur. Warner makes no claim that Mobil's PR efforts move public opinion on specific issues but thinks his company has gained recognition "that we're unique and different from the other entities in the industry."

Shell, the world's second largest corporation, certainly is different. For one thing, it has two home countries and makes every effort to obscure that fact. It likes to cultivate the "group" image and to present Shell Oil, Deutsche Oil, Shell Italiana, Shell Senegal, and the 114 other affiliates as so many modest local companies which just happen to have a committee of managing directors who are English and Dutch. From the beginning, Shell has been keenly aware of the frailties and susceptibilities of international discourse because, until the North Sea discoveries, it never had a drop of oil at home. Marcus Samuel was a Jew from London's East End, and —although Britain successively made him Sir Marcus and Lord Bearsted—the Admiralty, Churchill, and successive governments never quite trusted him to be totally loyal to king and country. Marcus was too cosmopolitan, too international. Over the years, the very precariousness of Shell's position astride nationalism gave its leaders an extraordinary vantage point and made them more open-minded, more aware of political nuances and shifts than BP and the American Sisters. From their dual headquarters in London and The Hague, Shellmen, as company officers like to call themselves, maintain an aloof distance from governments while trying to educate politicians in the eternal verities of oil. They see themselves as dedicated professionals with no sinister power who have fully resolved and clarified in their own minds their relationship to the world order. If they are told that Shell is precisely the kind of monolith that is largely beyond the control of any government, they will patiently answer that there is no such thing as an international corporation, that each member of the group is subject to the laws and sovereign will of the country in which it operates. If they are told that the center of decision making rests with the parent company's management, they will say that the Shell group's decisions are decentralized, even if capital expenditures above certain levels do require "discussion and agreement." Somewhat disingenuously, they will add that investment decisions in the oil industry are made in response to opportunities. Gerry Wagner, the chairman of the eight men who run Shell, is a Dutch lawyer; the second in command is Frank McFadzean, a Scottish economist who sees companies like Shell as beleaguered victims of tribal assaults throughout the world. A third of the $60 billion revenues are earned in the United States, but the group tactfully refrains from breaking down its figures by nation-states. The origins of its supplies, however, are no secret and are almost evenly split over the Middle East (14 percent from Kuwait, 11 percent from both Saudi Arabia and Oman, 10 percent from Iraq, and 7 percent from Qatar).

With oil from Czarist Russia, Marcus Samuel clashed with Rockefeller in the Far East before World War I; he managed to stand up to the Standard Trust by building storage tanks in key distribution points in Asia and a fleet of tankers of a new design, which, it so happened, fitted the stringent requirements of the Suez Canal Co. For sixteen years, the Far East trade was a three-way slugfest among Standard, Shell, and a Dutch East Indies concern called Royal Dutch. Standard had the millions to undercut anybody; Shell had the ships, the storage tanks, and oil in British Borneo; but Royal Dutch had huge reserves in Sumatra, and it had Henri Deterding, a brilliant and aggressive young bookkeeper. In London, Samuel was the epitome of the Edwardian *parvenu*, a stout and portentous figure who enjoyed being Sir Marcus and, for a year, Lord Mayor of the City. Rockefeller was an arrogant and aging millionaire, and Standard Oil was run by John Archbold, a jovial, popular Irishman who was said to have "laughed his way to the top." When Deterding was put in charge of selling Royal Dutch oil throughout the Far East, he was twenty-nine and determined to be the architect of Shell's ruin.

In 1903, when the world oil trade slumped and Archbold continued to cut prices and Samuel's tankers lay idle, Sir Marcus was forced to discuss a merger with Deterding on humiliating sixty–forty terms and the understanding that Deterding would be managing director. The merger went through in 1906, and today the top management is still sixty–forty Dutch–English, although the shareholders are 39 percent British, 19 percent American, and 18 percent Dutch. "The British public and most of the rest of the world except Holland still knew it as Shell and regarded it as a British company," Sampson wrote in *The Seven Sisters*. "But the British government now regarded it as being Dutch, and hence vulnerable to influence from Germans—a suspicion of which Sir Marcus became painfully aware." BP was nursed into prominence because the Admiralty and Churchill now trusted Shell even less. Sir Marcus was desperately anxious for his company to be accepted as part of the imperial service, but, from the beginning, "Shell raised the question that was to run through each company over the following decades: was it an international business, buying and selling oil between any nations, wherever the best profits were to be made or was it part of the special interest of a single nation?"[5]

Deterding ran Shell for thirty years. With Archbold's successor, Walter Teagle, Deterding was the "titan" of oil, and the two of them spent the better part of the 1920s and 1930s fighting over markets and territories. Deterding became increasingly autocratic and politically reactionary. In his seventies, he married Charlotte Knack, his German secretary, and became convinced Nazism was the only bulwark against a Soviet menace. His fellow directors managed to ease him out of the chairmanship, and he went to live permanently on his estate in Mecklenburg in Germany, where he died six months before the outbreak of World War II.

Shell has retained its original sixty–forty Dutch-British binationalism. All assets, interests, and dividends on the one hand and all taxes and expenditures on the other are divided sixty–forty by the two halves. Shell Petroleum NV in The Hague and Shell Petroleum Ltd. in London are responsible for the disposition of the group's capital, its investment policy, return on capital, and the related appraisal of results. The focal point of the whole organization and the ultimate seat of power is the committee of managing directors.

Unilever, the other big binational company, is a straightforward fifty–fifty union of Unilever Ltd. in London and Unilever NV in Rotterdam. Either one or the other owns all the capital in most of the subsidiaries. The two parents are separate companies but so closely linked that they work as one. Each director is on the board of both, and at the top there is a special committee of three execu-

[5] Anthony Sampson, *op. cit.*, p. 58.

tives to which the board has delegated most of its functions and which makes virtually all ultimate decisions.

"Does Exxon Have a Future?" *Forbes* asked in a teasing headline in 1977 before it proceeded to speculate that sheer frustration, not government edict, might force the world's mightiest company to liquidate itself partially.[6] Exxon would like to use its huge resources to develop other forms of energy, but if American public opinion should prevent the Sisters from developing sun power, coal, uranium, or "synfuels" because it considers the oil giants to be too big, Exxon might have to break itself up by paying out most of its riches to its shareholders. Two years later, when the company and the other majors declared sky-high earnings (Texaco 211 percent, Mobil 131 percent, Exxon 118 percent for the third quarter of 1979), Exxon seemed to edge closer toward self-destruction as politicians called for shackles on the oil companies, and it seemed unlikely that Washington would allow them to invest their hoards in *anything*.

Exxon *is* a breathtaking phenomenon. In 1974, it was stripped of most of its foreign concessions, but it seemed assured of getting its oil anyway because OPEC members needed Exxon as much as Exxon needed the cartel's crude. Four years later, OPEC members began selling more of their oil on the spot market to the highest bidder, and Exxon seemed to be the loser again. After the Ayatollah's revolution, it lost most of the half million barrels it was buying in Iran every day, and its recent searches for new oil have been disappointing. But the billions continue to roll in faster than Garvin and his brain trust can find ways of using them. Since OPEC is the supplier of last resort, every time the cartel raises prices, the value of *all* oil rises accordingly, giving the majors "inventory profits" and boosting revenues from oil that they own and produce elsewhere. When these increases outpace operating costs, profits soar.

Exxon tries to spend these profits—$5 billion in capital development and exploration in 1979 alone, while handing out only $1.5 billion in dividends to its stockholders. Still, $65 billion were racked up in sales, 73 percent outside the United States. Its dilemma, says Richard Gonzalez, a Houston oil consultant and former Exxon economist, "is finding a new game comparable in size to oil."

[6] *Forbes*, August 15, 1977, p. 36.

The old game is still responsible for 99 percent of Exxon's revenues. And what a game it was, full of ironies, suspense, and a cast of thousands of senior executives systematically recruited from the universities, earmarked and watched for promotion. The first irony is that it was the breakup of the Standard Trust that sent the stripped-down company overseas and eventually turned it into a major force on the world scene. The biggest irony, however, is that its earliest success in the 1860s was in finding a way to control the disastrous overproduction that periodically hit the budding industry in Pennsylvania and turned the lives of the men who flocked to the oil region from excitement to misery. The year after the first discovery, the price of a barrel of oil was twenty dollars; a year later it was ten cents. Rockefeller's ruthless genius was to put an end to the appalling instability of the ramshackle industry. By undercutting his rivals and getting rebates from the railroads to gain a firm hold over transportation, he established a monopoly to keep up the price at times of glut. By 1870, after only seven years in business, the thirty-one-year-old Rockefeller established Standard Oil Co. with a million-dollar capital, of which he himself owned 27 percent. Thirteen years later, he formed the Standard Oil Trust on a continental scale. The trust allowed him to get around laws forbidding a company in one state from owning shares in another, and for thirty years, he and his lawyers pretended all the Standard companies were independent. By the turn of the century, Standard Oil was almost untouchable by state governments and even by Washington, whose regulatory powers were minimal. Through bribes and bargains, it established "friends" in each state legislature. Its profits were big enough to finance its expansion, and as the oil industry grew and moved from Pennsylvania to Ohio, Kansas, California, and Texas, Rockefeller kept buying oil fields and refineries. By 1885, Standard Oil was exporting oil to Europe and the Far East; of the world's annual consumption of 35 million barrels, Rockefeller supplied 30 million.

The Theodore Roosevelt Administration began its antitrust suit in 1906. Rockefeller himself appeared to give testimony. To his own lawyers, he described how he had benignly built up his empire, but as soon as the special prosecutor began cross-examining him, his mind, as one newspaper noted, "was opaque as an oyster shell." The Supreme Court upheld the government in 1911 and ordered Standard Oil to divest itself of all its subsidiaries within six months.

Rockefeller lived to be ninety-eight, and when he died in 1937, the Standard Oil Company of New Jersey, which the government let him keep, was called Esso and, with Shell, dominated the world's oil. In the Middle East, it had come to be regarded as the leader of the American companies, dealing with the Saudi royal family as if it were a sovereign state. In Peru, it virtually ran American foreign policy. Walter Teagle was a friend of presidents, even of Franklin D. Roosevelt, and only ran afoul of public opinion when he wasn't fast enough out of Germany after Hitler invaded Poland. Although there was nothing treasonable about that—the United States wasn't at war with Germany for the first two years of World War II—Teagle was forced to resign at the end of 1942 (Renault was nationalized at the end of the war by General Charles de Gaulle for a similar crime).

Eugene Holman, who followed Teagle, was a geologist who prided himself on his planetary vision and global statesmanship. He engineered Exxon's entry into the Chevron-Texaco jackpot in Saudi Arabia. Monroe Rathbone took over in 1960 and faced a problem Rockefeller would have recognized—an oil glut. A chemical engineer who had come up through the traditional Exxon ranks, Rathbone was regarded as one of the more farsighted bosses. As Deterding had done in the 1920s, Enrico Mattei, the combative, aggressive, and exasperating head of ENI, bought cheap oil from the Soviet Union's big new Ural fields. Mattei, who invented the expression *le sette sorelle* and saw the Seven Sisters as a relic of the colonial past, was determined to launch an all-out war in Italy. Exxon and BP, the chief rivals of ENI's Agip filling stations, were forced to lower their prices, and Mattei's price war eventually forced them to cut their "posted prices" in the Middle East. Rathbone tried to make peace, and Mattei was invited to Washington, when he died in a plane crash in Sicily. Italian leftists have always believed Mattei was murdered by one of his many enemies, but ENI had already been prepared to make peace; it couldn't support the price war much longer.

Ken Jamieson presided over Exxon during the most difficult years. The tall Canadian from Medicine Hat, Alberta, took over from Rathbone in 1965. Over the next decade, he saw OPEC come into existence and become powerful enough to force the world's advanced countries to their knees. Exxon, Shell, Mobil, Texaco, BP, Chevron, and Gulf set up the producing countries and, over the fifty years of apprenticeship, taught the Saudis, Iranians, Venezuelans, Libyans, Algerians, and Indonesians the old discipline of any trust—the ability to withhold supplies to force up prices—and the new math of diminishing reserves. Mattei and other "oilmen without oil," such as Occidental Petroleum's Armand Hammer and Continental Oil's (Conoco) Leonard McCollom, persuaded the producing countries that they were being cheated and that they didn't need Exxon, Shell, and the other Sisters. Before Gus Long, it was Hammer who first caved in to Qaddafi on higher prices—Oxy had no alternative to Libyan oil fields—but it was Jamieson who saved the pieces once OPEC realized its power.

Garvin became Jamieson's successor in 1975, when he was fifty-three, and is expected to preside over Exxon when oil alone can no longer absorb its vast cash flow and it must decide on the next game. Garvin and the rest of the brain trust on the fifty-first floor of Exxon's tower on Manhattan's Sixth Avenue know what they would like to do with the cash flow—pump large amounts of the surplus funds into businesses with a brighter future than oil. "We're always interested in any new technology that has to do with energy," says the large, mildly loquacious Virginian. "I happen to believe that somewhere down the road, in thirty or forty years, we're going to be fundamentally an electrically based society." To prepare the way, or hedge its bets, Exxon has moved into leading edge semiconductors, bankrolling a Silicon Valley outfit called Zilog.

4

The Next Ten

Whereas the $10 billion-plus titans remain immovable juggernauts—impervious, it seems, to the ebb and flow of economics and history—the Next Ten reflect much more closely the ups and downs of international trade. With $7 billion in sales, Nippon Steel used to belong to this group of multinational corporations, but overcapacity and recession in the advanced nations have made governments resort to "orderly marketing"—negotiation of "voluntary restraints" with Japan, Taiwan, and South Korea and, in Nippon Steel's case, making its foreign sales fall below its domestic revenues.

This development is a significant departure from the goals of unfettered world trade that were enshrined in the 1948 General Agreement of Tariffs and Trade. GATT still embodies the basic ground rules for trade, but the rules are being bent by rising pressures in North America and Europe to protect workers in aging and arthritic industries such as steel. At the same time, the Less Developed Countries (LDCs), reeling under the impact of huge oil payments and mounting debt, are clamoring for help in stabilizing, if not raising, their earnings from raw materials that are so vital to their economies. Orderly marketing, another phrase for market sharing, is a form of creeping cartelization, and it has shown up in "voluntary" arrangements that the United States has negotiated with Japan, Taiwan, and South Korea, limiting their exports of television sets and shoes, and the European Economic Community's arrangements with Japan to restrain Japanese steel, shipbuilding, and other products to the EEC.

If Nippon Steel is no longer a multinational by the definition of earning more than half its revenues abroad, a cheap dollar and comparatively cheap energy in America have made Dow Chemical join the multinational club for the first time. The maturing world car market and the rise of the yen, on the other hand, have made the foreign sales of Toyota Motor Co. and Nissan Motors slip below the magic 50 percent mark. The pains of middle age are also giving P.S.A. Peugeot-Citroën and Fiat smaller foreign than domestic sales. Renault sells 46 percent of its cars and trucks outside France, but it is spending $350 million on plants in Mexico, Rumania, Yugoslavia, and Portugal. By 1985, one of every three Renaults will be built outside France, and if the earnings of Renault and everybody else stay relative to one another, the French automaker, which wants to sever its remaining financial tether to the Paris government, will slide in between Volkswagen and Hitachi among the $10 billion-plus giants.

ICI was born with a previous attempt at cartelizing world trade. Imperial Chemical Industries Ltd. was the conscious British answer to America's E. I. Du Pont de Nemours and Allied Chemicals and Germany's I. G. Farben. Founded in 1926, ICI was Britain's chip in the 1920s trade wars and in the chemical industry's decision to negotiate orderly marketing. A Du Pont official recorded for his company's confidential files what ICI chairman Sir Harry McGowan told him. "The formation of ICI is only the first step in a comprehensive scheme to rationalize the chemical manufacture of the world." [1]

The chemical industry was not the only one in the 1920s and early 1930s where companies agreed to limit their penetration of each other's backyards and to parcel out third-country markets. The usual pattern reserved Eastern Europe for the German leader in an industry, Latin America belonged to the United States leader, and the vast Commonwealth to Britain's leader (although ICI and Du Pont agreed to form jointly owned subsidiaries in Canada and South America). Ironically, what got Walter Teagle into trouble with American public opinion was that Exxon lived up to one of these understandings, which stipulated that Farben stay out of the oil business in exchange for Exxon staying out of the chemical industry, and to a joint Farben-Exxon agreement to exchange patents. Admitting there was nothing uniquely sinister about this, a Roosevelt Administration trustbuster said of Teagle and his counterpart at Farben in 1942, "What these people were trying to do was to look at the war as a transitory phenomenon

[1] George W. Stocking and Myron Watkins, *Cartels in Action* (New York: Twentieth Century Fund, 1946), p. 103.

and at business as a kind of permanent thing." After World War II, the Allies dismantled Farben for war crimes, and out of its ashes grew Hoechst, Bayer, and BASF.

If we except the binational Shell and Unilever, ICI is (after BP) the second biggest British company. With annual revenues of $12 billion (52 percent earned outside the United Kingdom), ICI is less than a billion dollars behind BASF and less than a billion ahead of Dow Chemicals. Like its American and German competitors, ICI lives on a fine edge of substantial gains and recurring overcapacity. In 1978, it moved heavily into the U. S. petrochemical market with a $700 million ethylene complex in Corpus Christi, Texas, in a joint venture with the U. S. subsidiary of the Belgian chemical giant, Solvay & Cie, and Champlin Petroleum Co. of Fort Worth. ICI likes to maintain an aggressive investment program. "It's a question of keeping our nerve while signs are that the world economy isn't going to pick up for a while," said treasurer Alan Clements when ICI raised $175 million on the New York bond market for the Corpus Christi venture. Company executives claim they see no reason for abandoning their long-term strategy of investing heavily in growth markets and in operations that exploit ICI's technical strengths. ICI has expanded its basic chemical capacity in Britain and Germany while shedding low-profit textile and clothing manufacture—as well as 10,000 employees from its 192,000 employee roster, despite acute sensitivity to rising unemployment everywhere. In recent years, ICI successfully launched the nonpersistent herbicide paraquat, which has quietly made the plow obsolete in many of its age-old applications (even if pot-smokers have been unhappy with the spraying of it on Mexican marijuana harvests). The company also developed fungicides that are taken up inside growing plants, insecticides that are selective in what they kill, beta-blocking drugs, an anticancer drug with benign side-effects, and fiber-reactive dyes. The dyes solved the problem of how to obtain the full range of bright, wash-fast colors and made possible the pop-art fashion in clothing that started in London in the 1960s.

ICI has had every reason to join the cleansing of the industry's image. It has had no Love Canal toxic waste nightmare, but in 1977 it accepted the claims of 2,000 victims of its drug Eraldin (practolol), a relatively new agent promoted as a unique contribution to cardiac arrhythmias and hypertension. The chemical industry ranks lowest in image of thirteen industries surveyed annually by New York pollster Yankelovich, Skelly and White Inc. Ronnie Hampel, ICI's commercial general manager, thinks it's unfair. "People accept the benefits of chemicals out of hand, but they don't believe the industry is doing enough to manage the risks. We believe we're acting responsibly."

BAT Industries is the largest foreign employer in the United States. It is also the largest British nonoil investor, and it is in America that it learned to sanitize tobacco out of its corporate name. And it is one of the few multinationals deeply implanted in the third world, from the Indian subcontinent and Central America to eleven black African countries.

Tobacco remains a disturbed commodity. World stocks reflect political rather than commercial pressures, and despite great advances in research and knowledge of how to minimize the hazards of tropical agriculture, world average yields improve by only 1 percent a year. Cigarette consumption, however, increases about 2 percent annually, except in North America and Europe where vigorous antitobacco campaigns coincide with ever-increasing taxes. Most of the world's tobacco is grown in the third world, and since increases in yields fall below increases in consumption, the only way to grow more tobacco is by planting more. This fuels a running controversy, since it often forces LDCs to neglect food crops.

Following Reynold's Tobacco Co.'s decision to become R. J. Reynolds Industries and Liggett Tobacco's move to change its name to Liggett Group, the seventy-four-year-old British-American Tobacco Co. became BAT Industries in 1976 (and even named its U. S. paper and cosmetics subsidiary BATUS). BAT makes cigarettes, paper, packaging and printing, perfumery and cosmetics products in 52 countries, from Australia to Uganda, Belgium to Zambia, and earns 83 percent of its $7.8 billion revenues abroad. It still buys up tobacco companies, like Brown & Williamson in the United States, but it has diversified into retailing. Gimbel Brothers and Saks and Company are BAT subsidiaries. Together with its tobacco business, its 21 Kohl Corp. stores in Wisconsin, and the 38 Gimbel and Saks stores, BAT counts just over 40,000 employees. In Brazil, BAT's subsidiary Souza Cruz has 83 percent of the cigarette market, making $100 million in profits a year.

BAT Industries likes to call itself a group, and, like Shell, Unilever, and Philips, it has gone a long way to globalize itself. In the developing world, its management is completely indigenous. Since the 1930s, Indians and Pakistanis have been on local boards (63 percent of BAT of India is Indian-owned), and much of the tobacco leaf research is being done in Africa. The local boards have considerable discretion vested in them, and in Brazil and several African countries, BAT Industries has a substantial local minority shareholding.

"Sharing the business with the local people is by no means easy," acknowledges chairman Peter MacAdam, who grew up in Argentina and came up through BAT's Argentinian subsidiary. "It is usually impossible for us to sell shares locally and remit the proceeds to the United Kingdom. In certain developing countries, it is very difficult to place a substantial issue, at least with a broad base of shareholders, either because there are not enough people with money to invest or because those who do have money expect to make much more than the normal dividend from an established industry, that is, by moneylending at exorbitant rates." MacAdam turns the table on the common third world charge that parent companies don't make the most modern technology available to their subsidiaries by saying the only case where BAT's most modern technology isn't made available is when countries put import restrictions on machinery. Likewise, if BAT has ever switched production across national frontiers, it has invariably been to escape punitive taxes, rather than for the sake of cheaper labor.

Saint-Gobain-Pont-à-Mousson grosses $7.5 billion a year (52 percent outside France) by making building materials. The company was organized in 1970 through the merger of the three-century-old Compagnie Saint-Gobain, famous for its safety glass, and the pipework and heavy engineering firm of Pont-à-Mousson SA. From his office on Paris' Avenue Hoche, chairman Roger Fauroux directs the activities of 160,000 employees in 20 countries. The construction materials include flat glass, insulating materials, and fiberglass reinforcements from Scandinavia to Argentina. There is engineering from Iran to Brazil, packaging in Canada. Fiberglass roofing materials are manufactured in the United States, Mexico, and Italy, and contracting in heavy civil engineering is sought and won all over.

Saint-Gobain has diversified away from declining industries and has gone into electronics, buying control of CII-Honeywell Bull, the mongrel French entry in the computer stakes, which has Honeywell of Minneapolis as the biggest single shareholder. Honeywell has retained technical preeminence, although CII-Honeywell Bull develops and produces most of its own computers. Fauroux sees Saint-Gobain as a data processing giant in its own right in the future. CII-Honeywell is the result of a 1975 merger between the faltering Compagnie Internationale pour l'Informatique (CII), created under de Gaulle in the mid-1960s, and Honeywell Bull, the French subsidiary which Honeywell bought from General Electric five years earlier. The Franco-American deal has proved to be of considerable value to both sides, which together claim 10 percent of total world mainframe installations. Tass, the Soviet news agency, bought CII-Honeywell's Iris 80 series when President Carter vetoed the Russians' $6.8 million order for a Sperry Rand 100 series to punish Moscow for harsh sentences imposed on dissidents. Since Honeywell and its French affiliate have full rights to each other's technology, the substitute computer gave the Russians back-door access to leading edge technology.

The fear of IBM made Fauroux propose marriage in 1980 to Olivetti, Europe's largest maker of electronic office machinery. The merger was unique since the usually stringent controls by the company taking charge were deliberately left vague. Some of the major provisions might give strong-willed executives elsewhere a case of jitters, if not ulcers, since Fauroux planned to link Olivetti with CII-Honeywell Bull. His hope: that by the mid-1980s as much as 40 percent of Saint-Gobain's sales could come from computers.

The fourth largest company of the Next Ten is Citicorp, as New York's First National City Corporation renamed itself in 1974. The bank is present in 93 countries, has 46,000 employees, $820 billion in assets, $62 billion in actual deposits, and is the world's second largest privately owned bank (behind BankAmerica of San Francisco). (World trade and investments are multitrillion-dollar-a-year activities, and the following chapter will deal with the stateless capital, money, and currency markets which have developed in a largely unplanned fashion and grown at a staggering pace.)

Dow Chemical is a newcomer among the more-than-half-foreign-revenues companies, a firm which has girdled the globe with bulk-chemical and petrochemical plants and is run by an Italian-born fiscal conservative with a sense of humor. During the fast-growth era of Carl Gerstacker, the company was leveraged to the hilt, and in the company magazine the boss called Paul Oreffice, his financial vice president, "a little old lady in tennis shoes" because Oreffice worried about liquidity. At Gerstacker's retirement party in 1975, Oreffice dressed up as that little old lady. Three years later when he was fifty, Oreffice was named Dow's president and chief executive officer in an upset move that surprised the industry.

"Our research and development expenditure is so great," says Oreffice, "the only way you can get a proper return is to go for a very big market. And no single market—not even the U. S.—can really do the job of giving us a good return." His appointment was a belated recognition that the era of easy expansion was over for Dow. In 1978, the board had to heed his arguments for reducing capital spending to 90 percent of cash flow. He still believes, however, that in chemicals the key to success is to large—and hence the lowest-cost—production. Headquartered in out-of-the-way Midland, Michigan, since it was founded in 1897, Dow, with Dome Petroleum Ltd., owns vast supplies of natural gas in western Canada, where it is building a $600 million ethylene and vinyl chloride complex. "We build plants 30 percent cheaper than anybody else," says Oreffice, "and we're the most internationally minded U. S. chemical company." The polyglot penchant runs in the veins of Dow presidents. At a 1972 White House conference, Gerstacker explained that he yearned for a lonely island on which he might establish the headquarters of an "anational company, independent of allegiance to any country."

With revenues of $6.9 billion, Dow ranks third (behind Du Pont and Union Carbide) among the American chemical companies, but chemicals are America's big export industry, and the Big Three, plus Eastman Kodak, Monsanto, and W. R. Grace, are sure to boost their foreign earnings, at least as long as energy, especially hydrocarbons, is cheaper in the United States. Dow, Du Pont, and Union Carbide run plants on natural gas, which is 30 percent cheaper than the oil derivative naphtha that ICI, Bayer, or BASF must use. This has put the Europeans at a disadvantage in important third markets, especially Latin America and the Far East, which together buy almost a third of American chemical exports. But the big threat to all of them is the oil majors moving upstream to build chemical plants in the Persian Gulf. Shell estimates that plants in the Gulf could produce cheap gas feedstock and in theory make ammonia fertilizers and ethylene (the biggest base chemical "building block") more cheaply than in Europe, even if the more sophisticated plastics, polymers, and fibers could not compete because of transport and high operating costs.

"Do you know how many people around the world are alive because of our products?" E. Bernasconi asks over morning tea. "Do you know how many lead normal lives, have a home and go to work, how many would have to be locked up if it wasn't for us? And, in the other end of the spectrum, how many people will eat because more corn can be grown because of us?"

Bernasconi is the president of Ciba-Geigy AG, and he takes his tea without sugar. He is a man dressed in stern gray, and his office in Basel reflects his severity. Ciba-Geigy makes drugs—psychopharmaceuticals, antibiotics, and medicine to treat cardio-vascular, hormonal, and rheumatic disorders. It makes herbicides—DDT is Geigy's most famous invention—food additives, textile colorings, photochemicals, film for X-ray machines, and cosmetics. Forty-eight percent of its $5.5 billion annual sales come from Europe, 37 percent from the Americas, and 95 percent of what it makes in Switzerland is exported. The Airwick air freshener you put in your bathroom and the Ilford film in your camera are Ciba-Geigy products, but more important to the company, so are a good proportion of the ethical drugs you are treated with. Together with Switzerland's two other drug giants, Sandoz and Hoffmann-La Roche, Ciba-Geigy files over 130 new drug patents every year, although Hoechst and its American rival Merck, of Rahway, New Jersey, dominate the world's pharmaceutical innovations, each filing over 50 patents a year. Because the price of pills is many times the cost of manufacturing them, the drug industry is an ideal one for a high-wage economy; the Top Ten pharmaceuticals are Swiss (3), American (3), German (2) and, one each, Japanese and French. A new drug requires years of painstaking research and testing. The safety checks often take seven years, and the interval from patent to market is just as long. And not every drug has a large market. Rocaltrol, launched in 1978 by Hoffmann-La Roche, is a synthetic substitute for calcitriol, a substance which is essential if the body is to absorb calcium and which the body itself normally manufactures from vitamin D. Rocaltrol can save patients with severely impaired functions of the liver, but it is needed only in minute doses; Hoffmann-La Roche estimates the worldwide demand at under 100 grams a year.

Corporations collect art, but Ciba-Geigy is the biggest of the corporate Medicis. PepsiCo may have Henry Moore sculptures strewn around the lawns of its vast Purchase, New York, headquarters and Seagram Ltd. a foamed-plastic sculpture by Horia Damian in front of its Park Avenue plaza, but Ciba-Geigy has art on all the office walls in Basel and those of various subsidiaries. The company has about 500 works, ranging from Willem de Kooning and the nucleus of the New York school of abstracts to contemporary lesser-knowns. When an employee wants a painting in his or her office, a request is made to an in-house curator, who tries to determine the person's taste in art and provides two or three works from which a choice can be made. A piece will generally remain in an office for about two years, before being rotated to give it the broadest possible exposure.

Ciba-Geigy spends $225 million a year on research, much of it for new laboratories and esoteric research-related equipment, and, together with the other billionaire drugmakers, is plunging deeper into biology and understanding disease. "We are studying the disease process to see what makes it tick," says John J. Horan, chairman of Merck & Co. "When you understand what's happening, you can create a substance that will alter molecular mechanisms." It is believed that the marriage of chemist and biologist will create the new and cheaper drugs that will be needed to qualify for in-

Tomorrow's Wonder Drugs

	1979 R and D Spending (in millions)	New Drug Patents Filed in 1978
Hoechst	$260	54
Ciba-Geigy	225	43
Hoffmann-La Roche	225	48
Merck	190	57
Eli Lilly	165	40
Sandoz	135	42
Upjohn	130	49
Takeda	90	n.a.
Bayer	80	n.a.

Source: Pharmpatent, Forbes.

creasingly chauvinistic national health plans in a myriad of countries, all trying to boost local development and production, even if it means small, inefficient plants that are costly to run. To qualify, drugs will have to be distinctly superior, in their ability to lessen pain and cure ills, to existing prescriptions.

Chase Bank is the seventh of the Next Ten, followed by Colgate-Palmolive. The maker of household and personal-care products rings up sales of $4.3 billion a year. Its subsidiaries include Helena Rubinstein in cosmetics, Hebrew National and the Houston Riviana Food chain, Kendall in textiles, and Bancroft tennis rackets. Colgate-Palmolive has ninety-four facilities in the United States and sixty-six in Austria, England, France, Germany, Italy, and Mexico.

Colgate-Palmolive is perennially outsold two to one by Procter & Gamble in the United States, but worldwide it is double the size of P & G (earning 58 percent of its sales overseas, compared to P & G's 23 percent). Since 1972, New Zealand-born Keith Crane, and his predecessor David Foster, have moved the New York City-headquartered company away from head-on confrontation with P & G to broaden its products in the United States and provide a potential source of new products for its huge and thriving international operation. "Our great disadvantage in the States is that we don't have the big brand names that can finance new products," Foster used to say. "We have no Tide, no Ivory soap, no Crest toothpaste." The move away from soap and toiletries has meant buying into textiles and hospital products, sporting goods, pet foods, and a Florida-based food chain. Like BAT, Colgate-Palmolive likes to finance local operations in local currencies and has been successful at doing just that in Argentina, Brazil, and Venezuela.

CPC International of Englewood Cliffs, New Jersey, produces and sells food products in twenty-six countries. It has regional headquarters in Brussels, Buenos Aires, and Hongkong and totes up sales of $3.2 billion, 63 percent outside the United States. CPC International was born Corn Products Refining Co. in 1906, and if its corporate abbreviation means little to most people, its brand names are famous on any supermarket shelf. They range from Skippy Peanut Butter and Knorr Soups to Mazola Corn Oil, Hellman's Mayonnaise and Gerber Baby Foods.

Under the chairmanship of James W. McKee, a shaggy-looking former Air Force pilot, CPC is ahead of both General Foods and

General Mills in profitability (and only second to Kellogg), and when it comes to leading edge biomass energy it's in the forefront also. Besides being a multinational producer of brand-name groceries, CPC is the world's largest wet miller of corn (so called because the corn is ground wet rather than dry) and possibly the world's largest producer of dextrose, corn starch, and corn oil. CPC has been making ethanol—as grain alcohol is technically known—for twenty years, and in 1980 was considering a joint venture with Texaco to switch its wet milling plant in Pekin, Illinois, out of starches and sweeteners and into ethanol which Texaco would mix with gasoline and market as gasohol. If the company decides to go ahead it will be because government incentives and special circumstances of CPC's Pekin plant make ethanol production attractive, not because international politics has made gasohol this month's panacea for solving the energy problem. "It looks as if making gasoline from petroleum is cheaper than making alcohol from corn, so it's going to depend on what the government wants to do in stretching our supplies with alternative sources," says McKee. This unflappable reaction is typical of CPC, which *Forbes* has called "one of the best managed outfits in the U.S." [2]

J. P. Morgan closes out the Next Ten, with $2.5 billion in revenues, 61 percent of it earned in international banking. The fifth largest American bank has $43 billion in assets and is constantly broadening its offshore activities; it is a believer in the German concept of the "universal bank."

To recapitulate, multinationalism is a characteristic of certain industries. The oil behemoths lead the field—Exxon, Shell, Mobil, BP, Texaco, Chevron, and Gulf—and are followed by the electronics giants, IBM, ITT, Philips, Siemens, and Hitachi followed by Volkswagen and Daimler-Benz in world carmaking. The food and household product companies are unevenly distributed up and down the sales ladder, Unilever and Nestlé among the over $10 billion firms and Colgate-Palmolive and CPC International toward the bottom of the Next Ten. Chemicals are big, from Bayer and BASF to ICI and Dow, and so is international banking, with Citicorp, Chase, and J. P. Morgan. Building materials are not normally a multinational activity, and Saint-Gobain remains an exception. BAT Industries is really the only vastly diversified

[2] Forbes, March 3, 1980, p. 43.

company that can claim to make over half its sales outside its national home base.

Growth—and inflation—are sure to push a number of firms into the league. Just below the 50 percent foreign sales limit and just behind the Next Ten are such household names as Bank of America (with 49.4 percent foreign revenues for a total of $6.9 billion), Coca Cola (45.7 percent of $4.3 billion), Xerox Corp. (47.2 percent of $4.4 billion), and Occidental Petroleum (41.5 percent of $6.3 billion). Big corporations in Europe and Asia whose exact foreign involvement is not known but believed to hover just under the 50 percent mark are Compagnie Française des Petroles ($11 billion in revenues), Montedison, Italy's chemical leader which is deeply entrenched in east-west trade but currently in deficit, the Hyundai Group, South Korea's Number 1 steel, ship, and automobile manufacturer ($3.7 billion sales), and Japan's Mitsui Group, which has $4 billion worth of natural resources investments in the Soviet Union alone. Just behind J. P. Morgan in the runner-up multinationals are two American drug firms, Pfizer (55.9 percent of $2.3 billion) and Merck (51 percent of $1.9 billion).

What multinationalism is made of, therefore, is energy, electronics, transportation, chemicals, drugs, and, to oil it all, banking, with a few traditional food and soap processors forming an odd niche of internationalism. None of the top corporations can be said to be new. Nearly all of them were born with their base industries, the oil, chemical, and food giants, before 1900, the electronics companies evolving out of early twentieth century electrical engineering.

Corporations Earning Over $10 Billion Annually, More Than 50 Percent Outside Their Home Base

		Sales in $ billions—1978	Foreign as percent of total
1	Exxon	60.3	73
2	Shell	45.2	n.a.
3	Mobil	34.7	59
4	Texaco	28.6	66
5	BP	27.4	81
6	Standard of California	23.4	60
7	IBM	21	52
8	ITT	19.3	51
9	Unilever	18	n.a.
10	Gulf	18	51
11	Philips	15	90
12	Siemens	14.4	51
13	Volkswagen	13.3	58
14	Hitachi	12.2	
15	Daimler-Benz	12.06	52
16	Nestlé	11.3	97
17	Bayer	11.3	70
18	BASF	10.7	51

The Next Ten:

		Sales in $ billions—1978	Foreign as percent of total
19	ICI	8.7	52
20	BAT Industries	7.8	83
21	Saint-Gobain	7.5	52
22	Citicorp	7.5	68
23	Dow Chemical	6.9	51
24	Ciba-Geigy	5.5	90
25	Chase Manhattan	4.4	63
26	Colgate-Palmolive	4.3	57
27	CPC International	3.2	63
28	J. P. Morgan	2.4	62

Source: Forbes, Securities and Exchange Commission.

The corporations are organic entities moving—mostly upwards —in relation to industrial shifts and world economic events. World inflation, for one, increases the number of companies earning over $10 billion a year.

The following table indicates the changes that occurred over one year.

		Sales in $ billions—1979	Percentage of change from 1978
1	Exxon	79.1	31
2	Shell	60	33
3	Mobil	44.7	29
4	BP	40.5	47
5	Texaco	38.8	34
6	Standard of California	29.9	30
7	Gulf	23.9	33
8	Unilever	23	4
9	IBM	22.8	9
10	ITT	21.9	13
11	Volkswagen	18	15
12	Daimler-Benz	17.8	13
13	Philips	17.5	2
14	Siemens	16.4	−3
15	BASF	16.4	21
16	Hoechst	15.8	12
17	Bayer	15.2	14
18	Nestlé	13.7	7
19	ICI	12	15
20	Hitachi	11.9	−10

Source: Forbes, Time, company reports.

5

Geobanking

When Generalissimo Francisco Franco died in November 1975, multinationals in Spain began a standard hedging on the national currency. In the face of political and economic uncertainty, they moved to protect themselves against the expected devaluation of the peseta. Their first action was to begin reducing their net asset exposure by "leading and lagging"—that is, by speeding up payments by Spanish subsidiaries to the parent company while the peseta was still worth something and delaying payments by the parent to its Spanish affiliate until after the expected devaluation. While Prime Minister Adolfo Suarez sought $1 billion in new loans to shore up the economy and called Spain's first election in forty-one years, multinational money managers and commercial bank currency advisers tried to figure out by how much the peseta would be devalued once the vote was in. Three months before the June 1976 election, the consensus was that the peseta would be devalued by 15 percent, but other estimates ran as high as 30 percent. Inflation was officially running at 20 percent, but the last two months before the election saw the consumer price index jump by more than 35 percent on a yearly basis; everybody realized the big crunch for the Spanish economy would come just after the vote. On July 12, the new Suarez Administration devalued the peseta by 19.8 percent, meaning that if a multinational doing a million-dollar-a-month business in Spain had both hurried its Spanish subsidiary's remittance and stalled on paying what it owed its affiliate, it had, in just the last month, made twice 19.8 percent, or $396,000.

The multinationals' ability to make money on money is considerable, since most of them operate in scores and scores of countries. No currency is immune. U.S. multinationals don't have their public relations departments tout it, but there is no reason why they shouldn't "lead and lag" on the dollar's weakness. "I have reason to believe the multinational firms and other holders of large asset portfolios have systematically substituted Swiss francs for dollar assets," Swiss National Bank president Fritz Lautweiler said during one of the periodic flights out of dollars.

But speculating on devaluations and revaluations is only part of the reason for the boom in the stateless money market—"stateless" meaning hard currencies held more or less permanently outside the countries that originally printed them, traditionally called Eurodollars and, since the commanding revaluations of marks, yen, and Swiss francs, referred to as Eurocurrencies or xenodollars. World trade and investments are so big that markets needed to finance them obviously have to be very large. The stateless money supply has grown at a staggering pace. Morgan Guaranty figures suggest the net size of the xenodollars grew from $14 billion to $50 billion between 1964 and 1969 and that a decade later, it was over $500 billion. How much currency is traded each day nobody knows.

It all began when banks began to chase after their big domestic customers abroad. After that came the glamorous and once exploding offshore, or strictly overseas, business of the Euromarkets; now international banking is moving onshore to go after each other's home business. Instead of local banks dealing in a single currency in a national marketplace, there is now a vast, global money and capital system, almost totally outside all government regulation, that can send billions of xenodollars hurtling around the globe twenty-four hours a day. The fact that this stateless banking system is sound at a time when the global economy is troubled and political tensions persist says a lot about private power and about the economic impotence of governments.

In general, it can be said that governments and central bankers hate the Euromarkets and that economists think stateless money performs functions on a scale which the International Monetary Fund (IMF) and the World Bank are not mandated to reach. Central bankers think of stateless money as an unruly monster, shattering their domestic policies and the whole exchange house of cards. Regardless of pros and cons, however, an ever-growing proportion of the world's financial requirements *are* being met in the Euromarkets. "These markets," says vice president John Hennessy of First Boston Bank, "have been growing at more than 20 percent a year compounded—a lot faster than our domestic capital markets."

How much money is out there? The linchpin remains the U.S.

dollar, accounting for an estimated 75 percent of the offshore money pool. Before World War II, the British pound was the international unit of trade, but foreigners never held as many pounds as foreigners hold U. S. dollars today. In 1978, *The New York Times* estimated the number of dollars held by foreigners to be over $200 billion in the hands of foreign central banks and over $500 billion in private holdings.[1] A move to unload those dollars could be ruinous for the American currency and the world economy, but, as *The Economist* has put it, foreigners are holding so many U. S. dollars "partly for the unnerving reason that they do not know how else to hold their foreign exchange."[2] Financings may be done in just about any currency, of course. What currency is chosen by a borrower depends on the availability of funds in each currency and the interest rates in one economy vs. the other. Eurobond investors tend to steer clear of dollar-denominated bonds, since they are afraid of further losses in the value of the dollar. Instead, they prefer bonds issued in marks or yen. "The only fixed-interest-rate issues that investors are willing to hold are in harder currencies such as marks and yen," says Geoffrey Bell, an adviser at the J. Henry Schroder Bank & Trust. This explains why Deutsche Bank of Frankfurt tops the list of banks managing Eurobonds.

Recently, the real action has been in syndicated bank loans. Here, major world banks band together to offer multimillion dollar loans, not only to corporations but to governments as well, in both industrialized and developing countries, many of which couldn't meet Eurobond creditworthiness. In 1978, Bank of Tokyo had more Euroloan volume than any other bank— $34.3 billion—but Citicorp was second with $24.1 billion. In all, banks put together more than $65 billion in such loans. Cash-rich multinationals have poured into Euroloans, but so have OPEC countries and even central banks.

Between one-third and one-half of most major banks' activities now take place offshore, and frightened governments try to erect exchange controls specifically aimed at slowing the movement of capital from country to country. But once the money has moved into the Euromarkets, there are no controls, and anyone can trade or invest. Banks that may be tightly regulated at home have no authority to answer to when they go overseas.

[1] Leonard Silk, "For Better or Much Worse, the Dollar Still Matters Most," *The New York Times*, April 30, 1978, p. E5.

[2] "1929 and All This," *The Economist*, October 13, 1979, p. 16.

International commerce is totally dependent on this system, and multinationals could not operate in a volatile world of floating exchanges without it. The system increases the efficiency of moving cash around the globe at a moment's notice. The dangers are that the growth of the market is too swift, that it unleashes new inflationary pressures, and that it may overwhelm the relatively few top professionals who guide the whole thing. The professionals have an answer to that, of course. Says Citicorp's chief Walter B. Wriston, "If governments and central banks intervene more actively to control international credit markets, there can be no doubt that another fruitful source of political conflict among governments will thereby be opened up."

Stateless money was born in London in the 1960s to serve the needs of companies going multinational and of international traders who needed free access to hard currencies. It came of age in the incessant turmoil in foreign exchange markets—partly in spite of, but mostly because of, tight exchange controls. An American example is Rule Number 8 of the Financial Accounting Standards Board (FASB-8) which requires U. S. companies to translate gains and losses in foreign currencies onto the income statement in the quarter in which they occur. FASB-8 has created a whole new reason for multinational business to jump quickly from one currency to another. The irony, as *Business Week* has underlined, is that each move by a national government to limit international money flows and to tie the hands of multinational business has given the system a new reason for being.[3]

The market is going electronic, and all anyone needs to buy or sell in Eurocurrencies is a computer terminal or a telephone. London accounts for 35 percent of the market, but rival centers have grown up in New York, Hongkong, Singapore, the Bahamas, Panama, and Bahrain. The supranational banks are hooked up in a computerized system that allows each to buy and sell certificates of deposit. Cash-short banks can purchase these certificates of deposits from cash-rich banks, and, instead of being forced to deal within the confines of their home base, they can tap a deeper liquidity.

Irresistibly, stateless money has begotten stateless banking. The ability to underwrite securities and place paper on a global scale has become essential to survival for banks and big investment houses, which sell Japanese bonds in New York and French bank

[3] "Stateless Money: A New Force in World Economics," *Business Week*, August 21, 1978, pp. 78-79.

certificates of deposits in Singapore. The big German banks have led the way in providing both commercial and investment banking services on a global basis, and, in the face of high inflation and rising interest rates, the system has invented floating-rate certificates of deposits and floating-rate notes, pegged to the cost of money in London and Singapore. "The global network is now in place," Hennessy said in 1978. "You have international investors who put their funds all over the world. And you have an international market for international paper."

All this success has caused bankers to bury quietly the old gentlemanly rule that you don't poach in your host's home business. Banks are leapfrogging over each other, not only to open branches in each other's money centers, but to buy up second-string chains and offer their services in the hinterlands. American and Canadian banks have gone after big industrial companies in the English Midlands while London banks snored and, via finance subsidiaries, have arranged mortgages for British home buyers. Sumitomo, Japan's third largest bank (behind Dai-ichi and Fuji Bank), owns the Bank of California chain. Another 100 foreign banks have some 300 outlets in the United States, accounting for over 20 percent of all corporate lending nationwide (35 percent in California and 43 percent in New York). Bank of Tokyo, Barclays, and Sumitomo are so big in the United States that they belong to the top league. But Bank of America, Citicorp, Chase, and Morgan cannot really grumble. They themselves have expanded much faster than foreign banks in the United States. The trend is always the same. Banks follow expanding national industries to other countries, but once the banks are implanted somewhere, they begin courting multinationals which do business locally or in third countries. Offshore banking centers come in varying sizes and reputations. Some are associated with somewhat unflattering terms such as tax gimmicks, brassplate mailbox banking, and bookkeeping fiction. Singapore and Hongkong are the two most dynamic in Asia, Singapore alone with an estimated $20 billion pool and forty banks licensed for foreign currency operations. Bahrain has granted over thirty offshore banking licenses. It has become the sponge for a lot of petrodollars and is a convenient time zone between Far Eastern and European markets. Singapore, Hongkong, and Bahrain provide addresses for registering businesses generated elsewhere. The liberal banking regulations in the three city-states, which have little or no income tax on interest earned by commercial banks on offshore loans and exempt foreign currency deposits from withholding taxes, result in advantages that are not inconsiderable; this explains why so many banks book a certain number of loans through these centers. But far more important is the fact that they generate their own business and draw from huge regional bases. Singapore is regarded as the capital of the Asian xenodollar market, or Asian currency market, as Singaporeans call it. Only the subtleties of geography distinguish an Asian dollar from a Eurodollar, and when commercial banks in Asia lend dollars locally, they normally transfer matching deposits from European branches. Hongkong is the *laissez-faire* capital which doesn't even have a central bank—its money is private script issued mostly by the Hongkong & Shanghai Bank. Here, even Moscow's Narodny Bank is in business (and in 1977 got burned in a $7.5 million real estate deal with developer Edward Wong Wing Cheung).

The first Communist bank with capitalist majority control opened in Budapest in 1979. Called the Central-European International Bank, this offshore institution—owned by Societé Generale (Paris), Banca Commerciale Italiana (Rome), Bayerische Vereinsbank (Munich), Creditanstalt-Bankverein (Vienna), and two Tokyo banks, Long-Term Credit Bank of Japan and Taiyo Kobe Bank, with the Hungarian National Bank as the biggest single stockholder—can engage in all kinds of banking business so long as it does so in convertible currencies.

Panama is a somewhat smaller Singapore, playing the role of capital market for Latin America. Nassau is the "nameplate" capital—Citicorp is the second biggest bank in the Bahamas—and has recently become a center for the recycling of oil surpluses. Some 270 financial institutions have a Bahamian home—that is one bank for every 800 inhabitants—and the money business is second only to tourism. The oddest participants in the Nassau market are the "cubicle," or shell, branches, consisting mainly of a license, a filing cabinet, and a desk ("although what's in the desk is another matter," one local banker commented). For a fee, several established banks manage the shells, which involves periodically bringing their accounts up to date. "Nassau has become significant in the overall tax planning and in minimizing the effective U. S. tax rates of the major U. S. banks," says John Shanahan, a banking specialist of the accounting firm of Peet, Marwick, Mitchell & Co. of New York.

The multinationals love it. If stateless banking means all banks can evade national monetary restrictions and offer the same global services, it also means their corporate customers no longer assume that their traditional bankers can best meet all their needs. In short, it means the multinationals can shop around.

They routinely use the Euromarkets to finance their operations at the lowest possible cost, and that often means making end runs around governments. In 1977, Olin Corp. saved a lot of money by using offshore Belgian francs to finance its Italian subsidiary. The Eurofrancs provided a cheap, efficient source of finance for the Stamford, Connecticut, company, but it bypassed Italian monetary policy aimed at lowering inflation by raising interest rates. A couple of years later, when the Carter Administration, through the Federal Reserve, tried the same thing, banks merely went to the stateless money pool to borrow the liquidity they needed to lend to their customers.

Stephen Sohn, the manager of project financing at United Technologies of Hartford, Connecticut, says all manner of banks are constantly pounding on his door, pleading with him to borrow from them. "Certain banks are better than others in a particular part of the world. We evaluate this expertise and many times we find foreign financial institutions or specialized consortium banks to be more apt to do a financing in certain nations. Probably 35 percent of all our financing is with non-line banks."

Bankrolling the subsidiaries' operations in the lowest currency at hand is perhaps the most popular corporate game. Olin has got its French subsidiary to bill its Italian subsidiary for goods in Belgian francs. Dow Chemical uses offshore loans to avail itself of the lowest interest rates. In Brazil, for example, cruzeiros could be borrowed at an effective interest of 11 percent in 1978 and dollars borrowed in Eurodollars for only 9 percent. "Our treasurer in Brazil is trying to decide things like this all the time," Dow treasurer Wilson Gay told *Business Week*.[4] The magazine said that a number of U. S.-based multinationals even considered financing operations in developing countries with xenodollars, while providing a hedge against their European operations in terms of FASB-8 currency exposure. "You can borrow Euromarks as financing for Mexico and still get a mark hedge outside of German exchange controls," says Robert B. Shulman of Conticurrency, a foreign exchange advisory service in New York.

[4] "How Multinationals Play the Euromarkets," *Business Week*, August 21, 1978, p. 79.

Beatrice Foods, the large diversified food company in Chicago which earns 22 percent of its revenues outside the United States, raised $100 million in five-year notes in 1978 to finance its purchase of Tropicana Products. A year later, Bayer raised $200 million in fixed-interest Eurobond issues.

To bankers, the unkindest cut of the multinationals has been do-it-yourself banking. Here, the big corporations bypass the banks altogether and set up their own foreign exchange dealing rooms and lend directly to one another. The biggest and most creditworthy companies can buy and sell IOUs from and to each other. If Dow Chemical, say, puts money in a bank and Mobil borrows it, Dow will receive an interest rate low enough and Mobil will be charged an interest high enough for the difference between the two to earn the bank a margin of profit. Commercial paper (short-term unsecured promissory notes) is an elitists' game. A company that doesn't merit absolute top rating by Moody's and other rating services might just as well borrow from the bank, since it will have to offer a high premium to attract lenders. During the post-Franco hedging on the peseta, multinationals "stayed loaned up" in Spain by lending to one another. National prejudices are disappearing from the commercial paper market. Nestlé and Philips have no more difficulty borrowing working capital in New York than Gulf Oil or Sears.

American banks in the offshore markets are virtually limited to New York, Chicago, and California banks, and after ten years of dramatic expansion abroad, they have reached a natural limit. The Eurocurrency market has become a borrowers' market, and few U. S. banks expect to repeat the kind of profits and growth they achieved in the 1970s. American banks are more sensitive to slim profit margins than nationalized French banks or German savings banks which have no private shareholders to think about, and the decline of the dollar and the parallel rise of the mark, yen, and Swiss franc have given banks in Germany, Japan, and Switzerland a new edge. Bank of America is reviewing the performance of existing overseas operations, instead of opening new offices compulsively all over the globe. Both Citicorp and J. P. Morgan have sold off unwanted bank premises, although Citicorp is still expanding in Africa and is also moving into countries which are opening their doors for the first time—Canada, Spain, and Argentina.

Stateless banking tends to provoke gory headlines. The fact that the big banks, operating through the Euromarkets, have quietly taken over roles as financiers to the world is unsettling. There are doomsday predictions that all this *must* end in a crash. Critics say there is something fundamentally wrong about excessive borrowing to live beyond your means, and most countries are doing just that, going deeper and deeper into debt, not to build productive assets but simply to pay their oil bills. The offshore banking system, in effect, guarantees OPEC against the bankruptcy of consumer nations, including Less Developed Countries that can't afford to pay for their energy imports without continuous borrowing. Very neat for the OPEC producers, the critics say. OPEC doesn't want the risk of selling oil on credit to poor nations; instead, OPEC members invest their surplus in the offshore system and let it take the risk of lending to the LDCs. By supplying credit and creating international liquidity without constraints and with fleeting regard to caution, the critics charge, stateless bankers have usurped the functions that formerly were the domain of official institutions such as the IMF and central banks.

But specialists hold conflicting views on stateless money. Monetarists tend to believe offshore banking's ability to create credit outside the supervision of financial authorities has been a factor in the worldwide surge in inflation. Since there are no reserve requirements, there is no real limit to the amounts of credit that stateless money can create. A single dollar on deposit can serve as the base for $10 or $1,000 in loans. Moreover, there is the multiplier effect among the banks that makes the pyramiding worse. One dollar put in Barclays by Mitsubishi Trust can be lent to the Hongkong & Shanghai, which in turn lends it to Crédit Lyonnais. They can all keep on building up liquidity, since on top of each dollar that changes hands, debt is created.

Defenders of stateless money say that precisely because there is no Federal Reserve to act as a lender of last resort in case of a credit crunch, the banks in the Euromarkets are cautious with credit. Others, such as Yale University professor Robert Triffin, say that U. S. banks in the offshore markets lend to the hilt, believing that the Fed "will never let one of their foreign branches fail."

Calls for central banks to impose reserve requirements on Eurobanks operating within their national jurisdictions have failed on two accounts. While the major countries could perhaps agree to impose such restrictions, it is hard to imagine every country doing so. Thus, Eurobanking would simply shift to the areas free of such controls. The Bonn government tried to squeeze German banks out of the system by forbidding the payment of interest to nonresident depositors but had to give up when all German banks simply shifted their Eurobusiness to their branches in Luxembourg. On a technical level, it would also be difficult to imagine how such requirements would be determined. Should the reserve requirements be the same as those imposed on banks in the country that prints the money, or as those imposed on the country where the money is held?

Money borrowed offshore by industry eventually ends up as factories and machinery somewhere. Academic opinion holds that the credit raised in the stateless markets tends to be a substitute for domestic credit, rather than a new addition to total credit. Thus, the Euromarkets are not the wild money machine of lurid news headlines that spawns credit and fuels inflation. "Inflation has not come about by excessive bank lending," says Milton Gilbert, the retired chief economist of the Bank for International Settlement (BIS), the central bankers' central bank and unofficial watchdog of the stateless money. "The source of inflation is not monetary, but rather the mismanagement of national economies."

Admittedly, governments often put into place tight credit policies that either send interest on loans soaring or dry up credit altogether. Admittedly, banks skirt such anti-inflation policies by going offshore for money, but economists argue that the speculation would have occurred in any event and that, at worst, the stateless money is guilty of speeding up the process. More important, the enormous liquidity of the Euromarkets tends to push down the net costs of borrowing. The pool of stateless money is an alternative, not only to the mammoth U. S. domestic market, but also to the German, Belgian, French, Japanese, and other capital markets.

And bankers and some economists fear that tampering by national governments can only be worse than the existing risks and freedom. Imposing reserve requirements—if they could be agreed upon—may overly constrain the markets, inhibit international financial flows, and do more harm than good.

What attracts corporate treasurers to the offshore money is not difficult to see. It is the mobility and speed with which a banking consortium can be put together and hundreds of millions borrowed in a week or ten days, compared to months on national capital markets. "Bits and pieces of world economic integration are running ahead of a broad range of political and public opinion," says Peter Oppenheimer of Oxford University. "And it's not only a problem for the Euromarkets. Multinational corporations also view the world as a single production base while national authorities try to grapple with individual units."

More and more banks are becoming multinational, all-around financial institutions involved, as we shall see in the next chapter, in tricky political lending. They do management consulting, export and investment promotion, trust and economic advising and face both exciting challenges and hoary risks. How big is the risk of lending to a Communist country, or a country run by a group of generals, or a country in the throes of civil war? Banks have developed highly sophisticated risk evaluation systems based on masses of the most detailed statistics that would surprise a lot of governments. But there has to be a degree of subjectivity in determining a country's political stability, and the harsh truth is that few bankers have enough experience or training to judge. Economists have long been important for banking institutions and hired at princely salaries. Of late, people with global views and experiences have been at a premium.

Global money has blurred the distinction between state-run and private banking as nationalized banks are forced to accept the dictates of modern, i.e., stateless finance and operate exactly like private banks. Global banking erodes both the ideology and sovereignty of governments, but then again, governments have

The World Bank League

Total deposits in $ billions, 1979:

1	Bank of America Corp.	$98.9
2	Citicorp	96.2
3	Chase Manhattan	63.3
4	Deutsche Bank	54.8
5	Banque Nationale de Paris	52.1
6	Crédit Lyonnais	46.7
7	Manufacturers Hanover	45.7
8	Societé Generale	45.5
9	Caisse Nationale de Crédit Agricole	45.2
10	J. P. Morgan	42.4

Source: The Banker, The New York Times.

not grown in international areas. The growth of government everywhere over the last hundred years has been in what we call national, or domestic, areas such as social security, family allowance, national health service, and public education.

U. S. Banks by Money Abroad

International assets in $ billions:

1	Citicorp	$44.1
2	Bank of America	30
3	Chase Manhattan	24.7
4	J. P. Morgan	19
5	Manufacturers Hanover	18.1
6	Chemical	12.8
7	Continental Illinois	10.5
8	Bankers Trust	10.3
9	First Chicago	8.2

Source: Company reports.

Leaders in Eurobonds

Total equivalent in $ millions:

1	Deutsche Bank	$2,578
2	J. P. Morgan	865
3	Crédit Suisse	740
4	Warburg	729
5	Union Bank of Switzerland	494
6	Westdeutsche Landesbank	464
7	Commerzbank	328
8	Dresdner Bank	321
9	Wood Gundy	242.7
10	Orion	242

Source: International Herald Tribune.

6

Now, About Our Little Bill

The way Paul Erdman had it in *The Crash of Seventy-Nine*, it all came tumbling down when Hitchcock, the American adviser to the Saudis, had his clients pull their billions out of the United States. The big Manhattan banks were frightfully overextended, but the President of the United States went on television and told everybody this wasn't 1929. It worked that day; people didn't start a run on the banks—mercifully, a weekend was coming up. But on Monday . . .

The real-life worry isn't that any $10 billion-plus multinational or any of the world banks go belly-up, but that countries do. Some years ago, an aggressive group of LDCs began demanding a new economic order. What they wanted was some formal restructuring to give poorer nations a bigger slice of the global pie. This implied that world leaders had some rational control over events. Inflation, energy prices, currency swings have all contributed to the upheaval in both advanced and developing countries and have shown how little control governments have over events. The rising tide of inflation has eroded public confidence everywhere and has led to a kind of defensive selfishness in support of parochial issues, lobbying for narrow advantages.

Yet the world is less protectionist than it likes to lament. In the decade "before OPEC," 1963–1973, world trade increased by nearly 9 percent a year, and trade in manufactured goods by 11 percent. After the price of oil increased fivefold, both figures were cut in half, but trade still kept growing well ahead of output. The crude tariff walls of the past are out of favor, and the new defensive barriers are more subtle. They range from dubious antidumping pleas and complaints like that of EEC fibermakers against the low feedstock costs of American chemical companies (only one step up from, say, the Libyan complaint against European butter on the grounds that Normandy or Devon get more rain than North Africa) through all manner of incentives, subsidies, regional policies, industrial restructuring, lame duck rescues of floundering big companies, and government procurement. Still, the rich countries' import of manufactures from poor ones grew by 15 percent in 1978; even textile and clothing imports grew by 9 percent. Both the United States and the EEC countries have trebled imports to $21 billion and $14 billion respectively. Japan textile imports have doubled, while the Communist countries have upped these imports from LDCs by only a pitiful $1 billion plus.

The World Bank, the 134-nation organization responsible for reconstruction and development, says LDCs outpace advanced nations, although it would still take one hundred years' for the poor nations to close the gap with industrial countries, even if the growth of the poor nations doubled while the rich economies stood still.

Free trade is not—as trade negotiators have to pretend—a great concession to allow foreigners to send you their good cheap products; it is a benefit to your consumers, but many fast-developing countries aren't eager to open their borders. President López Portillo's decision to have Mexico join the GATT free market agreement in 1980 frightened Mexican businessmen used to a long-captive domestic market. They had little appetite for the competition from Brazil, Taiwan, and Korea and for a while formed a tactical alliance with leftwing economists who argued that entry into GATT meant added Mexican unemployment.

If the less-rich got neither a new world order nor global chaos after the 1973 oil crisis, they got credit. The quintupling of oil prices was expected to impel the industrialized West to run up massive balance-of-trade deficits, but the recycling of petrodollars worked to the advantage of many advanced countries, leaving the major trade burden on those least able to afford it— the poor. And like strapped consumers unable to cut back purchasing and imports that had been fueling their growth, they promptly began borrowing. The Communist countries, with their own economic troubles, followed suit. And as one LDC after another approached default, international conferences were called. Yet the world came through much less scarred than had been feared.

Since then, debt has continued to grow. At the beginning of 1979, the LDCs were working under external debt, most to private banks and the IMF, estimated at $230 billion. This was more than a quarter of their total output and three times the level of their debt at the end of 1973. Jacques de la Rosiere, managing director of IMF, estimated the gap between LDCs' combined imports, oil included, and their exports as over $50 billion a year. Several countries have experienced severe strain. North Korea defaulted on its debt in 1977, and the Philippines and Peru have been forced to "roll over," or reschedule, their debt. Jamaica and Zambia are in almost as bad shape. Officially, Turkey was not in default in 1977 when its debt to foreign banks reached $4 billion, but it had built up large "overdrafts" at major New York banks. Two years later, Israel's external debt reached $20 billion.

New loans and rollovers aren't unusual in international finance, and the big polyglot banks say they are worried neither by the size of the debt nor its diversity. Petrodollar recycling has been accomplished by the banks through the stateless money markets, and most international bankers argue that it is misleading to look at aggregate figures. "There's really no such thing as a limit," says Harry Taylor, executive vice president of Manufacturers Hanover. "One can't look at a country in terms of an absolute ceiling. Each lending bank regularly reviews conditions in a particular borrowing country and makes a decision about what the country's lending limit should be. It is an evolutionary process, and country limits change along with conditions." Citicorp's vice president A. G. Costanzo agrees. "I just can't believe that everybody has lent to the hilt to the scores of LDCs. If so, we'd have figures at least ten times what's on the books. There may be some countries where banks would feel, 'Well, maybe I've got enough in this one basket and therefore in the future I'd want to relate any further lending more closely to the growth of the country's economy and debt service capacity.' When you put it into that context, I doubt if more than a couple of countries would fall into that category."

The U. S. Congress doesn't like to hear such talk. It is worried that American commercial banks become overextended and that eventually the U. S. government will find itself forced to provide aid to the debtor country simply to preserve stability of the American banking system. "Without wanting to cry havoc or shout fire in a crowded theater," says House Banking Committee chairman Henry S. Reuss, "I think the ability of the financial system to pyramid inflationary loans to developing countries is limited and those limits are being approached." The solution, he likes to add, "is not to lower the boom on the banks," but to give some fresh thinking to the global relationship between rich and poor countries.

Tall order. Overlending to countries with no earthly ability to repay on time may be innately silly, but the world's finance ministers have few fresh ideas, or recoil in horror when anything new is being proposed—such as allowing the IMF to go out and raise money in the Eurocurrencies to lend to deficit countries. The IMF represents more than 130 countries (basically everybody except the Soviet bloc). Its main responsibility is to provide loans to countries that cannot pay their bills, on condition that the countries accept often tough belt tightening, but member governments' rivalries and jealousies have kept its influence precarious and somewhat diminished its role as clearing house for coordinating economic policies.

In the absence of government ideas, bankers have become supervisors of shaky economies, laying down austerity terms, overseeing compliance, and playing fall guys to wounded national pride. Morgan Guaranty has had to criticize the Brazilian government for its "slowness" in correcting trade deficits and let it be known that future loans depended on such corrections. Peruvian officials have found themselves forced to follow Citicorp's advice in exchange for receiving continuous loans. In the words of Citicorp vice president Irving Friedman, "We had many conversations with them, to the point that we got accused of dictating. But we were just making it clear that they were not creditworthy."

One upshot of the Iranian crisis that third world sympathizers of Ayatollah Khomenei hadn't expected is that Euromarket borrowing has become more expensive for them. President Carter's freeze on Iranian dollar assets in 1979 reversed the trend toward thinner lending margins and longer maturities on loans, meaning that LDCs found borrowing more costly. Coupled with poor countries' soaring debt-service costs—something like two-thirds of dynamic Brazil's export earnings are consumed by debt servicing—this has nudged a number of hard-pressed LDCs closer to the edge. The LDCs' overall debt service has doubled to 14 percent of their GNP since 1976, despite a 50 percent increase in their exports over the same period. This has translated into a $25 billion rise in their annual debt-service payments since 1977, about half of which can be traced to higher interest alone.

How much more debt can be heaped on LDCs before they collapse into default? *World Business Weekly* asked at the height of the Iranian crisis. "A minority of Euromarket bankers, and many critics of international lending practices, suggest that the straw-that-broke-the-camel's-back stage has been reached, while others point to the LDCs' high overall liquidity—the product of better debt management and prudent Euromarket borrowing—in arguing that the day of reckoning is way off, if it ever comes," *The Financial Times of London*'s weekly answered its own question. "Since 1976, the international reserves of LDCs—the amount they have socked away in their treasuries to pay off loans and other foreign debt—has risen a healthy 43 percent to upwards of $128 billion, more than enough in theory to service their debt. The spectacular rise in the price of gold adds to this safety margin." [1]

The Washington-based IMF receives from LDC governments secret data on their total debt and economic posture. Reuss thinks it would be a great idea if banks could get hold of these figures. William Miller, chairman of the U. S. Federal Reserve Board, wants to see countries with large deficits—and those with large surpluses—forced to submit to full IMF review, whether or not they want to borrow money. But disclosure and the *threat* of disclosure is the IMF's best weapon when it wants to make sure countries don't manipulate currency rates. Besides, data has a way of trickling, mostly through central bankers, to their nation's commercial confreres. And, say the polyglot managers, lending is ultimately a matter of judgment. The dangers of not lending can be as great as those of too much lending.

For much of 1978, McDonnell Douglas workers feasted on 200,000 Yugoslav hams that the company received as partial payment for two new DC-10s that Jugoslovenska Aerotransport bought. Massey-Ferguson, the Canadian tractor company, is selling skis made in Poland, as part of a lucrative joint venture it is undertaking near Warsaw.

Over the past years, the Soviet Union and the European members of its Comecon trading group—Poland, Czechoslovakia, East Germany, Hungary, Rumania, and Bulgaria—have amassed a combined debt to the West of over $60 billion, and swapping hams for jetliners and skis for farm machinery are the devices they have come up with to boost trade. Poland is deepest in trouble, with public foreign debt climbing above $15 billion and

[1] *World Business Weekly*, December 24, 1979, p. 23.

debt repayments reaching $4 billion a year, a sum equal to Poland's total hard currency export for 1977. In a last-ditch effort to head off a debt crunch, the Warsaw government asked Bank-America to put together a syndicate for a seven-to-eight-year balance-of-payment loan of $700 million to $1 billion, the largest in the country's history. The offering had only reluctant takers in the Euromarkets.

The Poles have been trying to shore up their economy by implementing crash programs to relieve food and housing shortages, pushing production of coal and copper, expanding exports, and belt tightening on imports. They have pushed for rapid industrialization and improved living standards, importing Western technology and equipment. The growth of Polish exports to the West, however, didn't keep pace with sharply rising imports and mounting currency debt. Imports were maintained at peak rates for too long. Worker income grew rapidly while available consumer goods increased slowly. To appease workers, food prices were kept artificially low while their costs skyrocketed, production lagged, and subsidies rose. Poor harvests pushed up farm imports.

The Eastern bloc's debt has been accumulated with the willing collaboration of Western bankers and Western governments. Bankers were glad to lend to the Comecon countries some of the petrodollars which poured into their coffers after the oil-price jumps. Governments were glad to grant soft loans at below market interest rates in the hope that these credits would generate exports and maintain jobs. The headlong industrialization, set down in rigid five-year plans, continued in Eastern Europe after the OPEC crunch, partly because the Comecon countries basked under the protective umbrella of "friendship prices" for Soviet crude. The umbrella was ideological. Inflation was a capitalist sin, but in 1977 the Russians threw in the towel and increased the price of its crude to its satellites by 18 percent. In early 1979, they raised the price of a number of consumer goods from beer to restaurant meals, but Czechoslovakia and Hungary increased prices that took their neighbors' breath away: the Czechs doubled fuel prices, post and telephone rates; the Hungarians increased gasoline by 45 percent, electricity charges by 51 percent. The Budapest government took the trouble to tell the people why. Hungary's trade deficit with the West was huge and rising, doubling in one year to $2.2 billion, and the government spent $2 billion subsidizing retail prices. Yugoslavia ran up a

$6 billion foreign trade deficit and had to live with a 20 percent inflation and a $12 billion hard currency debt. The Rumanians pulled the toughest one on its Comecon neighbors. At the height of the summer flow of East European holidaymakers to its Black Sea resorts, the Rumanian government suddenly required them to pay for their gasoline in Western currencies. Thousands of the Communist states' *privilegentsia* piled up, baffled, at the Hungarian-Rumanian border. The East German government delivered a public and unprecedented protest, and the Hungarians imposed retaliatory sanctions. The Czechs, however, negotiated and obtained a ten-day respite for everybody. "We must buy our oil in dollars at the world price," said one carefully coached Rumanian border inspector. "Why should we sell it to the Poles for their zlotys or to the Hungarians for their forints?" For the first time, a Comecon country had broken the unspoken compact of the emperor's new clothes, implying officially that their currencies were, in fact, worthless to anyone but themselves.

"This is the last tenuous thread economically binding these nations together with Moscow, making Comecon and its various 'arrangements' vital to their economic survival," wrote David A. Andelman in *The New York Times*. "Where else could Czechoslovakia dump substandard shoes or machine tools but in Poland and Bulgaria? Where else could Poland buy grain for zlotys but in the Soviet Union?" [2] Rafal Krawczyk, a Polish economist, said something that could have been heretical a few years earlier: "I think it would be a good idea to let foreign capital into Poland in a big way. There is no longer any reason to fear foreign capital will take over Polish industry. And I think we could learn a lot from competition with west European firms in terms of efficiency and organization." In China, where people had come to regard stable prices as almost a natural right, the government mandated a 33 percent increase in food staples, the first since the early 1950s. To make matters worse, Peking decreed that the cost of 10,000 products, a fifth of those on sale, would no longer be fixed but, in a significant departure from rigid planning ideology, be adjusted according to supply and demand.

But before we examine how PepsiCo builds Pizza Hut fast-food restaurants in Bulgaria and how the Czechs and the Soviets woo Volkswagen, let us look at the advanced countries' debt.

[2] David A. Andelman, "An Oil Shock of Their Own Hits Members of Comecon," *The New York Times*, August 17, 1979, p. E4.

If some nations tried to spend their way out of the 1970s recession, Denmark tried to borrow its way to recovery. "Denmark is one big pyramid," one foreigner observer said in Copenhagen. "Everybody is borrowing from everyone else and the government is borrowing all over the world." The little EEC country (population: 5 million) with one of the world's highest standards of living ($7,600 per capita) had no difficulty raising money on the Euromarkets. Foreigners were willing to advance the Danes all the money they wanted because of their gilt-edged reputation for paying their debts and always muddling through what other countries would consider paralyzing crises, but in November 1979, when Denmark's balance-of-payment deficit reached $2.6 billion, Prime Minister Anker Joergensen slapped on the coldest wage-price freeze since Hitler's invasion of 1940. The tough policies didn't live long; Joergensen's Social Democrat coalition government was promptly enmeshed in political concessions because two years earlier it had tried to protect the krone from excessive devaluation by permitting unemployment to rise. When Sweden had been faced with the same predicament, it had devalued its money three times and hidden its rising unemployment by subsidizing companies to keep workers on the job in training programs or trying to stockpile inventories for a better tomorrow. Initially, Denmark tried to maintain the historic parity with the Swedish and Norwegian kroner but stayed out of the third Nordic devaluation, thereby gaining productivity and labor mobility. It allowed unemployment to rise but boosted unemployment benefits to about 90 percent of wages. Sweden, with the world's third highest per capita GNP ($9,530, behind Kuwait and Switzerland) joined the handout club in 1977 when its center-right coalition government began bailing out shipyards, the state-owned steel company, and L. M. Ericsson to prevent factory closings. Massive foreign loans and a real 2 percent drop in the GNP helped Swedish industry to its feet again.

Slow growth, high unemployment, large trade imbalances, and pronounced monetary instability, as well as a continuing failure to establish the cause of the sluggishness and then take concerted action, plague the entire developed world as governments pursue domestic policies without regard to their international consequences. Canada and the United States have run large and well-publicized trade deficits, and Americans have seen their dollar battered on the foreign exchanges by fluctuations and devaluations with ever increasing force. Japan has slipped out of the trade surplus column.

Nation-states gave up holding their currencies in any fixed relationship with each other in 1971, and since then the flows of money across borders and continents have become too large for governments to match with any confidence. They intervene to iron out small fluctuations, but they can no longer maintain even unofficial par values. Differing rates of growth of the money supply in various countries are responsible for currencies bobbing up and down. "There are two ways in which the money supply might affect exchange rates," says Hamish McRae, financial editor of *The Guardian*. "One is through international capital movements; put at its simplest, if a country prints too much money some of the stuff will try to flow abroad. The other way is through the effect of money supply on the domestic price level. This affects the trade account, increasing the price of exports and reducing the relative price of imports." The second of these propositions is not universally accepted, but there is general agreement that relative money supply growth must affect exchange rates to some extent.

Another debate centers on why the fixed-rate system broke down in the first place. The most obvious answer, as McRae has pointed out, is that the scale of financial flows against which governments had to intervene had risen enormously, but this merely begs the next question: why were governments' resources increased correspondingly? The answer is that the float of currencies that followed the breakdown was really a two-bloc system, with a number of currencies clustering around the dollar (the yen, the Canadian, Australian dollars) and a number around the mark (the "snake" currencies of the Swiss and French francs and the weaker EEC moneys); that is, clusters around the two largest industrial nations, the United States and West Germany, which each put different emphasis on inflation, overseas investment, and life-styles. During the first quarter century after World War II, Germany, like Japan, sought to build up direct exports of goods made in factories at home, while the United States permitted its large corporations to invest enormous sums abroad. The pressure of the developing world for a piece of the pie and the size of the Euromarkets forced Germany and Japan to adopt the American model for exporting industrialism. The fixed-rate system was essentially dollar-based. It self-destructed when the

United States began running deficits large enough to reduce confidence in its currency.

The Spread

Though the industrialized nations and the oil producers have only one-third of the world's population, they possess the bulk of the wealth. In more than 50 countries, per capita GNP is less than $500.

	Per Capita GNP in $
Kuwait	13,000
Switzerland	9,870
Sweden	9,530
Saudi Arabia	9,210
West Germany	8,400
United States	7,860
Australia	6,830
Japan	6,010
Britain	4,360
U.S.S.R.	3,990
Rumania	2,630
Venezuela	2,590
South Africa	1,450
Mexico	1,150
Algeria	1,100
Turkey	1,070
South Korea	880
Jordan	870
Nigeria	500
Philippines	460
China	390
Egypt	380
Indonesia	310
Pakistan	200
India	140
Afghanistan	130
Ethiopia	100

Source: U. S. Department of Commerce, 1979.

7

How Do They Do It?

Together with 97,000 of Philips' employees, chairman of the board Frits J. Philips is a Dutchman. And Dutch is the company language, although 275,000 Philips workers in 60 countries do not speak Dutch. The language of Svenska Kullagerfabriken (SKF), on the other hand, is not Swedish but English.

If the rapidly changing developing world has not yet been reflected in the upper reaches of global enterprise, the multinationals have become uniquely international. The need to attract and retain the best available talents regardless of nationalities makes some companies more polyglot than others, but the tower of Babel is irresistible. "International companies which reserve their top jobs for nationals of their home base will face, on a large scale, the same difficulties as family companies which reserved their best jobs for members of the family," Christopher Tugendhat wrote in 1972.[1] Less than a decade later, companies refusing to promote foreigners beyond a certain level are an exception. John Kenneth Galbraith, no great defender of corporate power, thinks total "internationalization" is the multinationals' best defense, with representatives from the countries in which they have subsidiaries sitting on their boards and integrated top managements.

Aramco may run its own housing, schools, stores, and recreation facilities in Saudi Arabia for its Americans, but such compounds are beginning to change, too. Bechtel Corp. and Fluor, the two big California-based heavy construction and exploration companies working on tomorrow's energy fields, have very mixed crews, to say the least, and payrolls in dozens of currencies at their work sites. The French presence in French-speaking Africa is sharply divided into Peace Corps-type government *coopérants*

[1] Christopher Tugendhat, *The Multinationals* (New York: Random House, 1972), p. 144.

122

and business expatriates. Africans have developed a higher tolerance for the private engineers and technicians, despite their more ostentatious life-styles, than for France's more idealistic government advisers and field workers. In the words of an Ivory Coast official, "We're getting tired of these European malcontents entertaining their world weariness at our expense." [2]

Integration and allegiance are not among the global companies' major problems. Without standing up and singing the company song *à la japonaise,* employee loyalty has little difficulty transcending national prejudices as long as the two are not in direct conflict. During the 1973 Arab oil embargo when the Seven Sisters were forced "to play God," they did just that, moving the supertankers around in their own mysterious ways and favoring no one, not even the United States, Britain, or Holland. If anything, Congressional post mortem inquiries wagged a finger at Exxon, Mobil, Texaco, Chevron, and Gulf for not being patriotic enough.

To say the multinationals are where they are because they are big is a trifle simplistic. To say they are where they are because they control production, financing, and marketing begs the next question: why aren't there any more OPECs? When former *Time* editor-in-chief Hedley Donovan made a swing through Latin American capitals after the 1973 oil crisis, he found everybody had heady visions of "other OPECs" but very little interest in the whole subject of how the advanced world got to be advanced. West German Chancellor Helmut Schmidt once reminded third world leaders demanding fast redistribution of wealth that the process of industrializing Europe "so far has taken 200 years."

The $10 million-plus corporations and the Next Ten are where they are because they control production, financing, and marketing, but also for more subtle reasons. They are there because of historic quirks and accidents, because they are good at what they're doing, and because they are clever at becoming something else. To be global has advantages. It means you can spread the risks. Recessions don't necessarily strike all markets at the same time, meaning that you can slow down some subsidiaries while keeping others elsewhere, working flat out.

Nationalists make the global corporations the villains of the world economy, especially in the poorer nations. In reality, the multinationals aren't very comfortable in third world countries

[2] Jacques Buob and Arlette Marchal, "Les Français de l'étranger," *L'Express,* October 20, 1979, p. 146.

and don't have that much business there. Zoltan Merszei, the man who spearheaded Dow Chemical's overseas expansion and is vice president of Occidental Petroleum, says big multinationals really work best in big industrial countries. "In many third world countries, the governments set up everything, and they don't know technologies are not available from the governments of industrialized countries. They have to get them from private enterprises, and unless they create conditions satisfactory to private enterprise, there is not much they will ever get. Less-developed countries that have natural resources are different. They recognize they need multinational companies to develop an industrial infrastructure, but the countries that have nothing are the most nationalistic, the least cooperative."

The products the multinationals make are often ill-adapted to the much simpler economies of LDCs. The problem is not simply that dishwashers, frozen convenience foods, and Kleenex tissues have less relevance; so does much of the high-tech emphasis on saving labor. The highly centralized management style is ill-adapted, as well, with its accent on return on investment and aversion to outside participation, but sensitive third world governments don't want to hear this. Nor do they want hand-me-down technology that is more labor intensive and really ideal for them. Their inferiority complexes and pride make them insist on "the latest and the greatest." In *Global Reach*, the best of the multinational-bashing textbooks of the early 1970s, Richard Barnet and Ronald Muller played on the words "obsolete technology" both ways. In the same breath, they say that in order to prolong the market life of their merchandise, the multinationals foist "last generation's technology" on poor countries and that selling them the labor-saving latest and greatest means converting the third world's only asset, its human resources, into social liabilities.[3] Such be-damned-if-you-do-be-damned-if-you-don't charges pervade much of the academic literature on the subject, often painting multinational enterprises as being in the position to shape the demands of any developing country, to determine its industrial technology, to avoid the restraints its government may seek to impose, to corrupt the ruling classes, and to magnify the diplomatic influence of their home countries.

Capitalism is not the only ideology stressing the creation of

[3] Richard Barnet and Ronald Muller, *Global Reach* (New York: Simon & Schuster, 1975), p. 276.

wealth. China under Mao Zedong, Tanzania under Julius K. Nyerere, and India during the short-lived coalition of Prime Minister Morarji Desai attempted a small-is-beautiful "appropriate technology" according to criteria that are admittedly more political than economic. Once associated with an almost Soviet emphasis on heavy industry, India's Janata Party government decided in 1977 "that whatever can be produced by small and cottage industries must only be so produced." Improved pottery wheels, small labor-intensive sugar refineries, methane gas burners using fresh manure, hand looms, and other cottage industries were tried; any company with more than $125,000 in assets was forbidden manufacture of the 800 plus items designated for the small sector. Proponents acknowledged that cloth woven on the improved village looms couldn't compete with fabric made in India's huge textile mills; the point was to create jobs and dignity for the country's forty million unemployed, to keep them down on the farm and away from already swollen cities. Opponents said India couldn't afford to slow down its economy with such experiments because of the increase in bureaucracy it took to protect "the tiny sector," made up largely of one- or two-man businesses.

Coca Cola has made efforts to make a nutritional drink that feeds as well as refreshes, and Volkswagen, GM, Ford, Toyota, Renault, and Fiat have pushed modern forms of GM's 1960s Basic Transportation Vehicle idea with various x- or world cars that can be assembled anywhere. Philips has devoted resources to the special technology problems of developing areas, but, by and large, multinational enterprise is an established part of mature, knowledge-intensive capitalism. In the tug-of-war with the globals, governments rarely bargain so hard as to drive foreign investors away. If they try to force the corporations to do certain things, the companies will pull out and concentrate on those "platform countries"—Hongkong, Singapore, and, tomorrow, apparently, Sri Lanka—where rules are bendable.

To most managers of global enterprise, the job at hand is to use a pool of resources—money, patents, trade names, knowledge, and organization—in the execution of a global strategy. "With the firm's resources spread out all over the world and the firm's threats and opportunities similarly dispersed, the managers have seen themselves as exposed and vulnerable," Raymond Vernon writes. "As they see it, the sovereign states can apply arbitrary force with little or no restraint. With impunity, they can break previous commitments, raise taxes, cancel patents, nationalize properties, and expropriate assets." [4]

The bargaining power between the multinational company and the developing countries is the most sensitive issue in the entire debate between rich and poor.

It is clear that the vast bulk of all Research and Development takes place in the advanced world—98 percent, by one UN estimate. As we have seen with drugs, a handful of companies— Merck, Hoechst, Upjohn, Hoffmann-La Roche, Ciba-Geigy, and Pfizer—file hundreds of patents a year and are responsible for four-fifths of the Western world's pharmaceutical innovations. Only 13 percent of *all* registered trademarks are held by nationals of developing countries, according to the UN Conference on Trade and Development (UNCTAD). The drug companies use patents and trademarks rights to limit the export of products manufactured under their licenses, say, from Mexico to Guatemala, and they demand that raw materials essential for the making of their drugs be purchased from the parent company.

The Group of 77 wants greater opportunity to purchase technology apart from this traditional direct package of capital, management, and expertise controlled by the companies. The group wants to "unbundle" this package, so that host countries can get more information about the merits of different technologies and shop around for the most efficient and cheapest available. The debate has reached near-theological heights, with LDCs wanting the industrialized world to declare, in effect, that knowledge cannot be the property right of anyone, and the companies replying that such unbundling would, at best, cause the price of technology to go even higher. The newly industrialized countries (the NICs), as might be expected, have taken a more ambivalent view. Singapore, for example, maintains not only that it has no problem with restrictive corporate practices, but also that too rigid a code would inhibit developing regions when it comes to attracting investments. Harvey Wallender of the Council of the Americas, a business group, maintains that wholly owned subsidiaries enjoy more automatic and perhaps even cheaper access to technology than do licensees or "arms-length buyers" of technology. "If host countries decided to take this system apart," he says, "they'd have to create a government organization to put it all back together again." Pfizer's Edmund Pratt, Jr., says that his New York-based drug company makes its most modern technology available to its subsidiaries in thirty-seven countries in the form of products, processes, and management "to the maximum extent consistent with local market requirements and the safeguarding of industrial property rights." Liotard Vogt says that if Nestlé didn't make the best suited technology available, its subsidiaries would gradually loose their competitive edge and disappear. "In developing countries, it is often the governments themselves that tend to show preference for technology that requires a large labor force," he adds. IBM has a worldwide product line that must be flexible enough to accommodate national requirements without basic changes in design. "Efficiencies of manufacturing the same product for worldwide use are central to keeping computer costs at reasonable levels," says Frank Carey. Philips is willing to supply the most modern technology to its subsidiaries, provided these services can be paid for and this knowledge protected.

Industrial companies transfer among themselves billions of dollars in royalties and fees every year for two-way exchanges of licenses. A smaller, one-way stream of cash in exchange for technology flows from LDCs, much of it to multinational parents from subsidiaries or licensees. In the mid-1970s, governments of the Group of 77 began tinkering with these payments for know-how. They would continue to pay handsomely for unique technology, they said, but they found the great mass of technical, design, and trademark licenses to be exorbitant. Most vulnerable were companies making pharmaceuticals, cosmetics, and processed food. "Where they are getting mad," Alan Spurney, business director of Electronic Industries Association, said in 1975, "is in soft goods where they are paying for just a trademark or brand name." Maddest of all were the Andean Pact members—Bolivia, Colombia, Ecuador, Peru, and Venezuela—and Mexico, which enacted laws setting up commissions to rule on contracts involving royalties for technology, trademarks, and even management aid. The new Mexican legislation outlawed a number of dubious practices, such as tie-in clauses forcing licensees to buy from the licensor only and restrictions on exports to third countries. Multinationals were told to rewrite existing contracts and present them to a government commission which was wading through 5,000 revisions that were eventually submitted. Argentina, Brazil, Yugoslavia, Israel, India, and Pakistan followed suit, and even

France and Japan tightened their . laws. The French discovered in the fine print that their nationalized power authority, Electricité de France, was paying Westinghouse $1 million in royalties per nuclear reactor. Canada went beyond strictly economic considerations when it came to getting maximum advantage from operations of global companies. Ottawa applied a formal set of criteria to foreign investment which sought a "psychic income" in job training or development of depressed areas.

A few years later, Latin America and Canada backpedaled a bit and talked about recognizing the need for bigger foreign investments. They still wanted local investors to participate in the activities of the multinationals, and the buzz phrase in Caracas, Bogotá, Brasília, and Ottawa was joint venture. "The real driving force in the economy is private enterprise," said José Martinez de Hoz, Argentina's minister of economy. "Profits are something that must be recognized as essential to the functioning of a market economy." Mexico's López Portillo took pains to reassure private investors: "The needs of the country are so great that the government has no choice but to push the private sector into the role it should play." Colombia pushed its Andean partners to adopt a relatively low common external tariff and, in a concession to multinationals, a Pact-wide scheme to create a wider market for large-scale operations by assigning manufacturing rights for some products to individual member countries. If Ciba-Geigy was making DDT in Venezuela, it couldn't also make insecticides in Peru.

Control over prices is a touchy issue. The standard theory of oligopoly—the market condition when there are few sellers—is simple. Companies dominating an industry with homogeneous products are said to recognize their mutual interdependence and to form monopolies. Opponents of multinationalism have easily adapted the theory to international commerce, including its assumption that only two constants rule the market—price and output. In the real world, corporate managers must take into account a wide range of variables—quality of product, product "mix," R and D efforts, tax structures in scores of countries, marketing strategies, and the dynamics of change. Numerous factors tend to break down the concentration-profit relationship and to provide stimuli for continued competitive striving, but the overall goal of worldwide profits is often viewed with suspicion. A modern multinational is acutely aware that anything less than exemplary citizenship would endanger its investment and lead to loss of opportunities, and, says Daimler-Benz's Joachim Zahn, "more important than profits is what happens to the profits earned.

"If the profits are taxed away or given away to stockholders, they are no longer there for further investment," says Zahn. "If they are to a large extent left for the further expansion of the company, as is our policy, the result is an entirely intentional growth effect for the revelant economy."

The multinationals' invasion and counterinvasion of one another's markets tend to break up monopoly positions. In 1962, direct competition in France by Firestone and Goodyear caused Michelin, Dunlop, and Kléber-Colombes to reduce prices of tires. Fifteen years later, Michelin's pioneering radial tires gave it the clout to invade the United States and, by 1980, to close in fast on troubled Firestone in *its* domestic market. The factors that give a firm a selling edge in scores of markets include experience and know-how of a particular line of business, a high rate of R and D, and economies of scale required by the nature of the industry—managerial economies of scale as well as physical plant economics of scale.

No critic of multinationals is without horror stories, telling how the globals charge different prices to different countries and how they defraud tax authorities in half the world. Barnet and Muller say the literature on how to run global corporations is filled with advice on how to set prices on intracompany transfers to maximize profits, and they quote figures showing the Colombian prices of Valium and Librium to be thirty-two and sixty-five times Hoffmann-La Roche's world price. Others quote a 1974 issue of *Business International* that listed "25 Steps to Minimize Taxes on Foreign Company Sales and Services Income," "10 Ways to Use Base Companies," "20 Examples of Nonforeign Base Income" and "8 Ways to Reinvest Base Company Earnings." All governments use taxes to stimulate export sales and, when they can get away with it, to limit imports, and most of the horror stories are either examples of clever bookkeeping or, more seriously, treatment of different products as though they were identical so as to make price quotations comparable. Of course, companies may well charge different prices in different countries. Demand may be very different among different countries; rapidly shifting exchange rates also affect prices. In Caterpillar Tractor's case, for example, profits are shared between subsidiaries and parent based upon evaluation of each affiliate's contribution—

the only fair stance Caterpillar says it can take before taxing authorities in countries of manufacture and countries where its bulldozers are only sold. All countries have tax rules to deter distortions in interaffiliate prices, and IBM applies a uniform cost-plus method—manufacturing cost plus a markup—that is simple and aboveboard and accepted by tax authorities in the countries where IBM is present and questioned only by Chile and Peru. Shell's policy is to treat intracompany sales as arms-length agreements that can be fully justified to governments.

Hoffmann-La Roche has been successful in defending high drug prices to cover research and development. In 1980, the West German supreme court found Roche's German subsidiary not guilty of abusing its market strength by charging extortionate prices for Valium and Librium. The court overruled both the federal cartel office and the superior court in Berlin to end six years of bitter litigation and dash any hope in Germany of pinning similar charges on other market-dominating firms. The German court victory gave Roche a virtually clean sweep of overprice cases against its popular tranquilizers. A year earlier, the Dutch supreme court reversed a government order that the company reduce prices on the two drugs. In 1977 a Danish court threw out a 20 percent slash in prices ordered less than a year earlier by a Copenhagen monopoly commission, and in Britain two years of court fights ended with nothing more than Roche agreeing to voluntary price restraints. (In Canada, ironically, Roche was accused of selling Valium and Librium too cheaply and found guilty by the Ontario supreme court of predatory pricing—setting prices so low competitors were driven out of the market.)

Control of itself and its subsidiaries is an essential feature of global enterprise. It is most obvious in manufacturing. Daimler-Benz do Brasil must make Daimler-Benz cars and trucks and cannot one morning decide to make hybrid Toyota-Fiats or Electrolux vacuum cleaners. The billion dollars that the four top pharmaceuticals spend a year on R and D must somehow be protected by patents and trademarks, or a new system will have to be invented. Innovations constitute a driving force in all business, and the link between novelty and increased profits is self-evident. Hitachi and Siemens are not only obvious benefactors of their own breakthroughs and closely identified with wholly new concepts and products, but Saint-Gobain, Dow, and Citicorp owe their success to innovation. In response to the energy crisis, building materials are undergoing dramatic changes. In chemicals, the turnover rate for products is quite rapid, and the Euromarkets phenomenon is an ingenious bankers' response to profound money market mutations. During the 1950s and 1960s, innovations among U. S. multinationals tended to be directed toward saving labor and satisfying high-income wants and tastes, while European and Japanese innovations were frequently aimed at saving materials, but the skyrocketing German and Japanese labor costs that have blurred this distinction are in themselves an altered state demanding new responses.

Trivial innovations come in for obvious criticism. Third world observers are shocked that grown men qualified in research are unashamedly "working on" softer toilet paper, more brightly colored comic strips, and cigarettes that are one silly centimeter longer. Spectacular advances require decade-long lead time and strategic decisions on the part of the innovating firm. Corning Glass Works of Corning, New York, opened its industrial laboratory in 1908 but didn't come up with the original Pyrex cookware until the 1930s. It is IBM's distinct corporate policy not to "dilute" its equity in its subsidiaries. When the Indian government asked IBM to start diluting its ownership in India to 74 percent, the company offered to split itself in two—one data-processing company would be 60 percent Indian-owned; the other, dealing with maintenance and marketing, would export all its manufactured production, but IBM would maintain 100 percent ownership. New Delhi pondered. Hitherto, IBM had only made card-punching equipment in India; now it was ready to manufacture computer peripherals and guarantee exports worth nearly four times as much as the old operation. In the end, the Desai government said no, ostensibly because the wholly owned company's marketing and maintenance work meant it would not be wholly exporting. So IBM pulled out, and Burroughs moved in, saying it would make computers in India with only 40 percent equity.

Central direction from the pooling of knowledge and experience is one of the major benefits of international corporations. Daimler-Benz has built plants in Iran and Nigeria and is leery of taking on local partners. Where there are national partners, it has found, decisions against the will of the subsidiary cannot be carried out and are therefore impractical. When applied to giant corporations, ownership and control have meanings that are complex and often changing. Majority ownership of common stock traditionally carries with it control of the corporation, but no single investor holds as much as 1 percent of such *Fortune* 500 companies as AT & T or United States Steel. Ownership, in the form of voting and participating equity stock of multinationals, varies from Electrolux, whose entire voting stock is held in Sweden, and Caterpillar and Nestlé, whose stock is quoted on stock exchanges in New York, Paris, Amsterdam, Frankfurt, Düsseldorf, Zurich, London, and Brussels, to BAT Industries, which has diluted subsidiary ownership in many developing countries to under 50 percent. Modern corporations are no longer in the hands of their owners but run by sizable, articulate, and influential managements.

Authority in a global enterprise is no different from authority in any other company. The head office is the brain and nerve center, and the component parts cannot be regarded in isolation. Cadillac, Buick, Oldsmobile, Pontiac, and Chevrolet could be independent automobile manufacturers, but they are divisions of General Motors. The headquarters in Detroit decides the global strategy, where new investments should be, and it allocates research programs and determines the prices that should be charged in interdivision exchanges. The general managers are powerful executives; much is left to their discretion and initiative and their input is needed, but the limits of their authority are set in Detroit and can be increased and diminished at will.

The driving force behind the globalization of industry is a managerial revolution that has made it possible to centralize planning on an international scale. The decision making varies a great deal. Decentralized decision making is the principal tenet of IBM's way of doing business in 127 countries. Equity control may be uncompromising, but all operating plans, including proposed profit and sales objectives, originate in the local IBM office. Olivetti, on the other hand, operates in a highly centralized manner. Mitsubishi says headquarters naturally must be in control, especially when things don't go too smoothly. Akzo says it gives its subsidiaries just enough freedom to be responsible but not so much as to be detrimental to the technological advance and the major synergetic effect of the group.

Global planning and decision making, whatever the control or elasticity, cannot be matched by governments. And governments are resentful of the corporations' ability to allocate markets, of faraway headquarters telling which subsidiary can export what to whom. They also dislike subsidiaries being forced to import parts that could be purchased locally and, in reverse, take offense when local affiliates accede to the wishes, laws, and policies of another country. This has been a constant irritant in Canadian-American relations, as when Ford of Canada complies with Ford Dearborn edicts not to export Ford trucks to Cuba, although there is no Canadian law forbidding trade with Cuba. It is the age-old conflict of king and bishop, lay and canon law, national and supranational jurisdiction. What set Henry II against Thomas à Becket in 1163 was the king's claim that the courts of the realm should try felonious priests and his desire to control English church appeals to Rome. Thomas defended the extraterritorial globalism of the Church and was murdered for it in Canterbury Cathedral.

The conflict makes for interesting dinner conversation, but it can be solved only if both sides will see the complementariness of purposes in a higher synthesis. After all, the point is to *make* something—cars, computers, or breakfast cereals. Rather than bemoan "parent direction," says Caterpillar's president Lee Morgan, governments should applaud the fact that Caterpillar bulldozers are made to the same standards the world over, that they have worldwide identity and can be serviced with replacement parts from any source.

In rich countries, the word multinational tends to evoke images of tax swindles. When the Navios Shipping Co. of Liberia brought iron ore from the Orinoco Mining Co. in Venezuela to the United States from 1957 to 1960, it overcharged for its services by 10 to 30 percent, a U. S. tax court ruled ten years later. But both Navios and Orinoco are subsidiaries of the U. S. Steel Corp. A case of the left hand not knowing what the right hand is doing?

No, the maneuver is known as transfer pricing. It has to do with where a multinational wants to see its profits to pop up in the system, but it has sparked intense debate as reformers try to eliminate global corporations' discretion exercised in their own interest. In the case of U. S. Steel, the tax court reallocated $27 million of additional taxable income in the four years to "prevent evasion or avoidance of taxes." After an audit, the Internal Revenue Service had the company assessed an additional $52 million, but U. S. Steel appealed. Although the higher court trimmed the IRS figure, it clearly found that U. S. Steel had followed a policy of keeping income out of IRS reach in the Liberian-registered subsidiary. The practice is common, of course, but few instances have been as thoroughly documented as the U. S. Steel court case. In 1977, Thomas Field, executive director of a public interest taxpayers' lobby in Washington, charged Getty Oil with a huge transfer pricing scheme. The state of Delaware, he charged, had been unable to collect income taxes on Getty's huge refinery in Delaware City because Getty's refining subsidiary served as a profits shield, allowing its profits to go to a Saudi division. "That siphons refinery profits out of Delaware and out of the United States and into a Getty operation that is amply sheltered from American tax by foreign tax credits," Field said. "And in addition it also overcharges the subsidiary for tanker services to move Neutral Zone crude from the Persian Gulf to Delaware City and into Getty-owned Liberian corporations that pay no corporate taxes to anyone." But Field, a Harvard Law graduate with ten years' government experience as an oil tax expert, *The New York Times* said in reporting the story, "can provide no documentary proof of the charges." [5]

Tax avoidance—if not evasion—by decent people has become standard, and governments are learning that the tax take cannot grow over a 200-year period from zero percent of personal income to 100 percent. Virtually everywhere inflation has caused income taxes designed as "progressive" to bite into the incomes of middle income earners they were never designed to catch. There is no swing against taxing business, but recession *has* caused governments to switch their concerns from the fewer golden eggs that enterprise can lay to the health of the goose itself. "Shear your sheep, don't skin them," *The Economist* headlined a review of the tax squeeze in advanced countries.[6] In 1945, British economist Colin Clark could say that when taxation of all kinds exceeded 25 percent of net national income, inflationary pressures followed. Most industrial nations passed the 25 percent threshold decades ago. In the United States, corporate taxes on consolidated worldwide profits are approaching 50 percent. Independent observers such as Raymond Vernon say we cannot hold the multinationals to account for running their computers to minimize their taxes, and economist Milton Friedman that with a near 50 percent tax bite, the U. S. government, not American companies, decides in effect what half the company investment will be.

[5] Clyde H. Farnsworth, "Tax Loophole for Multinationals," *The New York Times*, August 21, 1977, p. F9.

[6] *The Economist*, June 17, 1978, p. 12.

Such caveats don't impress the critics. How can we know that anything the corporations say is true, since we have only their figures? To which defenders of global enterprise say that multinationals, especially U. S.-based globals, are more accountable to more bodies, national and international, than ever before. Commercial bribery, shoddy products, and collusion on prices are not essentially a problem of multinationals, but a problem of the relationship between government and enterprise in general. "There is a lot of room for revision in this area, but it is not a problem of multinational enterprise," says Vernon, illustrating his point with the Lockheed Aircraft bribery scandal. "We ought to share a common secret which is that Lockheed is not a multinational corporation. It is a U. S. firm which happens to export airplanes."

Scandals overwhelm state monopolies and nationalized industries as well. In 1979, Italy's fragile Christian Democrat minority government suspended ENI president Giorgio Mazzani over a huge commission paid on a 91-million-barrel oil contract. In Britain, a prolonged muddle over inflation accounting has given public sector bosses the chance to name their own figures, often without blame from watchdog censors, and to add their depreciation write-offs as they see fit. A bigger accounting scandal came to light when Nigeria transferred from military to civilian rule in 1979 and the colonels wanted to show the new government it would inherit an aggressive oil policy. The military hired Coopers and Lybrand, accountants of London, who promptly discovered that the state oil monopoly had failed to record revenues of $5 billion on its books and that there were no records of dealings with Texaco and Ashland Oil, although such dealings were substantial.

But tax avoidance and even bribery are trivial irritants in the larger scheme of things. If we want to examine the deeper question of how giant corporations have come to be where they are, we must turn to their astonishing ability to become something else.

Obsolescence is the flip side of innovation. In some fields, the rate of obsolescence is so rapid that the innovators never find themselves required to consider overseas production. In civil aviation, the DC-7 was in production for seven years, but the Boeing 747 was introduced in 1969 and is still being made. Much automobile innovation is trivial from model year to model year, but the energy crunch compelled all automakers to reinvent the car and forced the least innovative—Chrysler and BL (formerly British Leyland)—to the wall. The trivial obsolescence the critics object to is what they see as corporate flimflam in retailing old needs to new customers and creating new needs for old customers. The rising middle classes in the NICs are a key target for established products such as cars. With population growth slowing in much of the advanced countries, the carmakers' market expansion is obviously the fast-industrializing nations, and, indeed, the middle classes in Brazil and Mexico are beginning to have sufficient income to discover that they cannot live without a car. But so are the *privilegentsia* of socialist regimes—the Soviet power elite is neatly compartmentalized by the cars they come and go in: black Volgas for plain political big shots entitled to state cars; Chaikas for the second echelon; and chauffeured Zils for the cream. The cravings of the upwardly mobile aren't necessarily foisted on them by first world throwaway technology. They are quite capable of corrupting themselves.

Yet entropy—the running down of a product or a process—is a problem. Overcoming it is one of the essential characteristics of global giants. A company that invests heavily in the development of a new product—pocket calculators, say—realizes that there will be an inevitable loss as competitors catch on. The leading company will no doubt try to prolong the product's life by holding off on still newer products, or by engaging in a frenzy of advertising to prevent the entropic force from pulling the product down to the commonplace and the blah. Governments watch this with a fascinated and sometimes jaundiced eye. "From the viewpoint of governments, the means that foreign firms select to hold off the effects of entropy are of considerable importance," says Vernon. "The objective of many countries has been to speed up the rate at which multinational enterprises surrender their old product lines to local firms. But the success of that strategy will depend on factors over which nation-states have little control, including future trends in the production of new products and processes and in the role of scale." [7] It is a signal of creeping entropy when leading firms begin to manufacture the product at so-called "offshore" facilities where labor costs and the tax structure are favorable to low-cost production: TV sets in Taiwan, pocket calculators in Malaysia.

What distinguishes multinational giants from much national

7 Vernon, op. cit., p. 90.

industry is their capacity to "roll over" from product to product. Hitachi and Siemens have moved from heavy machinery to semiconductors, Pfizer from penicillin to industrial chemicals and cosmetics, ITT from making telephones and operating telephone exchanges to almost anything else. Until the energy crisis, the Seven Sisters at the top of the $10 billion-plus list were basically all in one business, but they are beginning to metamorphose. The food and household companies constantly invent new products and processes, and the pharmaceuticals and chemicals are cross-fertilizing in biology. Since the future of the automobile may depend largely on radical changes in design and in the role itself of the car, the carmakers may be the first multinational casualties of entropy, unless they, too, learn to roll over.

What governments in developing regions don't like to hear is that raw materials can also suffer from entropy. The most durable and nearly universally propagated charge against the advanced world is the well-known contention of the LDCs that prices of raw materials tend to decline over the course of time in their relation to prices of manufactured goods. A ton of copper, according to the argument, will buy fewer tractors in 1985 than in 1975. Since OPEC, the ability to control the price of crude has slipped from the Seven Sisters. Western governments encourage the image of OPEC as an Arab cartel which has succeeded in holding them at ransom, but the reality is a little different. The OPEC system, supported by the oil companies, provides a mechanism in many ways more secure than the Sisters' cartel, Anthony Sampson has written, since it rests "on the assent of the producing countries." [8]

CIPEC was a 1974 attempt at "another OPEC." Made up of Peru, Chile, Zambia, and Zaire, the Council of Copper Exporting Countries was meant to force copper consumers to pay more. Ideological differences and past rivalries were set aside in the drive for the largest possible returns. The first order of business was to do what OPEC did, to establish a minimum floor price, but the four cartel members were economic invalids and never mastered the most elementary discipline for any cartel—the ability to withhold supplies to force up prices. Not only were the four in dire straits, but, having nationalized their copper industries, they had no "Sisters" and ran the mines as sources of jobs and patronage. At a meeting in Lusaka in June 1974, CIPEC's four

[8] Anthony Sampson, *Update, the New Crisis*, sixth printing of *The Seven Sisters* (New York: Viking Press, 1979), p. 381.

members were "unable to agree on any action" to implement the proposed floor price. Chile had publicly advocated a minimum floor price of £800 a ton, and the three others had supported the plan, but the classic problem was inability to reach agreement with the many smaller exporters outside CIPEC not to undercut the base price. Panama, Costa Rica, Honduras, Guatemala, and Colombia formed the Union of Banana Exporting Countries (UBEC) to wrest a larger share of the banana dollars from United Brands (née United Fruit), Castle & Cooke, and Del Monte. Malaysia, Thailand, Indonesia, Sri Lanka, and India, which account for 35 percent of the world's natural rubber output, held talks on forming a cartel; Brazil, Colombia, the Ivory Coast, and Angola tried a coffee cartel; Morocco led a phosphate monopoly attempt. Significantly, perhaps, the International Tin Agreement is considered a success because it includes *both* producers and consumers. Formed in 1956, the pact is governed by an international council made up of seven producing nations, led by Malaysia and Bolivia, and twenty-two consuming countries. The world's only *private* cartel is De Beers Central Selling Organization which markets industrial and gem diamonds for South Africa, the Soviet Union, Zaire, and Botswana.

A number of North-South meetings have been devoted to commodity cartels, or stabilization pacts, as they are euphemistically called in UN circles. Summit meetings have also addressed the question. The closing communiqué of President Carter's first summit with the leaders of Britain, France, Canada, Germany, Italy, and Japan in 1977 said, "The world economy has to be seen as a whole. We were reinforced in our awareness of the interrelationship of all the issues before us as well as our own interdependence." The leaders committed their nations to sustained noninflationary growth and to support for all the existing international economic institutions. It was a way of saying that they remembered the panicky pressures after the 1929 crash which led country after country to try to heal its own troubles by beggaring its neighbors—and wound up creating catastrophe for all. But it was also a way of saying they had not been able to figure out the new institutional arrangements that would assure renewed well-being and political stability.

8

End of Innocence

The company had subsidiaries all over Europe. It controlled mining in several countries, had a monopoly on copper, dominated banking, and had overseas earnings coming in from the West Indies, Mexico, and South America. It bankrolled imperial and papal elections, befriended governments, financed wars, and successfully defended itself against antitrust accusations.

The name was Ulrich Fugger & Bros. The corporate headquarters was in Augsburg. This Renaissance forerunner of diversified, multinational enterprise traded in textiles, metals, and spices; produced silver, copper, and mercury; and ran a financial institution so brilliantly that Jakob Fugger (1459–1525) was nicknamed "the rich." Jakob advanced the money for the Vatican's Swiss guard, paid for the Pope's army to fight the French, organized the Church indulgence business, and made his presence felt through sizable donations at papal elections. The company's influence on the Hapsburg dynasty was even greater. Anton, Jakob's nephew and successor as head of the company, secured Charles I's election as emperor with a 275,333 guilder payment to Charles's brother, Ferdinand, and a pension for life to the archbishop of Mainz. When members of the Hanseatic League—the North European transnational combine that lasted 600 years—complained to the imperial tax authorities about the Fuggers' monopoly practices and Charles seemed to forget how he had become emperor, Jakob wrote to him: "It is well-known and clear as day that without my help Your Highness would not have obtained the imperial crown." Proceedings against Fugger & Sons were dropped.

Greed is a constant in capitalism—if not in human nature; technology is not. If the collective wisdom of big business, during the rise of government and social reform, is, in hindsight, less than inspired, then Karl Marx's prophecy that the pain capitalism inflicts on its slaving masses will bring about its own doom is equally insipid. Behind the rise of U. S. Steel was not merely J. P. Morgan's greed but steel furnaces that could spew out forty miles of steel rails every hour. Behind American Sugar Refining Co. were whirling centrifuges; behind Swift & Company were refrigerated railway cars. What made possible the rise of American Tobacco Co. was the Bonsack machine that could roll 100,000 cigarettes a day. What made Henry Ford was the assembly line; what made Nestlé's "Roman legions" was Henri Nestlé's condensed milk. Technology begat efficiency which begat concentration. As companies saturated their local markets, they broadened their horizons and sought new markets. In the early nineteenth century, no single enterprise controlled as much as 10 percent of American industrial output. By 1904, twenty corporations controlled 76 percent of U. S. production. Today, a quarter of the world's commerce is intracorporate trade.

Multinationals have been around for a long time, but it is an article of faith among academic writers that high noon has both come and gone for global enterprise. If set in a narrow enough time frame and if only U. S.-based multinationals are examined, the claim can be argued. The 1960s were the go-go years for American expansion. During that decade, the annual growth rate in per capita GNP was roughly 20 percent higher in Europe than in the United States, roughly 235 percent in Japan. As a natural consequence of this disparity, the temptation was strong for U. S. corporations to invest where the growth was—to go multinational on a major scale. By the same token, the Japanese and Europeans had every reason to stay at home and reap the rewards of their own superior growth. By the 1970s, however, North American and European economies grew at roughly the same 2.2 percent annual rate. Japan's ferocious growth dipped to 4.3 percent, and only Korea, Hongkong, Singapore, and Malaysia achieved anything near the 7 percent annual growth that doubles real GNP in a decade. By 1978, the U. S. dollar was cut in half, and U. S. labor was no longer the highest paid in the world. Hourly wages were 14 percent higher in Germany, 20 percent higher in Sweden. Europe was no longer the superior economy to invest in, and European corporations began to look for opportunities elsewhere.

At the same time, the awakening third world demanded its piece of the pie. As a condition for setting up business, LDC governments demanded transfer of know-how, and technology was only one element in an expanding package of benefits that they extracted from multinational investors. Governments everywhere tried to get a bigger slice of the profits, jobs, markets, and skills that global corporations control. The aftereffects of the 1973 oil embargo were brutal. For advanced countries as a whole, the real output of goods and services stagnated. The GNP actually declined in the United States, Britain, and Japan in 1974—the drop in Japan followed a nonstop expansion that had lasted a quarter of a century. The task for the rest of the 1970s was to devise a world economic strategy that would boost the faltering growth rates and improve payment balances. This, however, was not possible. The growth remained sluggish and erratic. External imbalances became pronounced, giving rise to instability in foreign exchange markets and to a growth in protectionist sentiments.

The tag "multinational corporation" was invented in 1960—David Lilienthal is credited with having coined it—but the concept it describes has a long history. The Renaissance didn't just produce Fugger & Bros. but paved the way for the leaps in ideas, explorations, and organizations that lead to today's scale and vigor of trade. Britain and its empire were at the center of an enormous explosion in world trade over a 200-year period which saw England's population increase fivefold but its imports seventyfold in volume, even more in value. To pay for it all, Britain converted the raw materials it brought in from all over and sent them out again as manufactured goods. British bankers financed much of the world's trade, and statesmen like Joseph Chamberlain, a determined advocate of empirewide protectionism, profoundly affected the world by setting national goals.

As we saw in Chapter Three, nearly all of the twenty-eight multinationals were in place by the first decade of the century. They had looked for oil and built farm equipment and canned milk since the mid-nineteenth century. Siemens opened its first foreign subsidiary in Russia in 1853. Friedrich Bayer bought an American aniline factory in 1865, the same year Rockefeller bought control of his first refinery. Sweden's inventor of dynamite, Alfred Nobel, opened an explosives factory in Hamburg a year later, and Isaac Merrit Singer started his first overseas sewing machine factory in Glasgow in 1867. When he died, he left $13 million to the twenty-four children his two wives and three mistresses bore him and the recipe for turning out identical products in several countries. By 1900, Westinghouse's British subsidiary was England's biggest industrial complex, and by 1914, one out of every four cars rolling off British assembly lines was a Ford. Before World War I, Courtaulds Ltd., the British chemical company, controlled America's synthetic silk industry through an affiliate; Lever Bros. was well on its way to becoming Unilever; and two German firms, Bayer and Merck, led dyestuff and pharmaceutical production in the United States.

When founded in 1908, General Motors was itself a merger of several small automakers. Less than twenty years later, GM was assembling cars in Denmark, Belgium, France, England, Germany, Poland, Argentina, Brazil, South Africa, Japan, New Zealand, Australia, Spain, Sweden, India, and Indonesia. In 1925, it bought out the British Vauxhall Motors and four years later the biggest German carmaker of the day, Adam Opel AG. Standardized mass output began in processed food and beverages in the 1890s. CPC International developed its Maizena corn products in 1921 and went overseas at the same time as Coca Cola, General Foods, and Nestlé.

The internationalization of capital began after 1945. The Depression had unleashed a storm of cutthroat economic nationalism that so brutalized the industrialized world that the first quarter century after World War II was spent building defenses to make sure it wouldn't happen again. American corporations expanded on the coattails of the Marshall Plan which transferred $13 billion to Europe between 1948 and 1952. "In Europe and the United States, the two decades following World War II will for long be remembered as a very good time, the time when capitalism really worked," John Kenneth Galbraith has written. Everywhere in the industrialized countries, production increased, unemployment was low, prices were nearly stable. "After the Marshall Plan, there was hope that a similar infusion of money would also rescue the poor countries from their poverty. The rich countries weren't overwhelming in their generosity, but enough was done to show the problem." [1]

In the long perspective of history, the split of the world into rich and poor regions is very recent. It began at the end of the eighteenth century, with the Industrial Revolution in England. That revolution was quickly exported to Western Europe and to North America and Japan, but not to the tropics. Why this is so is variously explained by geopolitics and sociology. Western Europe and North America are said to have been largely self-sufficient in raw materials; indeed, their high farm productivity is supposed to have laid the foundation of the Industrial Revolu-

[1] John Kenneth Galbraith, *The Age of Uncertainty* (Boston: Houghton Mifflin, 1977), p. 225.

tion. The late John R. Commons' classic essay, "The American Shoemaker," demonstrating that it was the expansion of the market for shoes that led to the factory revolution in shoemaking, not technological progress, has been taken up by such third world economists as Sir William Arthur Lewis. The Jamaican Nobel economist stresses the relative dearness to the third world of goods produced in the industrialized world and the relative cheapness to the advanced countries of whatever the developing world produces. The explanation of this seeming paradox is that labor was more productive and better paid in the industrialized North and that the large cheap supply of labor in the South kept dragging down the wages, even of efficient industrial workers. The LDCs, Lewis contends, shouldn't have to produce primarily for markets in the advanced world. They should produce more for each other and be less dependent on the North. Why they don't, he doesn't explain. Gunnar Myrdal has tried the social explanation in attempting to find out why so many countries are so poor and what keeps them that way. Holding India, Sri Lanka, Southeast Asia and the ASEAN states (Association of Southeast Asian Nations) under his compassionate looking glass and carefully documenting and marshaling his facts, the celebrated social scientist came away depressed.[2] The vested interests are too great, and a kind of inertia seems to divert whatever comes in from the outside to the existing power structure, which uses it not to encourage but to suppress change. Ancient tradition, class structure, and especially the existing power structure are obstacles significantly underplayed in most Western and Marxist writing. When writing about the third world, most authors somehow cannot admit that the powerful have power, and that, therefore, very little can be done. Such social scientists as Friedrich Hayek have come to believe that social engineering is both futile and dangerous, that the idea of anyone standing above his civilization in order to judge it from the outside or from a higher viewpoint is an illusion. "It simply must be understood that reason itself is part of civilization," says Nobel laureate Hayek.[3]

By and large, the multinationals didn't go abroad in pursuit of cheap labor. Admittedly, low-labor-cost countries like Taiwan, Korea, Hongkong, Brazil, and Mexico have prospered, manufac-

[2] Gunnar Myrdal, *Asian Drama, An Inquiry into the Poverty Nations* (New York: Pantheon, 1968).

[3] Friedrich Hayek, *New Studies in Philosophy, Politics, Economics and the History of Ideas* (Chicago: University of Chicago Press, 1978), p. 32.

turing transistor radios, toys, shoes, and textiles on behalf of such companies as GM, Matsushita, Texas Instruments, Sony, RCA, and Levi Strauss. The Commerce Department figures, however, that only 7 percent of the more than $515 billion in sales that U. S. multinational affiliates generate each year comes back into the United States. The bulk of their output goes into their local markets and the rest, elsewhere in the world. This, truly, is what "multinational" means.

In 1950, U. S. private investment abroad amounted to about $12 billion, mostly in oil and mineral ventures in Canada, Latin America, and the Middle East. By 1970, the figure had sextupled to $65 billion, and the balance had shifted to a preponderance of manufacturing over natural resources extraction. By the mid-1970s, the figure had doubled again to more than $130 billion. That was the heyday of the American multinationals, the ITTs, Littons, and General Electrics, which came to be feared as insatiable gluttons as they learned to master the fragmentated overseas markets. In his doomsdaying book *Le Défi Americain*, Jean-Jacques Servan-Schreiber saw American companies and their recruits from the Harvard Business School devouring Europe the way the Israeli forces swept through the Sinai in the 1967 Middle East war. But West German, British, Canadian, Japanese, and Swiss companies also went abroad. Nestlé, Hoffmann-La Roche, Ciba-Geigy, and Brown, Boveri & Cie of Zurich invested twelve times as much outside Switzerland in 1975 than in 1960, the German multinationals thirty-five times as much.

But United States dominance in the world made the U. S.-based multinationals the most visible. The United States was the leader of a world economic system that produced wealth on a scale never before seen. Unlike earlier economic and political empires that were closed units based on tight territorial control and heavily regulated mercantile trade, this system was open, with its guiding principles of free flow of capital and goods. With the dollar as the world's reserve currency, the United States found that it was able to run continuous international deficits and—unlike all other nations—did not have to tighten up on its domestic economic policies to solve the problem. This also allowed the U. S. corporations to move abroad and buy into the burgeoning markets very cheaply. By the mid-1970s, overseas profits accounted for one-third or more of the overall profits of the top U. S. multinational corporations and banks.

For better or for worse? The debate, simmering all along, became strident in the 1960s, when multinationalization became the greatest single fact of world commerce and the economic, or even political, fate of countries could be affected by decisions made in executive boardrooms. The globals' impact came under close scrutiny. In the United States, where business' relations with government are usually adversary, Congress threatened to put a squeeze on international operations by slapping heavier taxes on income from foreign sources. In the Netherlands, Akzo and Philips had to operate under close trade union surveillance of their investment plans outside the country. Sweden, which has the biggest overseas investment per capita of any country, added labor union members to its foreign exchange control board and gave it the power to review foreign investment and its effect on employment at home. Nationalistic economic policies among the LDCs became more forceful, while in the newly developed countries like Brazil, governments backed, financed, and often wholly or partially owned industrial concerns that mounted fierce competition against first world globals.

Yet national boundaries were falling during the quarter century following World War II, partly through the realization of Adam Smith's dream of free international trade—postwar world trade far exceeded the wildest expectations—and partly through the investment by companies in operating subsidiaries abroad. In the mid-1960s, polyglot enterprises stood as the symbol and summary of what had happened over two postwar decades. Anything seemed possible for business. The world was its territory; outer space might be next. The year 1960 was the first when dollars held abroad exceeded American national reserves—that is, when a world run on the U. S. Treasury could have bankrupted it—but old ideologies were becoming obsolete and meaningless. The Russians were coming to the view that their own best interests were served, not by a capitalist West heading for bankruptcy and chaos as Marx had wanted, but by a capitalist West in a state of economic health, ready and able to supply them grain, manufactured goods, machinery, and technical skills. In Western democracies, governments were no longer business' implacable antagonists but its best customers. Everybody in government, including the huge establishment of regulators, now promoted industrial growth as being in the public interest.

The companies that went multinational were big companies, capital intensive for the most part, technology-oriented, and managerially intense. They were able to capitalize on the economies of scale afforded by volume production in large markets. "When they ventured abroad, they tended to go for the more dynamic phases of the foreign economies they settled in," *Forbes* wrote in a survey of the internationalization of business.[4] It was a game any number could play, of course, and European, Japanese, and Arab firms and banks gave Americans a taste of two-way globalism. The United States was no longer a refuge for the smart money or the fright money or the tax-evasion money seeking a haven for portfolio investments. Foreign companies challenged big American companies in their own backyard. Eurodollars—the profits from their exports to the United States—were used to build and buy factories in America. At the same time, American firms seemed to be retreating. W. R. Grace sold out its European consumer products business, Union Carbide its European chemical operations (while building new battery plants in Egypt and Nigeria), Liggett Group its European cigarette operation. Gulf Oil sold its Spanish refinery and SCM its German photocopier works. Firestone pulled out of Switzerland. In Scotland, Singer scaled back the now 112-year-old sewing machine factory by 80 percent; American Standard walked away from six plants in France; Reynolds Aluminum pulled out of British Aluminum, Kaiser out of Alcan Booth Industries. The most spectacular retreat was Chrysler's. It bailed out of Britain and France; it sloughed off its Colombian and Venezuelan operations to GM, all of its Argentinian capacity to Volkswagen, two-thirds of its Brazilian operations to VW, and a third of its Australian capacity to Mitsubishi.

The retrenchments, however, are deceptive and largely a part of the corporate rollovers or, in Chrysler's case, an inability to become something else. The causes ranged from bad judgment and bad luck to shrewd foresight. Grace vice president Charles Erhard, Jr., said his company made the wrong acquisitions—smaller companies that were second or third in their industries. "We didn't think there'd be as much competition in Europe, and we were wrong. The price/earnings ratios were just about as high as they were in the United States. One of the real mistakes we made was in thinking we couldn't get our chemical business growing fast enough to give us a major position in Europe, but that business has grown handsomely. If we'd known that, we might not have felt it so necessary to push ahead in a business we didn't know very much about." To stay afloat in European chemicals, Union Car-

[4] James Cook, "A Game Any Number Can Play," *Forbes*, June 25, 1979, p. 52.

bide discovered it needed its own ethylene facilities to supply its European petrochemical operations and decided it was cheaper to pull out than to integrate backwards.

The United States was buffeted by an unnerving series of shocks after the fall of Vietnam, shocks that were primarily military and political—the long agony of Watergate, the constant inflation, the energy squeeze—but the bottom line seemed to be economic. As the 1970s wore on, the dollar crumbled, and Washington's power to devastate half the globe seemed irrelevant. It was a time of American disillusion, of coming to terms with the disenchanting age of limits, of "things running out," of what sociologist and psychologist Thomas Cottle called "the haberdashery approach to economics: pull in your pants, tighten your jacket, pull up your socks." The simplest of all statistics told the story: since 1945, whatever else happened, personal income per capita, adjusted for inflation, doubled. Not that everything was bleak. The developing world, where two-thirds of humanity lives, also made progress. The underlying pattern was the same for everybody. Steady expansion of demand for goods and services resulted in increased supplies. Resources, especially labor, shifted from the primary sector (farming) to the secondary (industry) to the tertiary (services); productivity growth was fastest in industry, especially in manufacturing, so that regions which maintained or increased their industries' relative importance usually achieved the best overall growth.

Until 1973, it seemed as if the advanced countries had found the key to sustained growth, a key which others could also use. But OPEC's oil increases during the next two years carved about 2 percent out of the Gross World Product. Governments of industrial countries took fright and deflated; LDCs cut where they could and borrowed the rest. Inevitably, growth suffered.

Politically, the multinationals found the going roughest in the mid-1970s. To get a bigger share of the profits, jobs, and markets for themselves, governments used the big companies to promote a variety of their own objectives. Mexico arm-twisted Volkswagen and Ford to export more from their Mexican plants; Colombia wanted to put branches of foreign banks under majority Colombian control. Saudi Arabia asked Chevron, Texaco, Mobil, and Exxon to set up joint-venture refineries and petrochemical plants; France insisted that Motorola's semiconductor division set up an R and D department to qualify for investment incentives; Canada required companies to show that they would bring "significant benefits"; and the Andean Pact countries proposed a "fadeout" formula under which foreign investors would turn over their entire businesses to local ownership after fifteen or twenty-five years.

Multinational corporations as partners in development was a question Frank Carey addressed in 1975 when the UN accused international commerce of everything from exploiting labor to stealing natural resources. Quoting Henry Kissinger's utterance in the UN General Assembly that the economy is global, the IBM chairman said that if governments would harmonize their treatment of the big companies and honor the contracts they made with them, the multinationals could show they were "the most productive device ever invented for speeding development." Two years later, multinational bashing reached its hysterical height when the World Council of Churches called the global corporations accomplices of "repressive states, predatory local elites and racism." Meeting in Geneva, churchmen representing 293 denominations—but not the Roman Catholic Church—urged Christians to organize strikes and boycotts against the corporate felons. Tactfully, Nestlé, Philips, Shell, and Unilever sent spokesmen to Geneva, but they came away feeling the Council wanted to provoke a confrontation, not work out any agreement on how to make companies perform better.

The chilly winds of recession, slowed growth, energy uncertainty, and political uneasiness that buffeted the world toward the end of the decade toned down the rhetoric and made a number of governments put out the welcome mat again. One country after another pulled back from radicalism, and multinational executives, surveying the continents, could begin to see signs of reason, if not yet of glowing horizons. The Chinese joined the world, and their China International Trust and Investment Co. (CITIC) said it was possible for a foreign firm to have 100 percent ownership in high-tech subsidiaries in the People's Republic. Again, governments seemed to lose their nerve and self-confidence, while corporate capitalism, challenged by consumers, environmentalists, unions, and governments, learned to live with them all. On the world scale, it looked as if the old department store dictum applied once more: stock the stuff people are buying, and move to where people are buying it.

9

Energybiz

The energy crisis illuminates the world's most dangerous political issue. It shows the festering wounds of economic and social injustice, the brutality of national competition for resources. The energy crisis brought mesmerized governments crashing into a game with rules so complex and fast-changing that practically no one can understand them. Governments are promising bold decisions—to reduce consumption through taxes, to switch to alternative sources, to begin changing the patterns of transportation. But governments don't know how to *find* oil. Governments have learned to nationalize the wells the companies have brought onstream. They have learned, more or less, to run the wells and to make the companies bid for the rights to come and search for more, but looking for new energy is, astonishingly enough, not something governments do. Yet up it comes, pumped, transported, refined, and marketed by the oil companies. From Saudi Arabia to Sumatra, from Nigeria to the North Sea, 30,000 gallons are pumped from the earth every second, every day, twenty-four hours a day.

Oil fascinates. In every car and tractor, in every tank and plane —oil. Behind almost every lighted glass tower, giant industrial plant, or little workshop, computer, space launch, and television signal—oil. Behind fertilizers, chemicals, synthetic textiles, and a million other products—the same substance that until recently was taken for granted as a seemingly inexhaustible and obedient treasure. Few noted the considerable historic irony that the most advanced civilization depended for this treasure on countries generally considered weak, backward, and disunited. Still fewer noted that this critical energy source was controlled by a handful of companies richer and more powerful than most governments.

More powerful than most national governments? During the 1973 oil embargo, the prime minister of Britain called in the top managers of BP and Shell to request preference in divvying up the available supplies. The two companies said no. They felt obligated, they explained, to share what oil they had among their customers across the globe. During those frenzied months, BP, Shell, and the other Sisters were playing God, deciding who would be warm and who would be cold, who would drive cars and who would not. After the embargo, they were largely praised for their success. Six years later, they performed similar duties when revolutionary Iran confronted the United States. After the companies' profits topped 100 percent, they were cursed, but again they were found to have acted globally but responsibly. A secret review by the Department of Energy of international oil traffic concluded that the majors had acted responsibly in meeting U. S. energy needs, but not necessarily in the total interest either of smaller companies or American consumers. "We have found some examples in which American companies have been involved in selling foreign crude in back-to-back transactions on the same day and thus made handsome profits, but such cases have been few," said an Energy Department official with access to the data. "More to the point, we have found virtually no examples of this having been done by the American members of the 'seven sisters.'"

But Big Oil has always been more hated than understood. Outbursts against Exxon have been going on for over a hundred years. The British government sought to control Shell in 1893, and Winston Churchill fulminated against Exxon and Shell ("two gigantic corporations—one in either hemisphere—stand out predominantly . . .") in 1914. Nation-states look increasingly stretched over the oil barrel—producer and consumer governments alike unable to agree even on lasting international measures to conserve the precious stuff. The Sisters, on the other hand, have become global utilities, forced to play God while remaining shrewd and ruthless day-to-day traders, watching down the line for where profits can be maximized and shortages exploited. Now they are ready to roll over into newer forms of energy so that they can be around in the twenty-first century.

Every October, Clifton Garvin begins his exhaustive review of Exxon's budget, which indeed involves more money and longer forecasting than the budgets of most countries. It is a perplexing study of riches. Exxon's cash surplus is expected to reach $8 billion in 1982, a heady pile of assets for a company that is already virtually debt-free. Garvin and his brain trust try to spend the money, holding down dividends to stockholders to help finance capital projects. But what happens when oil no longer offers investment opportunities? Will Exxon be allowed to roll over? as *Forbes* asked in 1977. "If it turns out that we're going to be denied those opportunities to work in the energy field through a combination of government action or what-have-you," Garvin says, "then we have two basic choices. We could either take the cash flow that's coming in from current successful kinds of investments and give it all back to our stockholders so they may make the choices on what they want to do. Or we could make those decisions that would lead us in other directions, into other fields."

Garvin doesn't say so, but others say it for him: if Washington denies Exxon either of its choices—conglomeration or rolling over into alternative energy—the world's biggest company will, in effect, be liquidated. To see Exxon dismantled would make a lot of people believe that divine justice exists, after all, but their taxes would go up as a result. If the oil giants aren't allowed to plow their huge new profits into developing coal and nuclear and solar energy, only the government can raise the astronomical sums needed. But government cannot operate more efficiently than private industry, so the whole exercise would merely transfer the burden from energy users to all taxpayers.

And, anyway, Exxon and the rest of the industry have already started rolling over. They have diversified into alternative energy and into such apparent oddities as retailing (Mobil buying Marcor), home appliances (Chevron's Ortho garden supply line), newspaper publishing (Arco's *London Observer*), and office equipment (Exxon's Qwip word processors). Through a careful acquisition strategy that began nearly twenty years ago, eleven oil companies now own 25 percent of all the coal in the United States, and the oil industry has the future of coal in its grip.

Exxon is the fourth largest coal reserve owner, with 9.3 billion metric tons. It is developing its coal through two subsidiaries, Carter Oil Co. and Monterey Coal Co. The companies' production will shoot from 5.2 million tons a year to 36 million in 1985. Almost one-quarter of the total will come from a single strip mine in Gillette, Wyoming. Mobil produced no coal in 1978 but owns 3.7 billion tons of reserves and by 1985 expects to enter the ranks of major producers with an annual output of at least 15 million tons. Most of the production will come from mines in Wyoming.

Besides coal, Exxon owns lead, zinc, and uranium in the United States and Canada; copper in Chile; and solar energy systems (Day Star) in the United States. Shell owns coal in the United States,

Canada, Swaziland, Botswana, and South Africa; bauxite in Brazil; tin in Indonesia, Malaysia, and Thailand; solar energy in the United States; and zinc in Bolivia. BP has bauxite, coal, and uranium in North America and Australia; nickel in Indonesia; copper in Zaire; and so on. The smaller companies like Union Oil, ENI, Pennzoil, Kerr-McGee, Endeavour, and Tenneco are widely diversified natural resources operations. "Oil companies are smart," one longtime Alaska geologist said in 1979, "and so they're getting out of the oil business as quick as they can." According to the California Public Policy Center that year, the Seven Sisters and thirteen smaller independents own holdings outside oil production worth $35 billion.[1]

It makes sense. Mining draws on the same set of corporate skills as oil. It is an extractive industry, with a strong risk element and the need for a lot of political negotiations. It requires the conversion of geological data into feasibility forecasts and discounted cash flows, and there is even an increasing technical overlap in such new alternatives as oil shale, synthetic crude from tar sand, and the upgrading of heavy oil. Several trillion barrels of crude lie trapped in tar sands and additional vast quantities of a similar form of viscous oil are set in deep reservoirs where it is too heavy to be recovered by conventional means. In western Canada, a partnership of four oil companies, Alberta province, and the Ottawa government is producing 100,000 barrels a day (b/d) from oil sands near the Athabasca River. The deposits are believed to contain as much as 967 billion barrels of oil—far greater than the total oil reserves of Saudi Arabia—but the problems of getting it out of the ground are colossal. When Ahmed Zaki Yamani, the Saudi oil minister, toured Athabasca and was told it cost $20 to produce a barrel of tar sand oil, he replied, "It costs us 40 cents a barrel." On the Alberta-Saskatchewan border, another form of unconventional oil is being extracted. It is not locked into sand formations but lies in underground pools and is too thick to be pumped by conventional methods. The Alberta firm Husky Oil is exploring ways of speeding up the flow by heating it below ground to increase its fluidity. One experimental technique involves lighting an air-fed fire at the bottom of the well. When the oil is sufficiently heated after about a year, it is forced out of the ground with injections of air and water.

[1] Michael Rogers, "The Great Alaska Raid," *New West*, July 16, 1979, p. 24.

The rollover in coal also means modern techniques. The eleven oil companies developing 25 percent of American coal reserves have leapfrogged forward over deep mining—epitomized by the soot-blackened miner, tangled labor relations, backward management, declining productivity, and black-lung disease—to strip mining in the West, which resembles huge construction sites. These mines are not labor-intensive but rely instead on draglines—giant earth-moving machines. Oil companies argue they are best able to finance, develop, and manage such operations which require heavy up-front capital than anyone else. "The companies will go into the West and act like oil companies, not coal companies," says Mel Horwitch of Harvard Business School. "They're much more capital-oriented." About 60 percent of all private money spent on coal research and development comes from the oil companies.

If Exxon went all out, Garvin estimates it could build a synthetic fuel industry in ten to fifteen years. It would be worth it, he says, because there are really no alternatives. Exxon lost $8 million on its mineral operations in 1976, $9 million in 1977, and another $9 million during the first half of 1978 but hopes to produce 3.2 million metric tons a year by 1981. Its main copper project is the $1 billion expansion of the Disputada mine in Chile—a project so big no mining company could tackle it. It will be the most expensive copper mine in the world when it enters production in the mid-1980s.

"It's too early in the game to say there are not opportunities, and ample opportunities, to spend a lot of capital money," says Garvin. "We've made it clear that going into the coal business is one of our strong desires. It's motivated by several things. One, in the short term, in its use in power generation, but longer term there is no doubt in my mind we're going to see an awful lot of coal converted into liquids and gas. It's almost impossible to get any substantial amount of energy through these sources during the next 10-year period. It's the next stage beyond that. The capital costs are great, at least $2 billion for every 50,000 to 75,000 barrels a day of production of oil shale, and it's even more in the case of liquefaction. So if you want to get two million barrels a day in a decade or so, just add it up and you'll see for yourself that you are talking several hundred billion dollars."

Shell's rollover is bold and original. It is diversifying, but on the acquisition front it is also moving deeper into oil. In a 60–40 partnership with Nigeria's oil monopoly, Shell still lifts 1.5 million b/d from Nigeria, while its prospectors look for coal in Botswana, South Africa, and Canada. Shellmen are mining coal in the United States and South Africa, and the company's metal interests are centered on its wholly owned Billiton Group, with total sales of $1.1 billion in 1977. Turnover doubled between 1975 and 1977 because of the acquisition of Union Carbide's tin interests in Thailand. Billiton has one of the world's biggest bauxite mines—in Surinam, with an annual output of over 2 million metric tons—and stakes in a major zinc and lead mine on Baffin Island in arctic Canada, and interests in the Cuajone copper deposits in Peru. Its uranium interests are confined to the United States, but its chemical interests are also in Germany and Belgium. With an awesome $3.7 billion bid for Los Angeles-based Belridge Oil Co., a tiny producer but the owner of potentially vast but hard-to-recover heavy oil deposits trapped beneath its 33,000 acres of Kern County in Central California, Shell became the owner of nearly 200 million barrels. To get it out of the ground, Shell geologists, petroleum engineers, and data processing experts at the Houston research center are using computer simulations to estimate the effects of certain enhanced recovery techniques that they have pioneered. The precision afforded by these models has raised Shell's confidence in predicting what recovery will be possible.

Texaco is in chemicals but not in minerals, and, as we have seen, it may be the one Sister suffering from entropy. The smaller oil concerns are diversifying out of oil as fast as the majors. Occidental Petroleum owns Island Creek, one of the biggest U. S. coal companies, and is building up a 5-million-metric-tons-a-year production of phosphates as part of an elaborate deal with the Soviet Union. Compagnie Française des Pétroles is involved in uranium, and the other French oil company, Elf-Aquitaine, has a share of Imetal's big nickel operations in New Caledonia. ENI also has uranium interests, and Kerr-McGee, which was the first American oil company to get into uranium, is now a big producer. Atlantic Richfield owns Anaconda, America's third largest copper producer and fifth largest aluminum group. Worldwide, roughly two-thirds of the oil giants' capital and exploration expenditures go toward exploration and production of oil, and an increasing percentage is spent on other forms of energy, *The New York Times* established in 1979. In all, they poured more money into their business than they reaped in profits, although the investment figures would be slightly lower if cash flow, including depreciation and depletion, were used instead of profits.[2]

Understandably, the companies try to stay out of the tangled knot of energy politics. Each crisis seems to clash with the solution of the others—pollution controls reduce energy supplies; energy conservation costs jobs—but the companies all agree that the faster we get at synthetic fuels, the better we will be. Punitive actions against the oil majors by governments of every stripe will not solve anything, Garvin says, but make matters worse. "If you ask a company what its corporate strategies are in the energy business in that kind of background, any manager who says to you that he clearly knows where he's going doesn't know what he's talking about," Garvin said in 1979, when the sky-high profits provoked governments and public opinion to seek to shackle the companies.[3]

The crisis of public and political confidence can be blamed partly on the majors themselves. Oilmen are the people you love to hate. They are perceived as liars, cheats, profiteers, and worse. They have made many mistakes and paid for a number of them, yet they have been pilloried as well for things they haven't done. Many people simply don't believe their denials, in part because industry pronouncements are often tactless and their timing frequently inept. Despite high-powered lobbies and the command of huge financial resources, the industry appears indecisive and ineffectual in combating charges that the majors are hoarding oil, waiting for prices to rise, that they are in cahoots with OPEC or international bankers, and that they are reaping an embarrassment of riches from crises of their own making.

The consensus among lobbyists and government officials in Washington is nevertheless that the smaller independents—the explorers, producers, pipeline operators, jobbers, and refiners—are more effective than the majors, mainly because there are so many of them. "When the call goes out to Texas," one Washington official has said, "the sky gets dark with Lear jets if they don't like what's going on here." Big Oil thinks that attacks on them satisfy a basic human urge to find scapegoats to explain away complex problems. "People feel if you could just find the

[2] Anthony Parisi, "How Oil Industry Cash Is Spent," *The New York Times*, November 26, 1979, p. D1.

[3] *Forbes*, August 15, 1977, p. 39.

villain in all this and expose him, then everything would be okay," says Robert Stobaugh, head of the Energy Project at Harvard.

Yet the industry's defensive posture also provides an example of how money and manpower alone cannot win friends or influence people. Hundreds of company and trade association lobbyists roam Washington, buttonholing Congressmen, offering information and advice and doling out election campaign contributions —more than $500,000 to members of the Senate Finance Committee alone in recent years. This battalion of "government relations specialists" is backed by divisions of corporate and outside public relations people, lawyers and consultants, yet for twenty years the oil lobby has been unable to overcome objections to new refineries.

The emergence of the so-called "spot" markets has hurt the Sisters' image because they benefit from this major structural change in the oil business and because they are involved in it. Big Oil can also play independent traders, but the spot markets have sprung up as a result of government-to-government deals, new state monopolies, independent jobbers and speculators. Shell, BP, and Exxon have affiliates in Rotterdam watching the market, although they don't trade as actively as Bulk Oil, Transol, Vitol, and Vanol, the four largest Dutch independents. In the long run, increased spot market prices work against the majors by encouraging producing countries to introduce surcharges and withhold oil from long-term contracts for quick profits. "Control will perform no useful function, however," says Johannes Wellberger, the former president of Deutsche Shell. "Controls would mean that the spot trade would just be pushed to another area. But the numbers would be the same."

As with stateless money markets, governments are divided on what to do. The immediate future will be delicately balanced, vulnerable to the next political or economic shock. Energy ministers of the biggest capitalist economies meet regularly to put precision into the vague promises their heads of government agree to. When the EEC ministers met in 1980, however, they couldn't agree on whether British North Sea oil should be counted as part of EEC's agreed target of 9.5 million b/d by 1985. David Howell, the British energy minister, would like to charge $30 a barrel, but Yamani urged him to be more modest: "A historic moment in the developing of the world oil industry,"

The Economist commented, "an OPEC minister urging a member of the OECD to keep its oil prices down."[4]

Since the 1970s, the worldwide yearly use of oil has exceeded the discovery of new reserves, and the beginning of the end of oil is said to be in sight. Futurist Herman Kahn and Standard Oil of Indiana chairman John Swearingen, however, say no one really knows how much oil is locked into the earth's crust. "It's like trying to guess the number of beans in a jar without knowing how big the jar is," says Shell's energy economics forecaster Sheldon Lambert. "God is the only one who knows—and even He may not be sure."

What really counts is all the oil and gas that might be recovered, including deposits yet to be found. There is general agreement that there is a minimum of one trillion barrels—nearly twice the world's proven reserves—still waiting to be discovered, and a rough consensus puts the total at 1.6 trillion barrels. As far as natural gas is concerned, the sky may be the limit. "No one really knows how much gas we have," says Swearingen. Some estimates range upwards of 230,000 trillion cubic feet, enough for 4,000 years.

So the industry keeps looking. For political reasons, the senior members of the sorority keep bidding for onshore and offshore leases in the United States, and in 1980, nearly 3,000 drilling rigs were boring into the American subsoil. Since the oil companies tirelessly contend that higher earnings will motivate them to search harder, steel drilling rigs—eight and ten stories high—are rising at muddy, cluttered sites from the Rocky Mountain foothills to Louisiana's Cajun country. Although production is not expected to rise, there is always the possibility, however slight, that oilmen will hit another Spindletop or Prudhoe Bay. In 1978, opinion among Exxon's top management was divided on whether to invest what eventually became $460 million in a futile search for oil in the Baltimore Canyon off the New Jersey coast. Though preliminary seismic studies were not encouraging, Exxon went ahead for PR reasons. The decision, *Time* reported, was made partly on the grounds that Exxon couldn't be seen as declining to explore in an area so close to the petroleum-hungry Northeast.[5] But 1,600 miles further north, Chevron found a whale

[4] "Problems of a European Oil Sheik," *The Economist*, January 12, 1980, p. 65.

[5] *Time*, May 7, 1979, p. 78-79.

of a well off Newfoundland in 1980, sending geologists back to their charts and computers to see if the trough running along the entire east coast of North America was of the same geological formation, or whether Hibernia trough has nothing to do with the Baltimore Canyon depression.

The Sisters will drill for anybody, including state monopolies and governments who don't believe in private enterprise. Exxon explores for Petroleos de Venezuela, which nationalized the affiliates of the majors in 1976, and for Pertamina, the Indonesian national oil concern. Pullman has been a consultant on Pemex's pipelines, Brown & Root of Houston on the Mexican monopoly's onshore fields in Veracruz and Tabasco. In the South China Sea, Chevron, Texaco, and Mobil are drilling for Peking, Exxon is off Hongkong, BP in a sector off Shanghai. "I'm pessimistic any oil company is going to do well in China," an American representative of the seismic surveyors said in 1979. "But considering the state of the world market, it's a game we can't afford not to be in." If any of them strike it rich, Peking is expected to adopt the Brazilian formula, whereby the companies will be paid in oil only if China's domestic requirements are met first. Otherwise, they will be paid in cash. In 1979, Japanese companies were trying to get the multinationals to join them in financing exploration of gas deposits in Yakutia in eastern Siberia. The Japanese have worked with the Russians, prospecting for oil reserves off the island of Sakhalin where oil was struck in 1977, and Occidental Petroleum has a twenty-year barter contract for Soviet ammonia, based on Siberian gas, for superphosphoric acid supplied by Oxy's phosphate properties in Florida. Energy, it seems, is too important to be held entirely in the hands of politicians and governments.

Yet governments are very much in the picture—according to the oilmen, much too much in the picture. In the United States, which proclaims itself a believer in private enterprise, nearly half the 19,000 employees of the Department of Energy (DOE) write and enforce regulations. In Houston, the DOE keeps forty full-time auditors in residence at Shell headquarters, and other companies also have their in-house bureaucrats hovering in the hallways. Yet even the U. S. government relies totally on the companies for figures and statistics. The President, Congress, and the DOE must base their judgment on only such information as the target industry will release. The government gets little help from the U. S. Geological Society, whose predictions have fluctuated wildly over the years and have often seemed suspiciously like propaganda aimed at supporting the industry's latest crisis. "In general, government officials have racked up an almost perfect record of inaccurate predictions," Robert Sherrill has written. "In 1970, for example, the President's Cabinet group studying imports concluded that if the import quota system was phased out rapidly, the U. S. and Canadian oil industry [it was fair to think of them as a unit since about 75 percent of Canada's oil was controlled by United States companies] would be so productive that in 1980 it would be able to supply 92 percent of North America's needs without rationing and more than 100 percent of the needs with rationing even if the two countries were cut off from all, yes all, Middle Eastern and Latin American imports." [6]

If anything, the Sisters have not lost but gained power since the 1973 oil crisis and subsequent heavy involvement of governments in energy. In 1974, when Senator Henry Jackson began his Senate Energy Subcommittee investigation of oil, he said, "We meet here this morning in an effort to get the facts about the energy crisis. The facts are . . . we don't have the facts." For the next four days, he and the other members of the subcommittee grilled the oil executives and came away virtually as ignorant as when they started. If anything, government involvement has taught the oil giants new bookkeeping—their most creative area, industry critics say. American companies operating abroad enjoy the U. S. tax code's foreign credits. Unlike most nations, the United States taxes not only domestic income but all earnings of American taxpayers. For oil companies, the tax credits produce perversely beneficial results. Instead of simply holding their U. S. tax liability to the national rate of 46 percent of profits, these credits sometimes let companies pay no taxes at all on foreign profits. How? Because if a company has to pay taxes of more than 46 percent of profits in some country, the excess is counted as a credit. The company can use the credit to reduce or even wipe out income taxes owed the U. S. Treasury from profits earned in other countries where the rate is lower than 46 percent. Income taxes in some OPEC countries not only are much higher than 46 percent but are sometimes based on the price of the oil. That gives the companies large credits that they can use to "shield" profits from, say, refineries in Caribbean tax

[6] Robert Sherrill, "The Case against the Oil Companies," *The New York Times Magazine*, October 14, 1979, p. 32.

havens where there are low or even no taxes at all. Aramco has
been one of the big beneficiaries of this tax law. In 1978, it earned
$580 millions in profits but paid no U. S. income taxes at all
on its Saudi bonanza. In fact, Aramco has paid no such taxes
since 1950.

Aramco's many critics also complain that the company is altogether too cozy with the Saudi government. Why, they ask, have
the Saudis failed to complete the 1975 nationalization? Has
Aramco persuaded the Saudis to go slow, since a full buy-out
would burden the four corporate shareholders in America with
enormous U. S. capital gains taxes? Company officers are extremely wary of divulging details of their business, and Aramco
is not required to publish financial records because its stock is
not publicly traded. Slips can prove costly for the four Sisters.
Much of the Saudis' ability to restrain fellow OPEC members
from driving up prices depends on whether they can convincingly
threaten to boost production enough to create gluts. High
Aramco officers are among the few people who know the real
size of Saudi capacity. In 1979, Exxon and Chevron divulged
to the U. S. Justice Department that Aramco had little spare
capacity. That statement helped to undercut Saudi influence
over cartel prices, and Yamani punished Exxon and Socal for
their indiscretion by ordering Aramco to cut back deliveries to
the two by 20,000 b/d.

Successive American administrations have asked Congress for
legislation to tighten Aramco's tax loopholes, but Aramco's owners argue that they need the benefits to stay competitive in world
markets. The industry's advantage is that it can provide more
"facts" more quickly than any of its critics. Exxon is unique,
one Washington oil lobbyist says. "They get together a task force
of people, do a position paper, fly it up from Houston overnight
and send an expert to explain it."

Governments can bully and cajole, decree and legislate but,
ultimately, they have a hard time finding oil. With the possible
exception of Pemex, the outfits looking for the stuff are not
government agencies, and the men who find it are not civil servants. The few governments who do explore, like the Soviets,
would love to have the majors come and help them in elaborate
joint ventures. As long as nation-states haven't defined where
they fit into the world economy themselves, the most precious
commodity is likely to remain in the hands of the global utilities.

Multioil

*(excluding state-owned oil companies
operating in only one country)*

$ billion sales 1978

	Exxon	$60.3
Seven Sisters	Royal Dutch/Shell	44
	Mobil	34.7
	Texaco	28.6
	BP	27.4
	Standard of California	23.3
	Gulf Oil	18
	Standard Oil (Indiana)	15
	ENI	12.5
	Atlantic Richfield	12.2
	Cie Française des Pétroles	10.8
	Continental Oil	9.5
	Petrobras (Brazil)	9.1
	Elf-Aquitaine	8.3

Source: OECD.

10

The Enterprising State

Insurance against nationalization, ayatollah, revolution? This way, sir.

Julian G. Radcliffe has his offices in London and the family estate in western England. If a company wants to buy peace of mind, the address is 9 Crutched Friars, EC 3. Radcliffe's Investment Insurance International, which he runs as part of the old-line Hogg Robinson brokerage group, will insure you against *coups d'etat*, ayatollahs, even war. Across the Channel, the Compagnie Française d'assurance pour le Commerce Exterieur, or COFACE, will do the same. Nearly 300,000 telexes flow from 32 Rue Marbeuf, where Jean Chapelle oversees nearly half a million dossiers on individuals and firms around the world. COFACE will insure against such calamities as collapsing governments and revolutions, and both Radcliffe and Chapelle are quite cheerful. "Unless there is anarchy for a hundred years, no country is totally uninsurable," says Radcliffe. "Of course, you're better off if you're putting in something that's basic to the economy than if you're building palaces for the royal family."

If all this is too late and revolutionaries are at the gates of your plant, you get in touch with Vinnell Corp. at 1145 Westminster Avenue in the Los Angeles suburb of Alhambra. Vinnell trains such forces as the Saudi National Guard and can be contracted to handle everything from "insults in the *souk* to final evacuation" of your personnel.

Businessmen are notoriously optimistic, and, says Radcliffe, they don't want to know whether the risk in Malaysia is greater than in Nigeria; they want to know about *their* particular risk in these countries. Radcliffe's rates range from 0.1 percent to 10 percent of the sum insured. Not counting oil rigs, ships, and planes, worldwide private premium volume for political risk coverage is about $50 million and growing fast.

Experience shows that when the payoff is near-term, to use corporate jargon, private industry usually does a better job than government, but governments like to be all things to all men. Multinationals are a threat to the sovereignty of governments, but so are national corporations, although we rarely hear about it. The cost of state intervention and state ownership—subsidized full employment, subsidized losses—is not only onerous, it is usually a smoke screen covering economic problems that have a tendency never to get solved. The state as stockholder of last resort, as employer of last resort, is a worldwide phenomenon, although some examples are more glaring than others. For years the Italian state has been taking over factories because so many old industrialists find it more convenient to cede them to the government for handsome settlements than to preside over their own bankruptcies.

Public or private ownership doesn't normally alter a company's activity; it must still be managed by professionals in whom the state places its confidence. Francois Bloch-Laine, president of France's nationalized Crédit Lyonnais, says he has never received instructions or guidelines from the government that weren't the same as those sent to private banks. "Where the stock of a corporation is owned by the government, there is likely to be more public knowledge of its operations," says John Kenneth Galbraith. "Management cannot so easily assert that something is the proprietary information of a private business. There is also, one imagines, somewhat more concern for public and legislative opinion, but the differences—as Renault, Rolls-Royce, the Tennessee Valley Authority all show—are not that great." [1]

Nationalization is the big bugaboo, even if there is less than meets the eye in many government takeovers. Multinationals want their foreign branches to contribute to profits; governments want them to contribute to local development. The enduringly profitable multinationals seem to be those who understand the broader focus of host countries, and the governments which attract the most beneficial foreign investments are those which never forget, as *The Economist* has said, "that boardrooms in New York and Tokyo contain some of the least sentimental people in the world." [2] In the first world, nationalization is rare nowadays and limited to protecting employment in lame-duck industries. Na-

[1] John Kenneth Galbraith and Nicole Salinger, *Almost Everyone's Guide to Economics* (Boston: Houghton Mifflin, 1978), p. 121.
[2] *The Economist*, June 23, 1979, Survey, p. 3.

tionalized firms are poor economic performers, and innumerable horror stories can be told about this or that government getting itself into an incredible fix. There is France's attempt at a national solution to semiconductors that led the Giscard d'Estaing Administration to bankroll competition against itself. There is Peru's nationalization and subsequent denationalization of its anchovy fleet, the world's largest, and there is the heavyhanded nationalization of oil in Indonesia and Malaysia that led to billion-dollar losses and shattering corruption.

The idea of state ownership springs from political theory. Many nineteenth-century socialists felt that the means of production, distribution, and exchange should be owned by a collective of the people, and modern nationalized industries are saddled with a historically determined range of activities and, increasingly in Western Europe, with a historically determined work force. Business, of course, can also be pretty liturgical about its opposition to state ownership. As Galbraith puts it, "No business convention ends without the ritual hymn of praise for rugged individualism and private enterprise, even though the individualism is now manifested by good, conformist organization men who themselves have liquidated the power of the old capitalist free-enterprisers."

Nevertheless, if corporations check with Radcliffe before moving into a new country, it is no wonder. With impunity, governments can break previous commitments, raise taxes, cancel patents, and expropriate assets—but more about that when we come to the UN and its code of conduct for multinational enterprise.

The Newly Industrialized Countries have often found state capitalism a better solution than messy nationalizations of local subsidiaries of global corporations. Instead of expropriating the local operations of U. S. Steel, Bethlehem Steel, Pfizer, and August Thyssen-Hutte, Brazil created Companhia Siderurgica Nacional and, with public money, turned it into the world's sixteenth largest steel producer.

If Argentina and Italy are examples of mixed economies going nowhere, Brazil and South Korea are examples of aggressive government-prodded dynamics reaching for the brass ring. Social democracy seems to work best in its early stages when it still has a hungry and willing work force and when real productivity can be built on previous generations' habits of work and saving. "By now even those showplaces of social democracy, the Scandinavian countries, are finding it increasingly difficult to maintain economic productivity," writes Ashby Bladen, senior vice president of Guardian Life Insurance Co. of America. "Since there no longer exist adequate incentives for working hard it is necessary to find disincentives for not working. In Sweden they are trying to figure out how to put a tax on leisure." [3]

But while it goes, how sweet it is! The GNP shoots through the roof, cheap, unskilled labor flocks to the cities, and nobody worries about the environment. The mood is upbeat, and little time is spent on organizing efforts to redress grievances. In Brazil everything is huge, especially the land area (the fifth largest in the world, 8.5 million square kilometers, a surprising number of them still virgin), the population (approaching 120 million, the world's eighth largest), the GNP (the world's tenth largest, approaching $200 billion, trebled in real terms since 1964). During the go-go years between 1964 and the 1973 oil crisis, Brazil's growth hovered near 10 percent a year. Internal demand mushroomed, and, despite the 2.7 percent annual increase in population, real GNP per capita more than doubled to $1,600. Brazilians cultivated optimism and could be said to share the North American dedication to life, liberty, and the pursuit of happiness, but in the reverse order.

Foreign capital and technology poured in, confident in the strong-arm rulers and the vast natural and human resources. Although the economic "miracle" meant little to most of the population, Brazil is now the eighth biggest Western economy, management by government technocrats running ever larger state concerns whose efficiency and profitability at times rival or surpass private enterprise.

Sixteen of Brazil's twenty largest firms are run by the state, which owns 86 percent of the total assets involved. Besides Companhia Siderurgica Nacional, the world's sixteenth largest steel producer, there is Companhia Vale do Rio Doce, the iron-ore producer that has made Brazil the second largest iron-ore exporter (after Australia) but is also involved in shipping, reforestation, marketing, engineering, consulting, geological prospecting, and mining. Its various joint ventures with European, American, and Japanese companies include metal-pelletizing plants, bauxite and aluminum production, pulp manufacture, and an iron-ore project in the Amazon jungles that is being touted as the world's biggest

[3] *Forbes*, October 15, 1979, p. 128.

mining development. Vale do Rio Doce is the first state concern to have ventured into the international stock market, issuing debentures on the Frankfurt, New York, and Tokyo Euromarkets. "We are going to need fabulous quantities of money," says its president Fernando Roquette Reis. "We are involved in projects that require the building of hydroelectric plants, hotels, houses, even jails. Besides that, we have to attract engineers and specialized people to regions like the Amazon by paying them three times as much as they would make in São Paulo or Rio. I'm not a defender of a state takeover of the economy, but I believe there are sectors and activities where only public enterprises can go in."

Going after foreign capital is what makes the Brazilian state companies unique. Governments of other emerging countries routinely step into industrial development, but only Brazil's big state enterprises have successfully attracted foreign capital. And Petrobras (the oil enterprise), Electrobras, Embratel (telecommunications), Embraer (aircraft manufacture), and the other state monoliths are forging ahead, come hell, high water, and 100-percent-a-year inflation. Their ambitious, multibillion-dollar projects to develop energy, mineral resources, and transportation are meant to make Brazil self-sufficient and to create export earnings. But all this wasn't so much planned as the result of a lack of courage, vision, and financial resources of the country's private sector. As in most developing countries, local entrepreneurs invested in projects that were low in risks and quick in returns. Real estate in particular had been a favorite outlet for private capital, and all those luxury high-rises along Rio's Ipanema and Copacabana beaches and in São Paulo's frenetic downtown may be more lasting monuments to Brazilian private capital than factories, mining, and farming. Also, say the technocrats, too many native capitalists all too happily sold out to foreign multinationals instead of competing with them (one-third of U. S. companies entering Brazil in the 1960s did so by directly acquiring existing Brazilian enterprises).

The much-vaunted Brazilian miracle was helped by the vast pool of labor from the immense and arid northeast. People moved in droves to the overcrowded cities in the south, becoming a 3,000-kilometer human pipeline of cheap labor and creating a geographical absurdity—65 percent of the country's population became urbanized. The big development projects in the Amazon took their toll as thousands of workers died from disease and the climate. The buses were sent by southern industrialists to pick up the penniless workers of the sunbaked, exhausted land of the northeast. Yet, as *The Economist* has remarked, the human costs have almost certainly been lower in Brazil than in the two countries which have undergone a similar process at as great a scale and at as fast a speed—China and the U.S.S.R.[4] Critics of the breakneck development wonder whether the boom has made the most of the country's resources or whether Brazil's new riches were built, like Argentina's in the 1930s, on the sand of fickle world demands, and not on the rock of Brazil's enormous natural wealth.

South American governments rarely keep out of the way. Until 1974, Brazil's military rulers had moved away from protectionism, away from nationalism, toward internationalism and control via the money supply. But the oil shock made President Ernesto Geisel move toward "planned investment," and his government began, to quote a Hudson Institute report, "printing laws like cruzeiros." Subsidized loans became the law, and every loan-worthy individual said he was a farmer or a resident of a poor region or a deserving industrialist about to invest in the northeast. These borrowers promptly lent back to the government on index-linked bonds, and inflation shot up from 15 to 55 percent. Geisel had started all this because he thought such policies would bring better balance to the economy and help the poor. When the interventionism produced the opposite effect, he doubled the dosage.

Conselho Administrative de Defensa Economica (CADE) moved against the multinationals. The heavy electric-equipment companies—Brown, Boveri & Cie, Siemens, Hitachi, AEG-Telefunken, Toshiba, General Electric, and Westinghouse—were guilty of strangulating local electrical firms, CADE established, without saying that the less efficient domestic businessmen had disliked competing with the globals and cheerfully sold out to them. Workers got 132 percent pay raises, quickly dissipated by roaring inflation. When West Germany's Chancellor Helmut Schmidt was begged by a bishop in São Paulo to "instruct Volkswagen do Brasil to pay the same wages as Volkswagen in Wolfsburg," he haughtily replied, "Excellent idea, then VW Brazil would close, transfer some production back home and marginally ease my unemployment problem in West Germany."

CADE wrote a "law of similars," which threw up tariff barriers

---

[4] "A Survey of Brazil," *The Economist*, July 31, 1976, p. 56.

against goods for which local substitutes existed at comparable prices, then rewrote it to make it tougher and added a measure requiring parts of the proceeds of foreign loans to be held in idle, noninterest-bearing accounts for various periods of time. The state companies still stumbled, but Petrobras achieved a breakthrough in gasohol. Sensibly, the Petrobras technocrats said it takes the sun 15 million years to convert its energy to oil, but only six years for sunshine to become methanol via eucalyptus or other trees and about six months to become alcohol in the form of sugar, *cavassa,* and other fast crops. The Ministry of Industry says that six million of the country's nine million cars and trucks will soon be running on a 20 percent alcohol mixture, a feat *The Economist* said "shows that Brazil has broken through to become one of the liveliest of young technological countries and that it can flexibly use the price system to put new technologies into effect." [5]

If nationalism demands a Brazilian solution to everything, ebullient economics minister Antonio Delfim Netto isn't above buying foreign know-how when it is critical. Petrobras has had no difficulty hiring those Texans who drill for everybody else. Netto says Brazil must go for fast growth "while trying to live with tolerable inflation." The country's debt may go over $130 billion by 1984, but he doesn't seem to lose any sleep over it. A cartoonist's delight with his portly shape and owlish look, Netto is the man closely identified with the phenomenal 1964–1974 boom. "Reducing production is not the way out," he said in 1979 when he unleashed the money supply by 60 percent—approximately the inflation rate plus the GNP growth.

Less than six months after he took office, however, Netto announced still more measures, including a 30 percent devaluation of the cruzeiro and an end to credit subsidies. The irony of Brazil's breathless forward plunge between 1964 and the oil crisis of 1973 and its reverses since has been its cheap borrowing. The state enterprises accumulated most of the debt; two-thirds of the national foreign debt is theirs. In an about-face on going-it-alone nationalism, Netto recognized that the motor of the country's miracle had been its industrial exports and that 62 percent of the 100 biggest exporters were the multinationals. This recognition came too late, however, to keep IBM do Brasil in place. In

1978, the screws of the law of similars were tightened, and IBM, Burroughs, Hewlett-Packard, NCR, Olivetti, Four Phase, and TRW decided to bow out of the Brazilian computer market— expected to be worth $800 million by 1990—rather than build "similar" microcomputers that would eventually exclude them. The CADE guidelines in effect asked them to extend their hand, then to cut it off themselves. After months of tortuous negotiations, the government awarded control of the industry to four national companies, principally Computadores Sistemas Brasileiros, or Cobra. The decision didn't come without controversy, and *Jornal do Brasil,* the leading national newspaper, called it "one of the most abrupt and deplorable forms of state intervention in the economy." [6] The fear, which the technocrats dismissed as unfounded, is that Brazil may have condemned itself to obsolescence in a field where dramatic changes occur very fast. "Since the government will allow no other manufacturers, what is to keep these companies from producing in 1987 that which they produced in 1977? It makes no difference to them—the one who pays is the consumer," the paper editorialized. The ostensible reason for the go-it-alone decision was the same as the cause of India's scuffle with IBM—the endemic balance-of-payment deficit —but the technocrats at Cobra, stung by the criticism, decided to double the UN standard for minicomputers, decreeing Brazilian computers would have to have not 65,000 bit memories, but double that. When IBM pulled out, however, Brazil lost exports of $100 million over five years in IBM do Brasil hardware exported to Japan and other Latin American markets.

The executives at Cobra and the other state enterprises are not afraid of spending money. With the army, they are the biggest spenders in the Brazilian economy, and their methods of bookkeeping and losses are regarded as a bad joke, even in the accountancy profession. The technocrats channel credits, import privileges, and handsome salaries their way. The presidents of the public sector corporations often get more than $100,000 a year, more than their capitalist colleagues in multinational subsidiaries.

All of which doesn't mean Brazil is a textbook case of an aggressive NIC government beating global corporations to mincemeat. The ultimate corporate clout *is* technology, and while the

[6] *The New York Times,* February 19, 1978, p. F3.

last chapter of the Cobra saga has not yet been written, Brasilia will have time to ponder the cost of nationalism in carmaking. For years, the Brazilian government insisted on a high percentage of local components, but in 1979, Ford and GM said that if Netto continued to insist on high local content, they would continue to build costly, outdated models. But if Netto lowered the requirements, they would build cheap, modern vehicles. When the two American automakers confronted Nigeria with the same choice, Lagos turned a deaf ear and kept insisting on an increase in Nigerian content from 30 percent in 1979 to 100 percent by 1992. Netto, along with finance ministers in Argentina, Australia, and Mexico, was willing to listen. Protectionist Argentina was converted by a Ford study showing that Argentinians paid twice as much for cars as they should.

If Brazil's growth is the envy—and, say its technocrats, a model for other NICs—it is ho-hum compared to South Korea's sizzling pace. Seoul's eight million citizens consider a sixty-hour workweek routine and move at a pace that makes Tokyo's legendary workaholics seem in slow motion. Since 1961, the GNP has been growing at about 10 percent a year, and manufacturing has risen about 17 percent every year. The per capita income of this one-time colony of Japan was $82 in 1961, roughly the same as China's, and in 1979, $1,242, at least three times the People's Republic level. And all this is taking place within a system that sets its goals from the top but encourages private enterprise to carry them out.

A country without resources where, at the end of World War II, the poor ate bark off trees to keep from starving, South Korea had little in its 4,300-year history to suggest its people would accept rapid industrialization. Traditional Confucian society may revere government service but holds merchants in low esteem; yet, in 30 years, this small country of 37 million has mastered an economic growth rate that has replaced Japan's as the wonder of the world.

In 1961, when a young general named Park Chung Hee seized power, it was still fashionable in Washington to think of South Korea as "the basket case destined to rest indefinitely on the U. S. doorstep," in the words of Jim Mahn Je, president of the Korea Development Institute, Seoul's largest think tank. Little more than a month after taking power, Park centralized planning in a new Economic Planning Board and, to show the importance he attached to its activities, made its head the deputy prime minister. Since then, the government has set the policies, and businessmen follow in an unusual blend of state direction and private enterprise that is quite different from the Japan Inc. model, which implies a government-business partnership in which policy reflects consensus between equals.

In South Korea, the government's strongest weapon is its control of credit. The government can—and has—put companies out of business by shutting off their credit, and it has kept companies out of some fields or forced them into others through this control of funds for expansion. "Whereas large Japanese industrial groups often have their own banks and get funds from them," Norman Pearlstine has written, "Park confiscated all privately held banks soon after taking power. Although Park has vowed that he'll keep them out of the hands of Korea's big industrial groups—aides say he thinks Japan's industrial groups are too powerful for that country's own good—top economic officials say that most of the country's commercial banks will make share offerings to the public in the early 1980s. Control, however, is likely to remain in the government's hands for years to come." [7]

Since Park's assassination in 1979, Seoul's powerful business community has been in favor of a return to parliamentary democracy as the best guarantee for a free-market economy. "Market forces pull away from dictatorships," says Chung Ju Yung, the controlling stockholder of the Hyundai Group, Korea's most profitable multinational ($324 million profits on $3.7 billion sales). Hyundai, a manufacturer of steel, ships, and cars, is the backbone of Korean heavy industry.

Business leaders have to keep the economy kicking over rapidly to maintain cash flows, service debt, and even pay wages, a fact that made the armed forces take the back seat after Park's murder. Foreign bankers, briefcases in hand and looking assured, flooded the lobbies of Seoul's international hotels less than four weeks after the assassination, and by the end of 1980, Korea's Commerce and Industry Department forecasts that the country will be the world's largest exporter of textiles.

The Mexican government is a powerful, centralized one. It has a big role in Mexico's drive to industrialize, but what makes

[7] Norman Pearlstine, "How South Korea Surprised the World," *Forbes*, April 30, 1979, p. 56.

it similar to Japan and South Korea and different from Brazil is its heavy reliance on private enterprise. To develop, Mexico must sell oil, but, thanks to OPEC, it won't have to sell very much. Like Brazil, it has started with basics. Steel production at the end of the 1980s will be 29 million metric tons as compared to 8.4 million tons a decade earlier, petrochemical output 49 million tons vs. 7.4 million tons. Cars are assembled by Volkswagen, GM, Ford, and Chrysler, and Mexican companies are beginning to make electrical motors and turbine generators, pumps and forged metal products.

Monterrey, the steel and factory city 200 kilometers south of the Texas border, contains 3 percent of Mexico's population but produces 20 percent of its $100 billion GNP. Monterrey's industrialists are legendary, particularly four powerful, family-linked holding companies known as the Monterrey Group. Grupo Industrial Alfa SA, one of the four, has rolled over into petrochemicals, fibers, television sets, capital machinery, and farm equipment from its base in steel. Its top management is schooled at the Wharton School of Economics in Philadelphia, Harvard, and the Massachusetts Institute of Technology and wants to be compared with the big Japanese industrialists. Alfa's whole outlook is geared to the government's plan to raise exports of increasingly sophisticated consumer and industrial goods. It thinks it can build electrical motors of the quality of Hitachi at 75 percent of Hitachi's cost. The government greatly encourages capital investment by private industry with tax credits up to 20 percent and no taxes on capital gains. The official corporate tax rate is on a par with that of the United States, but because it invests so heavily year after year, Alfa usually pays at the rate of 18 to 19 percent of profits. Alfa has joint ventures with Hitachi and Ford and bought out Massey-Ferguson's Mexican business after the government pressured the Canadian farm equipment company to "Mexicanize." World bankers are eager to lend to Mexican companies like Alfa. In 1979, First Boston floated $65 million of debt for an Alfa subsidiary in a private placement to five U. S. insurance companies. BankAmerica has headed a syndicate that included Deutsche Bank in a $75 million loan to Alfa.

Tijuana, Juarez, Nogales, and other towns along the U. S. border are becoming so many day-and-night industrious Taipeis, booming with 600 foreign plants called *maquilas* or *maquiladores* (literally cosmetics, hence subcontractors). Here, the federal government has taken the opposite tack. In Monterrey, it is spending oil money to build industry; in the border towns, it lets the foreigners build *maquilas,* supply the machinery, and pay the salaries.

All of the border *maquilas* take advantage of U. S. tariff regulations. If the components are American and the product returns to the United States, duty is paid only on the value added by foreign assembly. "Our workers are approaching the productivity of our workers in Taiwan and Hongkong," says Ron Tosta, who manages two electronics assembly plants for Ampex Corp. in Juarez. Ampex is not alone in Juarez, just across the Rio Grande from El Paso, Texas. GM, General Electric, Westinghouse, and Chrysler are also there with their *maquila* shops, as are Matsushita and Sony.

Mexico is a partnership between free enterprise and a powerful central government that has produced results, whether it is with heavy state investment in industrialization in the interior or *maquilas* along the U. S. border. The question is whether the results can come fast enough for a land where half the work force is underemployed and 40 percent of the people live on subsistence agriculture.

While the verdict is still out on state capitalism in newly developed countries, there seems to be no doubt that government monopolies are a failure in more mature economies. The president of Crédit Lyonnais may never receive instructions or guidelines different from those sent to private French banks, but nationalized industries are more often bedeviled by lack of clear objectives, and having them overridden by political considerations, than by a hands-off approach by governments. State companies are rarely allowed to buy outside expertise for difficult and costly developments—Pemex, Petrobras, and the other national oil corporations are the exception—but, worst of all, they cannot roll over. The process of change and development that helps an organization to continue to grow even when its basic operations are in decline is denied state companies. Their objectives are fixed, and they are effectively barred from evolving.

Some Third World "Biggies"

	products	Sales, $ million 1977
National Iranian Oil	oil	$22.315
Petroleos de Venezuela	"	9.628
Petrobras (Brazil)	"	8.284
Pemex (Mexico)	"	3.394
Haci Omer Sabanci Holding (Turkey)	textiles	2.902
Hyundai Group (South Korea)	shipbuilding transportation	2.590
Indian Oil	oil	2.316
Chinese Petroleum (Taiwan)	"	1.920
Zambia Industrial & Mining	mining, copper	1.862
Lucky Group (South Korea)	oil, electronics	1.744
Steel Authority of India	metal refining	1.447
Turkiye Petrolleri (Turkey)	oil	1.376
Kuwait National Petroleum (Kuwait)	"	1.375
Korea Oil	"	1.341
Samsung Group (South Korea)	industrial equipment electronics, textiles	1.305
CODELCO-Chile	mining, copper	1.231
Koc Holding (Turkey)	auto construction	1.207
Philippines National Oil	oil	0.986

Source: Harvard Business Review.

11

Ali Baba

In Kuala Lumpur you need Ali Babas. In Rio you need *despachantes*—expediters who, for a fee, jog along the bureaucracy so you can get that import license, permit, or other indispensable piece of paper. Not surprisingly, many *despachantes*—there are two pages of them in the São Paulo Yellow Pages—are relatives of bureaucrats.

The multinationals are, in the popular imagination, the corrupters, vast power structures awash with cash and ready to debauch third world innocents and pay off politicians in advanced societies. Christianity and Marxism notwithstanding, poverty is not particularly ennobling. The meek may inherit eternity and the grand tomorrow, but in the here and now it is mostly you against me, whether it is one-to-one for the best streetcorner to sell umbrellas, or tribal, one ethnic group settling old slights by warring over those new ministries and bureaucracies in the new capitals. The Ali Babas in Malaysia's hot and humid capital fall into the latter category.

Besides being the world's largest supplier of tin and rubber, Malaysia exports a modest amount of oil from its north Borneo fields. It has followed Indonesia's example in setting up a national oil monopoly, Petronas (with Exxon and Shell as its partners). Under the New Economic Policy, Petronas requires that any company bidding on oil- or gas-related projects must be 51 percent locally owned. The policy has become the cause of deep concern for scholarly, soft-spoken Prime Minister Hussein bin Onn, but he is deeply committed to *bumiputra*, the "son-of-the-soil" affirmative action that is supposed to unravel the racial tangle by 1990 and make up for a century's neglect of ethnic Malays. The *bumiputra* laws frankly discriminate against the industrious Chinese, who make up an uneasy 38 percent of the population, and the highly educated and qualified Indians, who form just over 10 percent.

Malaysia's nominal democracy—its liberal, bourgeois, entrepreneurial, property-owning stability—rests upon a delicate alliance among uppercrust Malays who run the government, Chinese who run the money, and Indians—mostly Punjabis—who are in business or hold down all sorts of jobs in the public service. Prime Minister Hussein admits that *bumiputra* has curtailed investment, but the policy was virtually imposed by traumatic race riots in the 1960s. If there are now over a hundred *bumiputra* millionaires, few Malays have made it in business. They have become Ali Babas—front men who for a fee will have relatives and themselves constitute the 51 percent sons-of-the-soil majority.

The multinationals with interests in Malaysia have, on the whole, coped with the job of Malaysianizing themselves. Shirt-sleeved Scotsmen still run the companies and have been labeled "non-*bumiputra* residents." But Ali Babas *are* expensive. In one documented case, a Malay offered to be the Ali Baba for an American providing catering services to the oil-rig workers. In return, he wanted free-of-charge shares worth $125,000, a questionable loan to purchase another $200,000 worth, plus a $175,000 "service fee." But Malaysians, whatever their race, have become richer during the past twenty years—the GNP advances at a steady 7 percent clip every year, and as a Chinese Malaysian has put it, "Now that they've got their Hondas, they are less likely to smash up my Mercedes."

Across the Strait of Malacca, *bumiputra* is called *pribumi,* but the idea is the same: to give indigenous Indonesians a larger role (and the ethnic Chinese minority a lesser role) in the economy. Indonesia is the most densely populated and poorest of the OPEC members. Oil and gas earnings top $10 billion a year, but there are disturbing signs that the military government of President Suharto will again miss the opportunity to industrialize Indonesia as it did after the 1973 oil embargo price run-up. Suharto's base of support is undermined by widespread corruption that reaches to the cabinet and to the first family—earning Mrs. Tien Suharto the nickname, in Jakarta gossip, of "Mrs. Ten Percent."

The hitch in the *pribumi* program is the scarcity of local capital and entrepreneurs. Many companies are nominally headed by *pribumis,* while financial and management control is still in the hands of Chinese. Such an arrangement is often the means by which foreign companies, including many of the 200 Japanese firms that have taken on local partners, have Indonesianized. The curbs on Chinese businessmen are draining capital and management know-how out of the country, and the schizophrenia about investment from abroad makes it increasingly unlikely that Indonesia will attract the kind of labor-intensive "offshore" plants that have served as springboards to industrialization for Singapore, Malaysia, and the Philippines. National Semiconductor Corp. and Fairchild Camera and Instrument Corp. are the only chipmakers to have located in Indonesia, even though rising wage costs have made Hongkong and Taiwan increasingly less attractive.

Nothing galls governments of emerging countries more than seeing their national resources being exported, fresh from mine or field, to be exposed to the mercies of a volatile commodity market before being processed and packaged in faraway affluent places. The pressure is naturally on the multinationals to transfer technology, to move their factories upstream to the source so that the countries of origin can share in the benefits.

On the surface, it seems the governments hold all the marbles, that with their array of carrots and sticks they can get the global corporations to produce more locally and, in the case of Brazil, Mexico, and other NICs, force them to export to the rest of the developing world. But the trump card is the multinationals' ability to decide where they will put their plants—that is, to decide who will work and reap the benefits of technology and who will not.

This ability to withhold services is a formidable weapon that, even in the aftermath of the 1973 oil embargo, Exxon, BP, Shell, and Mobil were able to wield against Indonesia and Malaysia.

In 1975, when Pertamina, Indonesia's state-owned oil corporation, found itself in a $10 billion jam, resulting from what it later called "uncontrolled" management and overspending, President Suharto unilaterally tore up contracts with the four oil majors. As the eighth largest exporter of the thirteen-member OPEC, Indonesia was not without clout, and the oil companies knuckled under. Previously, Pertamina had taken 65 percent of the profits, after deductions for recovery costs, with 35 percent going to the companies. Now, Suharto's law was an 85–15 split and stiffer cost-recovery terms. Prodded by panicky governments in Washington and London, the oil companies agreed but stopped exploring for new oil. Two years later, Suharto got nervous and tried to stimulate exploration by offering marginal incentives on such items as depletion allowances and pricing details. When the oil companies didn't bite, he tried again in 1978, this time calling executives from the United States, Japan, and Europe to Jakarta and telling them that Indonesia was seeking "mutually beneficial" relationships in new contracts. "Everything is flat out again," said John Dailey, president and general manager of Stanvac Indonesia, the Mobil-Exxon joint venture, when the Suharto government came around and provided incentives again.

Corruption and hostility toward foreign investors among lower-echelon bureaucrats create a basic ambiguity among Indonesians as to what kind of industry the country should have. "The small-is-beautiful battle is going on in government right now," said H. W. Wilson, senior regional representative for Bechtel Inc. which built more than $2 billion worth of Indonesian installations in 1979. Says Masao Koizumi, president of the Japanese Chamber of Commerce in Jakarta, "Unlike other countries in this region, Indonesia still is in conflict between the modern and the traditional. There is a lot of conflict between the technocrats and the nationalists."

Multinationals are caught in this conflict in many parts of the world. In 1979, the Suharto government ruled that new companies must be at least 20 percent *pribumi*-owned and that all companies must set up training and promotion programs to Indonesianize their operations within ten years. Kaiser Aluminum and Centrex, a Japanese-Indonesian textile venture, were the first to comply by selling shares to the public. BAT Indonesia followed suit, offering 30 percent of its equity for $26 million. "There is a lot of ambiguity in the attitude of government officials toward investment," concedes Anwar Ibrahim, deputy chairman for planning and promotion at Jakarta's investment coordinating board. "They want to stand on their own two feet, but they recognize they need know-how and technology."

Considered in its proper context, the choice of local vs. foreign ownership is more often than not a choice between a foreign-owned enterprise and no enterprise at all. Malaysia has made sure it gets enterprise. It has set out to provide itself with an industrial sector and has benefited from the transfer to low-wage countries of low-technology industries, especially textiles and the assembly of electrical gadgets. There is no minimum wage—$100 a month is a reasonable rate for a production worker in many of the rural locations in which multinationals set up. Tax concessions to "pioneer" industries are generous, electricity and other services are in most places reliable, and, although all foreigners have to get work permits, there is little bureaucratic hostility. Also, the rules about *bumiputra* participation don't apply to pioneers.

Foreign investment in developing countries is always the result of a bargain struck between a company and the host country. Good or bad, all bargains are influenced by numerous considerations beyond the control of the two parties—tax, insurance, and exchange policies in third countries vying for the plums of industrialization, the world trade climate. Multinational enterprises differ from other foreign links that new and often insecure small states must secure. A subsidiary of a global becomes deeply involved in the internal economy. Developing countries feel unsettled, insecure, and suspicious. They want Ali Babas, local investors, and talent to participate in the activities of the multinationals. They want joint ventures—almost a buzz phrase in third world rhetoric—and they expect technology to come to their doors, along with the money. Zaire threw out all foreigners in 1973 and tried to lure them back in again two years later. In November 1973, when copper prices were high and the economy was booming, President Mobutu Sese Seko announced a program of placing all business, commerce, and agriculture in the hands of Zairians. A year later, the government stepped in to nationalize some key industries, arguing that they were being mismanaged. The program was more sweeping than in most other African countries. It crystallized an urge to break the ties of dependence on the former colonial overlords. Politically, the move reaped great rewards for Mobutu, comparable to those won by President Idi Amin of Uganda when he expelled Asians in 1972, but economically, it was a disaster since there was no educated, entrepreneurial class to keep the business running. Agriculture suffered. Stores ran out of stocks and closed. Transportation broke down. Zaire's wealth, far from spreading to reach a great number, was concentrated in the hands of a rapacious elite.

When Mobutu decided to seek to lure the foreigners back, his government offered the original owners 40 percent of their former businesses. There were few takers. A year later, the offer was increased to 60 percent, with the foreigners retaining full management control and able to choose a Zairian Ali Baba partner who would pay the owner the remaining 40 percent. This time, the major companies came back.

Foreign investors demonstrate an unsurprising preference for a stable and friendly economic environment. Much has been made of multinationals cozying up to dictatorships, when not actually having tried to subvert progressive regimes when they have come to power. Unconsciously, perhaps, managers of global companies will weigh in with regimes that give them the fewest headaches, and that is often governments which don't have too frequent elections. But the multinationals' alleged affection for reactionary regimes *can* be overdrawn. Venezuela has as practicing a democracy as anyone has been able to devise in Latin America; Colombia has a very modified kind of democracy and Brazil a military junta; yet multinational companies play identical roles in all three. They are pervasive in all three and have influence in all three. But, if anything, Brazil has never been quite as wide open for global corporations as both its advertisements and its angry nationalists pretend. One ineluctable fact in a system of nation-states is that the objectives of different states are often mutually incompatible. The overall goal of global corporations is, if nothing else, consistent.

12

Stuck in Neutral

Theoretically, labor should have no difficulty countering the challenge of global enterprise. In reality, however, unions are stuck in neutral, benevolent monopolies too chauvinistic and too parochial to accommodate to modern economics. Although their early leaders called upon workers to unite, unions pay only lip service to the brotherhood of the laboring masses when it comes to risking jobs to support workers in other lands. In thinking, structure, and goals they are rooted in the last century.

Their argument is that the basic stuff corporations are made of—technology, capital, and marketplace savvy—is mobile. Workers and their unions are not. The $300 billion that American corporations invested overseas during the last quarter century have reaped handsome profits, but they have also resulted in a decline in American jobs and in a shift in the distribution of wealth. Transfer of technology means transfer of wealth, ultimately.

The American Federation of Labor-Congress of Industrial Organizations (AFL-CIO) holds the largest U. S. companies responsible for "the dimming of America" by emptying American factories and giving away American technology, thereby turning "the greatest industrial power into a nation of hamburger stands!" European unions are more militant than organized labor in America but appear to understand even less than the AFL-CIO the nature of the challenge. Unions in the third world belong to the elite, and unions in socialist countries are a farce. When the Soviet Union joined the International Labor Organization (ILO), headquartered in Geneva, Moscow got around the ILO's right-to-strike credo by saying Russians don't want to strike because the factories in the Soviet Union already belong to them.

Labor doesn't lobby national governments for relaxed immigration practices so that laid-off Siemens workers in Germany can work in understaffed Siemens plants in Sweden, or out-of-work Olivetti employees in Brazil can temporarily assemble Olivetti typewriters in Mexico. Transnational bargaining is *verboten* in many countries because it tends to turn into secondary boycotts, and labor thinks that's just fine.

Trade unions formed international organizations long before governments got together to create the League of Nations. The International Metalworkers Federation was established in 1893 and now claims ten million members in affiliated national unions; the International Federation of Chemical and General Workers' Union dates from 1907 and counts three million members. However, as the International Labor Organization, itself born of the Versailles Treaty of 1919, admitted in 1976, "It would appear that transnational collective bargaining in the strict meaning of the term is not for the immediate future." [1]

Multinational corporations tend to live in or create their own special worlds. They show a marked preference for training people for the use of their technologies, rather than adapting technologies to the available work force. They are often highly professionalized in their labor relations, and their pay scales and fringe benefits are usually in the lead. Their internal communications are highly developed, and their managers naturally tend to look to headquarters for their wider career aspirations. An employee's wages, job evaluation, and performance are often rated according to criteria reflecting company experience elsewhere. But, the ILO estimated, multinationals have created between thirteen and fourteen million jobs worldwide—twelve million in developed countries and two million in LDCs.

Created or exported jobs? Predictably, American unions are no favorites of *maquilas* and have lobbied Congress to change the customs laws. "They deprive American workers of jobs," grumbles one textile union spokesman, but Mayor Aureliano Gonzales Vargas of Juarez says Mexican workers have never been competitors to American workers. In the early 1970s, the AFL-CIO was engaged in a statistical battle with the Emergency Committee for American Trade, the Department of Commerce, and the Harvard Business School over the loss of American jobs. Between 1966 and 1969, the labor organization charged, American global corporations were responsible for a net loss of half a million jobs. Harvard's Robert Stobaugh, on the other hand, had figures show-

[1] *Social and Labor Practices of Some European-based Multinationals in the Metal Trade* (Geneva: International Labor Office, 1976), p. 67.

ing the internationalization of American business had contributed to the *growth* of employment in the United States—528,000 new jobs. The totally different conclusions were based on different assumptions. The labor study assumed that a worker is infinitely employable in the United States if only a company will keep its capital in the country. The management figures assumed that if a worker now employed by a global corporation was not working for the corporation, he would be unemployed. As Barnet and Muller pointed out in *Global Reach*, the company statisticians operated on the assumption that foreign investment was "defensive"—that if a company didn't locate a factory in a cheap labor market, the displaced American worker would be unemployable, while union statisticians acted as if comparatively high labor costs in the United States made little difference in competition with foreign companies.[2]

It is all a matter of perception and national priorities. If North American and European governments spend part of their GNP to bandage lame duck industries, Japan and other aggressive East Asian governments push their industries to roll over and to move "upmarket" at every opportunity. Every year Japan's Economic Planning Agency comes out with a list of goods of which imports from South Korea or Taiwan are rising, indicating that these are the industries Japanese corporations should roll out of. In 1980 it was general textiles, transistor radios, rubber and plywood goods, Christmas electric bulbs, stringed musical instruments, and general shipbuilding. Death sentences are approaching for some electrical equipment, synthetic resins, and industrial pharmaceuticals.

In North America, the United Auto Workers is the only union even to think of internationalizing contract termination dates for possible strike action in several countries at the same time. The UAW is also the only union to realize that wage parity among GM workers in the Philippines, Germany, and the United States will not only be fair but ultimately stop the export of jobs by making such exports uneconomical.

Despite the socialist rhetoric, unions have little sympathy for their brethren in Less Developed Countries. Malaysians agreed to and financed a fairly big scheme to prefabricate wooden housing components for export to Australia. Then Australian unions objected, refusing to unload cargoes that would have given their

[2] Barnet and Muller, *Global Reach,* op. cit.

fellow countrymen good cheap homes, and the Australian government obeyed its unions' voice and slapped on a tariff. In France,
unions are dead set against exporting capital; they feel it means
exporting jobs, and, while France is the fourth biggest exporter
in the industrialized West, it comes in a poor sixth in foreign investments. And the gap separating France from other advanced
countries is not closing; that is, French workers don't have a
higher employment rate than British and West German workers,
although both Britain and West Germany invest twice as much
abroad as France. When the Conservative government of Mar-
garet Thatcher abolished exchange controls in 1979, allowing
Britons to buy and sell any amount of foreign currency, former
Labor Chancellor of the Exchequer Denis Healey called the move
a "reckless, precipitate and doctrinaire step" because it allowed
rich people and institutions to stuff their money into overseas
property rather than into cash-starved British companies, thus
exporting jobs and hastening England's deindustrialization. But
money cannot be forced into unprofitable companies, and
cooped-up money won't be invested in industry unless the real
rate of return in manufacturing can be raised.

Britain has been a notorious example of multinationals "voting
with their feet" when confronted with intractable union demands. George Turnbull, the chairman appointed by Chrysler
UK's new French owner, P.S.A. Peugeot-Citroën, got workers in
two Scottish plants to accept 5.5 percent pay increases, instead of
the 20 percent the union wanted. But workers in two Midlands
plants chose to walk out and to stay out. Turnbull told them the
company was losing money: "Five point five percent, that's it—
and, if you insist, Peugeot-Citroën can always make the cars in
France." Despite a "no" from shop stewards, a mass meeting
accepted.

Hopping over national borders raises irritating questions. Can
a multinational, faced with a strike in one country, properly bring
in employees from another, as Hertz did from West Germany
when Danish employees stopped work? The biggest labor complaint is that companies don't keep unions informed, above all
about layoffs and restructuring in various subsidiaries. European
unions have notably raised the example of Poclain, the French
excavating company, but their list includes Bendix in Holland,
Siemens in Belgium, and Philips in West Germany. Philips is one
of the very few that has agreed to transnational talks with worker
organizations. The company got in hot water when it agreed to

meet the European metalworkers but would not agree to an observer from the metalworkers' international. It also refused leave of absence for British shop stewards to attend an international meeting of Philips workers. The reason, said Philips, was that it didn't conduct multinational bargaining—as distinct from multinational talking. In 1980, the metalworkers were at it again, trying to hammer out a master contract for ITT employees in twenty countries.

Such transnational bargaining attempts, however, have been few and far between. In 1969, Saint-Gobain workers in Italy, Germany, and the United States coordinated their negotiation efforts with the company by setting up a steering committee in Geneva. They were joined there by worker representatives from Saint-Gobain plants in Belgium, Norway, Sweden, and Switzerland and agreed that no negotiations should be concluded in any country without the approval of the standing committee and that, in the event of a strike in one country, all unions would provide financial assistance. IG Chemie-Papier-Keramik, the German union, was offered a handsome package, including an 11 percent pay raise plus various benefits. With the standing committee's approval, IG Chemie accepted but warned the company that its promises to the sister unions still held good. Saint-Gobain employees in Italy and the United States coordinated their strike deadline; before the Italian union could call a seventy-two-hour strike, Saint-Gobain/Italia settled, giving in to nearly all the union demands. In the United States, Saint-Gobain claimed it could not agree to the demands of the Glass and Ceramic Workers on the grounds that the American subsidiary had been a money loser. The Geneva steering committee, however, sent the Glass and Ceramic Workers details of Saint-Gobain's worldwide profits and the details of the German and Italian labor contracts. After a twenty-six-day strike, the U. S. Saint-Gobain workers secured a three-year contract with wage increases of nearly nine percent plus benefits. The only losers were Saint-Gobain's French work force. The main French union, the Communist-controlled Confédération Générale du Travail (CGT), didn't participate in the overall plan. It accepted an offer of a 3.5 percent pay increase.

The Saint-Gobain affair shows how cross-border cooperation in negotiating can produce dramatic results for unions confronting a single employer while pursuing and bargaining for individual contracts. Besides the International Metalworkers Federation, the only unions seeking common objectives for workers of different nationalities remain the North American "internationals" (read: Canadian-U. S. unions). The UAW bargains for a master contract for autoworkers regardless of on which side of the Detroit River they live and work, and entertainment unions in Hollywood and Toronto have developed joint negotiations for "continuous jurisdictions" to treat the U. S. and Canadian film and television industries as a single market.

The unique Canadian-American relationship and the two countries' near equality in standards of living and economic organization help North American unions to harmonize their objectives and demands. Elsewhere, national unions too often find themselves bidding against one another, as when Ford shopped around in England, Germany, and Belgium before settling on Austria for its new European facility. Besides the metalworkers' attempt with Philips and ITT in Europe, bargaining coordination has made little progress since the Saint-Gobain affair.

Most of the globals live on a high-tech frontier and have already one toe in a tomorrow when menial jobs will disappear and upwards of 90 percent of the entire work force will be in jobs that involve the accumulation and processing of information. "We are riding toward the end of the industrial society," says Paul Strassmann, vice president of the Informational Product Group at Xerox Corp. Most futurists agree that some products will still be recognizable in fifty years—some corporate names, too—and many of the services performed in industry today will still be performed, but some of today's major producers of consumer goods, such as apparel and home appliances, will virtually disappear in their current form. Tomorrow's business leaders will be those who think in global rather than domestic terms.

Unimation Inc. of Danbury, Connecticut, is making the already-here futurist robots that are taking over the most backbreaking and tedious industrial jobs. The Condec Corp. subsidiary makes $120,000 robots for Goodyear Tire and Rubber and for Australian sheep shearers. For GM, Ford, and Chrysler, robots pick up furnace-hot castings and weld them to car bodies and paint difficult-to-reach corners of auto assemblies. For General Electric, automatons put together small appliances; for Minnesota Mining and Manufacturing, they assemble tape cassettes and for Olivetti, typewriter cartridges. In Sweden, Magnussons AB has robots feeding parts for stainless-steel elbow tubings to polishing machines. On weekdays, Magnussons, located in the southern Swedish town of Genarp, has sixteen workers in the plant, but on weekends, the robots work alone, with an employee coming in every twelve hours to load their parts magazines. Both Texas Instruments and IBM are exploring possibilities of getting into robots. Japan uses far more intelligent automation than any other country—42,000 robots, about 3,000 of which can be taught to do their jobs by remembering a series of movements and 1,000 of which can obey complex orders given by a computer. Hitachi makes its own robots, while Kawasaki Heavy Industries uses technology from Unimation.

To industry, the most endearing trait of robots is that their "labor" keeps growing cheaper in relative terms. Robots range in price from $10,000 to $120,000, and auxiliary equipment can easily double installation costs, but robots don't get hangovers, can work around the clock in noxious fumes, stifling heat, and next to blast furnaces. Most important, they have a zero inflation rate in their "wages."

Latter-day Luddites have destroyed automating machinery at *The Washington Star* and *The London Times*, and labor is uncomfortable with high technology. Visions of participatory management and employees deciding their working conditions and procedures disturb them as much as stagnant managements. Some union leaders are aware of their own queasiness when it comes to the future. Sol C. Chaikin, president of the International Ladies Garment Workers Union, wondered in 1976 (when Henry Kissinger was Secretary of State) whether the "leapfrog bargain for more, more, more" will continue to be the right response. "We in labor have got to have a policy or the Kissingers and the multinationals will determine policy for us." UAW's Irving Bluestone thinks unions must broaden their social involvement and foresees long-term wage-price controls and joint management-labor decision making.

But capital, not people, is the scarcest commodity. Ninety percent of increased productivity is provided by capital and improved technology, and only 10 percent by better-trained, faster workers. The more modern and dynamic an industry, the greater its reliance on high technology, which always replaces workers in new production processes to reduce the unit cost. If Texas Instruments pocket calculators are still "made in USA," the reason is that they are 75 percent assembled by robots. Companies will spend staggering sums—$7 billion between 1979 and 1982 by Daimler-Benz and Volkswagen alone—further to automate assembly lines.

The irony is that high tech not only eliminates jobs, it also changes the work for those it retains, management included. The electronics that are beginning to dominate business offices not only organize, screen, and deliver data, but also process, analyze, and store it for later use in ways that force a company to mix and match both human and automated resources in new systems. Automated information allows for shorter development cycles, but it also forces management to sharpen up.

Unions are afraid of desk-top terminals and computer printouts. They feel they already have a hard time being informed about a company's strategies and even about its actual financial status. But when labor organizations actually investigate multinationals, they are forced to concede that to work for a global firm generally has more advantages than drawbacks. These firms usually compare well with those of comparable national competitors, the ILO reported after one exhaustive study. When a big international corporation moves in somewhere, it usually joins the "appropriate" employers' association and usually recognizes local unions—exceptions that are a source of irritation in the labor movement are unions in the United Kingdom and, to a degree, the Netherlands.[3] What the ILO doesn't publicize is that the winds of change that foreign-owned subsidiaries often bring with them are more than disturbing to national unions. In Belgium, the "human relations" practices of some multinationals have alienated the workers from their unions.

A decline in the political clout of organized labor is apparent in most countries that have settled into their modernity—mixed welfare economies and even social democracy. Only Eastern Europe evokes images of morbid collectivism—shoddy, shabby, and unfree. Elsewhere, labor is stuck in knee-jerk opposition, while business seems to have found new influence. In contrast to Italy's horror show of state industries and the gloom of large private business complaining bitterly of low productivity, labor disorder, and high absenteeism, northern Italy is dotted with small, dynamic enterprises (whose figures seldom reach tax authorities). Their advantage, says The Economist, "does not just lie in the magical virtue of smallness but in their flexibility, above all in the use of labor. Italian industry is far from fully unionized, and a small business is the least unionized part. Tough regulations, union power, and political pressure make it hard for any big

[3] Multinationals in Western Europe, the Industrial Relations Experience (Geneva: International Labor Office, 1976), p. 68.

company, state or private, to redeploy or lay off labor. Small companies can shed labor overtly or—still more effective—quietly increase or decrease their resources to the flourishing tribe of moonlighters. Few small companies would accept the 12–15 percent absenteeism common in big ones."[4] In Japan, unions have given up organizing the two-thirds of the work force employed by small firms and are sticking to the job of representing the third working for the major companies. They have no comment to make on the fact that the nonunionized majority is having a tough time because of Japan's system of widespread subcontracting, which in itself ensures that the first brunt of a recession doesn't fall on employees of big corporations but on those countless, often small, subcontractors. In the United States, the decline of labor's clout has helped make room for the expansion of business influence—as has the weakening of other power centers such as political parties, Congressional leadership, and even the Presidency itself.

Labor's burning issue in a maturing economy is job security, and it is not only Japanese unions that put guaranteed employment before wages. Labor federations in many countries are edging toward the German solution—codetermination. Many companies, and some unions, have difficulties accepting the idea of their workers participating in corporate decision making by means of board membership, but here again multinationals are, if not the greatest enthusiasts, at least the companies first exposed to it. *Mitbestimmung* became law July 1, 1976, when the Bonn parliament decided that the supervisory boards of Germany's 650 biggest companies would be composed equally of worker representatives and corporate executives. Codetermination thus came not only to Siemens and Daimler-Benz, but to GM Deutschland, Deutsche Shell, and all the other German subsidiaries; if anything, the results have been improved management because unions have been forced to see the logic of the market economy. Says BASF president Bernard Timm, "Codetermination makes the atmosphere of distrust disappear." In Norway, "soft" codetermination has given worker representatives a third of board seats, while in Sweden, the unions moved into a no-lose position. Under new legislation, they have to agree to any new participatory mechanism—and if they don't, they still have to be informed about all major changes in corporate decisions. In Holland, stock-

---

[4] "Which Italian Economy?" *The Economist*, December 8, 1979, p. 62.

holders and employees jointly choose the controlling board, but plans to give unions a considerable share in profits or equity has gone nowhere in Denmark, Sweden, and the Netherlands. Chrysler UK offered two seats to workers in 1976 in an effort to obtain labor peace, but the British unions turned it down, preferring the role of senior gadfly to junior board member. Three years later when a near-bankrupt Chrysler USA invited UAW leader Douglas Fraser to join the board, he accepted.

In America, codetermination could come through a concerted union effort to demand representation for the huge amounts of stock owned by employee pension funds. Pension funds own a majority of the stock in most of the *Fortune* 500 corporations and within a few years are expected to own as much as two-thirds of the big business stock. Stockholders, however, are notoriously weak in codetermining anything in a modern corporation, and true *mitbestimmung* is more likely to come via Congressional fiat than pension fund clout. The UAW sought to bring union involvement into industrial policymaking at the top in a 1976 contract with Chrysler. The union was rebuffed, but both sides emerged from contract negotiations with plans for intensified cooperation in worker participation in job design and job enrichment at the plant level.

Codetermination, says *The Economist*'s Norman Macrea, could be fatal for corporations—and society. To the proponents of worker participation who say that the arguments for it are the same as those for universal suffrage in the nineteenth century, Macrea says, "Exactly, the arguments for it belong entirely to this land of look-behind. Voter control of anything in the 20th century, like monarchy in the 19th century, is where the world is coming from, but not where it is going to." [5]

Where it is going is toward widening horizons which will make corporations more entrepreneurial and allow individuals different life- and work-styles. American business generally thinks the Japanese method of filtering information downward and weighing all responses equally leads to agonizingly slow decisions, but executives envy the immediate implementation of decisions that Japanese "consensus management" provides. Technology may allow business to have the cake and eat it, too. Aggressively applied information systems can speed up the consensus forming and "time-phase" the solutions. "The autocratic instincts of many

[5] "The Coming Entrepreneurial Revolution: A Survey," *The Economist*, December 25, 1976, p. 44.

American executives are such that they would rather go under than become more democratic," says James O'Toole, a writer on work organization and head of the forecast project for the Center for Futures Research. "The only way to increase efficiency is to get workers to be more responsible," he says. "You don't *order* people to be more responsible." Volkswagen's Toni Schmucker, who knows what he is talking about, says codetermination is a never-ending effort of communication. "Where there are areas of potential conflict we have to persuade people in terms of our long-range goals."

Employees of future corporations will expect—and get—a much greater say in how they do their job, most forecasters predict. Guaranteed employment and lifetime benefit policies will increasingly make white- and blue-collar costs fixed for a company; the big globals, especially the binationals like Shell and Unilever, are already seeing a trade-off in a very high company loyalty. "The number of organizations where people cooperate with people of different nationalities will increase dramatically," predicts Howard Perlmutter, a professor at the Wharton School of Economics in Philadelphia.

13

Mutations

Sitting Bull, who lived both in the United States and Canada, is quoted as having said, "The meat of the buffalo tastes the same on both sides of the border." James Wilkie and Kenneth E. Hill are a pair of latter-day Sitting Bulls who, independently of each other, have come to the conclusion that it's time to erase again the lines white men traced across North America. Professor Wilkie, a Latin American scholar at UCLA, has submitted a proposal to the Joint Economic Committee of Congress to throw the U. S.-Mexican border wide open. Hill is a Wall Street energy consultant who thinks Canada, the United States, and Mexico should recognize current realities and pool their human and natural resources and form a North American common market.

"Do away with immigration laws, do away with any limitations of what U. S. tourists can import from Mexico, do away with all tariffs on Mexican goods, let everything come in freely," says Wilkie. "Not only would it attract people to Mexico who would invest money, but it would attract foreign capital in ways that are undreamed of to go down there and take advantage of lower wages, and to be able to sell in the American market. It would give Mexico such economic health that it would attract population back."

Wilkie insists his idea is rooted in pure economics, but as *Forbes* said in reporting his proposal, it is at once both too radical and too sensible.[1] Hill, who prepared the North American common market idea for Blyth Eastman Dillon and Co., admits that substantial political and emotional barriers will have to be breached and that one of the prerequisites will be an American willingness to deal with both its neighbors as economic and cultural equals.

Let's take advantage of geography, says Hill. A common mar-

[1] James Flanigan, "North of the Border, Who Needs Whom?" *Forbes,* April 15, 1977, p. 41.

192

ket would make possible much better joint utilization of energy resources. Alaska has large oil deposits, but its natural gas can be shipped to the lower forty-eight markets only at very high costs. Canada's gas fields, on the other hand, are much closer. In the South, a pipeline could be built from Mexican oil fields to the nearest crude oil trunk line in Texas, while natural gas pipelines could be used to route gas produced in Texas and Louisiana for consumption farther north. Refineries in Canada's Maritime provinces, which operate at 60 percent capacity, could be fully utilized with pipelines into New England. Canada is traditionally the United States's biggest trading partner, and Mexico isn't far behind. As for free movement of people, open borders would merely legalize a fact of life. The current "push" in Mexico, with its unemployment and overpopulation, coupled with the "pull" in the United States of riches, provide a motive for movement that no law or border patrol can defy. For many Americans, Canada is "the last best West." Americans now make up the second largest group of Canadian emigrants, with their numbers only exceeded by emigrants from the British Isles. Every year upwards of eighty million people cross the U. S.-Canadian border, and Canadians are the fourth largest resident alien group in the United States. Americans have not migrated to Mexico in comparable numbers, but an estimated 100,000 U. S. citizens are permanent residents of Mexico. Free immigration from Mexico, says Hill, would provide the United States with a valuable labor force, but on a recognized, legitimate basis rather than the present illegal flow, whose exploitation and mistreatment has strained relations between the two countries for years. As *Forbes* puts it, "Americans must ask themselves what they want—machine guns and barbed wire along the frontier, or an acceptance of a minor sacrifice involved in sharing some of their great affluence with their proud, talented but economically needy neighbor to the south. The logic of free trade and reasonably open immigration seems overwhelming."

The economic links are irrefutable. The United States takes 70 percent of both Canada's and Mexico's exports. The visible trade between the United States and Canada is approaching $70 billion a year, more than between any other two countries on earth. Some 80 percent of all foreign investments in Canada comes from the United States, and Canada is the second largest foreign investor in the United States.

In the early stages of the 1980 election campaign, presidential hopefuls, from John Connally to Edward Kennedy, attempted to drum up support for a Mexico-United States-Canada common market, but only California's Governor Jerry Brown understood that the idea just couldn't be a quick fix for Americans to lay hands on secure and abundant energy supplies. Brown, an ardent supporter of increased regional cooperation, said, "The real relationship will have to be based on mutuality and interest," and the Carter Administration conceded it would have to give up the idea because "there is no benefit to either Mexico or Canada." One Toronto newspaper columnist put it succinctly, saying the notion resembled a "wife-swapping agreement with someone who has no wife," reflecting the common Canadian view that the United States doesn't have much to offer in any energy barter. In summing up the prospects for a North American economic community, *The Los Angeles Times* said it will take decades to achieve, as it is "highly unlikely that political stumping—no matter how slick—will persuade Canada and Mexico it is in their interest to move hastily toward a closer union with the United States." [2]

As usual, politicians and public opinion were behind the times. Three virtually free-trade-zone agreements have existed for decades. The auto pact, concluded in 1965, has meant benefits for both countries—it has had mixed but generally favorable results and increased twentyfold to more than $20 billion since implemented. Defense production has been shared since 1941, with current duty-free trade in military hardware in effect since 1959. In farm machinery, an effective but informal free-trade agreement has existed since the early 1970s. If a free-trading mood develops, there are several candidates for new bilateral agreements, including petrochemicals, pulp and paper, and textiles.

But if North Americans think they have substantial political and emotional barriers to overcome, they should put themselves in the shoes of their European cousins. The core of the European Economic Community (EEC), the world's most successful customs union, was formed in 1958, a mere thirteen years after its principal members stopped slaughtering each other on the World War II battlefields. Today, France and Germany are the "indispensable" down-to-earth partners of a new interdependence, and Brussels is beginning to resemble the federal structure of Washington, even if it is not yet the capital of the United States of Europe.

[2] *The Los Angeles Times*, April 8, 1979.

As in Washington, Eurocrats are realists, and *le trade-off* has entered the Community lexicon. The member nations haven't given up their sovereignty, but through highly refined habits of working together, talking things out, finding the compromises, they have forged impressive common policies in monetary matters, agriculture, taxation, and trade. The community has its own resources—$15 billion drawn chiefly from part of the EEC-wide value-added tax, and in less than twenty-five years, Europeans have created a zone of stability and growing prosperity and developed a sense of continuity.

West European critics of the EEC, mostly of idealistic persuasions, call the Common Market a spiritless association of grocers, and they do have a point. The Common Agricultural Policy has created huge surplus stocks of basic foods all over the EEC. It has protected farmers who continue to produce wine that can't be sold. It allows the dairy farmers to sell tons of butter to the Soviet Union at prices far below those paid by housewives in Brussels, Copenhagen, Frankfurt, and London. Its system for paying subsidies to farmers is so distorted that the largest share goes to German farmers, who form the smallest agricultural sector in the richest economy. A succession of EEC commissioners has warned that the Common Agricultural Policy is an open financial tap that could, if it were not closed, drain the EEC dry, but the nine member countries are considering only modest changes in the system.

Whether old enemies make better partners than fellow victims of colonialism is an interesting question. Things fell apart early for the East African Community, which united Kenya, Uganda, and Tanzania. In 1967, the three former British colonies signed a fifteen-year treaty of economic cooperation and created a joint currency, a joint airline, and a joint development bank. Ten years later, the East African Community was in shambles, however, the victim of Kenya's success, Idi Amin's megalomania, and Tanzania's cottage industry collectivization.

More fortunate regional groupings are the Andean and ASEAN blocs. The Andean Pact includes the five nations of the northern reaches of the towering Andes Mountains—Bolivia, Colombia, Ecuador, Peru, and Venezuela. Created in Cartagena, Colombia, in 1969 as a countervailing economic unit to Argentina, Brazil, and Mexico, its goals included rationalizing regional development, establishing common external tariffs and, like the EEC, eliminating internal ones, adopting common policies for foreign capital, and giving preferential treatment to the group's two poorest members, Bolivia and Ecuador. The pact was avowedly against multinational corporations. The rules on foreign investment were quite stiff but at least enabled investors to know where they stood. The Decision 24 allowed foreign companies to repatriate the value of their investment over a period of time, plus a maximum annual profit of 14 percent of the investment. Local interests were supposed to take over at least 51 percent of any foreign investment, but Decision 24 was eventually watered down. Like the EEC, the Andean officials stuck largely to trade problems during the first decade, but the five countries have recently tried to move toward joint political action.

Solidarity on political issues is less of a novelty for the Association of Southeast Asian Nations (ASEAN), grouping Indonesia, the Philippines, Singapore, Thailand, and Malaysia. Born under the shadow of the various Vietnam wars, the ASEAN group has developed what Singapore's Prime Minister Lee Kuan Yew calls "a common determination to prevent these catastrophes from spreading to us." In 1976, the five ASEAN heads of state met for the first time in a summit conference in Bali and agreed to move toward preferential trade agreements and regional industrial projects that would use resources in each member country. Economists predict that the rapidly developing "Pacific Basin"— the ASEAN five plus Japan, Korea, and Australia—will have an increasing impact on the world economy in the last decade of the century. As if to emphasize this, businessmen from sixteen countries in the area met in Manila in 1978 and signed a Pacific Basin Charter on International Investment. The ASEAN members have tried to parcel out some big projects, which are becoming the main or even sole suppliers to their joint market. Thailand got a soda ash plant, the Philippines one for superphosphates, Malaysia and Indonesia urea plants, and Singapore a diesel engine factory. To smooth the way, the ASEAN countries also got a $1 billion loan promised by the Japanese government. Rivalries take time to disappear, however, and the Singaporean diesel engine plant was abandoned when the other ASEANs were reluctant to trim their own diesel engine ambitions.

The EEC formalized part of its relations with fifty-seven developing countries through the Lomé II Convention, named after the Togolese capital where it was negotiated. The convention is based on equality between the two regional blocs, the EEC and the fifty-seven African, Caribbean, and Pacific (ACP) states, and, like all such trade pacts, covers a sufficiently wide ground to provide something for everybody. Following Lomé I, which ran from 1975 to 1980, the pact includes a shadowy area called industrial cooperation. Here, the fifty-seven have come as close as they can to "another OPEC" that takes into consideration the interests of its consumers. With a $370 million fund from the EEC, an agreement covers copper, cobalt, phosphates, manganese, bauxite, aluminum, tin, and, in due course, iron ore. But payments from the fund will only be made if production is endangered, not simply if commodity prices fall. Lomé II contains a whole chapter on EEC financial and technical assistance, including provisions for risk capital and mineral development and a joint declaration encouraging private investment in energy and minerals in the ACP states. This is still a long way from solid government guarantees for new investment, but Lomé II has reduced the distrust of some ACP states and some companies.

Regional pacts have created new capitals where multinationals have found it advisable to set up shop. Although the Europarliament sits in Strasbourg, the EEC capital is Brussels. It is in the Belgian capital that Europe's technocrats sit in glass towers. Floor after floor of corridors lined with identical offices are filled with toiling but well-paid Eurocrats. The Babel factor means catering in six official languages (translators make up 38 percent of the staff), holding over 8,000 meetings a year, and translating and revising half a million pages of documents a month.

Multinationals have felt it necessary to open offices in Brussels. Historic Waterloo and the neighboring suburb of Rhodes Saint Genese are the ghetto for multinational managers, and, not counting the Eurocrats, resident foreigners with their families number 120,000, 10 percent of Brussels' total population. "If you've been here as long as I have, you begin to see a real internationalization of the American businessman," says Stephen Freidberg of Chemical Bank's Brussels office. "A lot of guys came over here in the 1960s, after Britain's first bid for the Common Market failed. They learned languages and customs, and they really are a new breed—maybe in Singapore three years, Milan two years, here in Brussels four years. They understand what international business is all about. They realize you can't successfully negotiate the same way with Italians, Germans, and Russians. They recognize that what succeeds in one market may fail for exactly the same reasons in another."

American horror stories about not understanding local markets include Nabisco's thirteen years of trying to crack the $700 million German cookie and small-snacks market. Nabisco lost $25 million before it pulled out. Sears, Roebuck lost $20,000 a day on Galérie Anspach, a Brussels department store it bought in 1971, and Siemens and Burroughs also closed Belgian subsidiaries. Reverse transatlantic woes include German retailing giant Hugo Mann Gmbh buying the $1 billion Fed-Mart chain for $22 million, losing $11 million the first year and sinking another $60 million into the San Diego-headquartered discount and food supermarket chain before realizing that U.S. Sunbelt shoppers don't necessarily go for the impersonal and austere minimal service, minimal prices style that Mann customers are used to. Cavenham Ltd., a British food processor and retailer, bought Grand Union, one of eastern United States' largest supermarket operators, then acquired Colonial Stores of Atlanta, the largest Southern supermarket chain because it didn't feel confident over its Grand Union purchase. Continental Can became the first multinational to be hauled to court by EEC trustbusters in 1973. In the first antitrust suit brought by the Community, Continental Can won its case, more or less, but the European Court of Justice, in a startling decision, gave Brussels sweeping new powers to crack down on acquisitions and mergers by large companies, powers that the EEC has never really exercised.[3]

Generally, multinationals have been shrewd in choosing Brussels. Most companies fear that if their office is in Paris or Bonn, it will seem to be their French or German subsidiary, rather than their European subsidiary. With 10,000 employees of international organizations, 42 percent of Geneva's population is foreign (and rapidly spilling over into Fernay-Voltaire, Geneva's suburb in France where life costs half as much), but business is beginning to prefer Brussels. Multinationalism has created a growing cadre of polyglot managers who are able to work in any country and who are at a premium. The incomes of expatriate executives keep pyramiding, and, says Burton Teague of the Conference Board, "there is always a shortage of really competent management executives everywhere in the world."

The world community still has far to go before customs unions mutate into regional federations. Critics of Lomé II say that the EEC's concessions to the ACP states are purchased at the expense of other LDCs. The Andean pact started with towering hopes,

[3] Peter Vanderwouken, "Continental Can's Intercontinental Tribulations," *Fortune*, August 1973, pp. 74–79.

but each has been toppled. Under pressure from Brazil, Bolivia wanted the rules of foreign investment bent, as did Peru and Colombia, who both want American investment. Ecuador and Venezuela, which export oil and have strong balances of payment, didn't agree. Completely free trade among the Andean countries and the integrated long-term industrial planning for an Andean market of 75 million people have not been achieved.

But progress *is* made. Despite its strictly circumscribed powers, the new European parliament has found quirks in the EEC laws, allowing it to flex its muscle. Within months of its creation, EuroMPs staged filibusters and discovered the power of the purse. An unlikely alliance of Socialists, British Conservatives, and Communists blocked an attempt by two groups most sympathetic to farmers—Liberals and Christian Democrats—to push for stop-gap spendings to buy up food mountains and boosted social, regional, and industrial spending by $2 billion.

Nation-states may not be able to roll over and become regional federations, but evolution and economics are subtly redrawing the maps. Joe Garreau, a *Washington Post* editor, has imagined a nine-nation North America, membership based on economics, resources, topography, history, and, most important, on the way each nation views itself and the other eight. His map has New York City as a border town, the trade and diplomatic center between New England and the Foundry, and that "other expensive anomaly," Washington, D.C., a border town between the Foundry and Dixie. The West is divided into the Breadbasket, the Empty Quarter, Mexamerica, and Ecotopis, the last a small-is-beautiful believers' dream running from northern California to British Columbia. The border between the Empty Quarter and Mexamerica runs through central Arizona and New Mexico in the north and Sonora, Chihuahua, and Coahuila to the south. California ecologist Raymond Dasmann has designed his own bioregion map aimed at reorienting boundaries toward "ecological realities," and Peter Schwartz, an adviser to Governor Brown and a researcher at California's Stanford Research Institute, thinks bioregional ethics will take hold in small regions within a large state, in which the residents of that region feel exploited or unnecessarily controlled.[4]

Cracks surfacing in the American consciousness are seen in the sunbelt vs. frostbelt rivalries for jobs, influence, and money and

[4] John A. Jenkins, "The Nine Nations of North America," *TWA Ambassador Magazine*, September 1979, p. 109.

for the giant outlays needed in resource development. These fissures reflect notions of a finite economy and lowered expectations, barriers that Americans, apparently culturally and ideologically united, are surprised to discover. Only a reversal of migration or a deliberate federal policy seems to be able to halt regional rivalries. The states muscle one another in attempts to entice an industry to pull up stakes and move all or part of its operations elsewhere. Since 1970, population in the sunbelt has grown six times as fast as in the Great Lakes region and ten times as fast as in the combined Atlantic and New England regions.

Once underway, migration of people and capital gathers a momentum that is self-sustaining, whether within one country like the United States or a regional bloc like the EEC. The migration shifts incomes and accelerates growth in the favored region (the sunbelt, southern England, the Parisian region). As new markets spring up, the region begins to attract a broad array of industries, from manufacturing to all of its support services. This rapid growth of taxable activity assures adequate revenues for maintaining or expanding public services without boosting taxes. In the stagnant areas (the U. S., Northeast, Lorraine, Italy's Mezzogiorno), the declining tax base leads to higher rates of taxation or to cutbacks in public services. As people and companies realize this, the rush to move out intensifies. Most economists believe economic differences, rather than ethnic incompatibility, are behind separatism, at least in developed countries.

Corporations have learned to exploit the regional scramble for investments and jobs. Volkswagen sat back and let Pennsylvania and Ohio outbid each other for its first American assembly plant. Ohio offered a vacant military tank factory, but Pennsylvania won with a $71 million package that included a $40 million loan and $25 million in upgraded highway and railroad access to the plant. GM had half of Europe's governments vying for the location of its new engine and assembly plant before Austria won with $110 million in concessions (or $75,000 per future job).

It is not easy to see how nation-states will disappear, but the EEC, ACP, Group of 77, and other acronyms and, at the opposite end, separatism and bioregionalism are trends away from the more frenzied forms of nationalism. Schwartz thinks the "geographical schizophrenia" of neatly boundaried, multicolored schoolroom globes is already yielding to the pictures from space, showing earth as "a dynamic, vibrant, living organism demarcated by plant and culture groups and geographical features." Modern social and economic development doesn't automatically favor a trend toward internationalism and a world community, but it is always difficult to foresee change. Frenchmen and Germans killing each other in the trenches of World War I would have a hard time imagining that, toward the end of the century, Europe's real *entente cordiale* would be Franco-German, with a parliament sitting in Strasbourg. The Andean bloc is actually a rediscovery of Simón Bolívar's vision and, in one lyrical moment, dedicated "to unite the weak nations he freed with his sword." There seems to be no chance of nationalism being depoliticized as Christianity was after the religious wars of the seventeenth century, but if we can grasp both the regional tensions and the layers of unifying flavor and interests, we may be able to understand the high and low pressures of global affairs that may have the makings of radical change. Alvin Toffler foresees a "Third Wave" in the near future which "will topple bureaucracies, reduce the role of the nation-state, and give rise to semiautonomous economies." [5] Most people no doubt think radical change will never take place. Americans, for example, are too set in their ways to imagine an altered continental map. They probably said the same thing in 1776.

[5] Alvin Toffler, *The Third Wave* (New York: William Morrow & Co., 1980), p. 27.

14

The UN's Leaning Towers

Global business has little affection for its government equivalent, if that is what we may call the United Nations and its agencies. The resentment felt by poorer countries toward richer countries easily spills over into the belief that the rich got rich by exploiting the poor and not, as Chancellor Helmut Schmidt suggested, because industrialization in the advanced world is now in its second century. Given that the UN is composed of 152 sovereign states, varying enormously in size, economic wealth, structure, culture, and political interests, the remarkable feature of the General Assembly is that it ever speaks with anything like one voice on any topic. The world organization deals in diversity and works best in the negative. It can say no emphatically—no to Iran's seizure of American diplomats, no to Vietnam's attempt at legitimizing a regime it installed in Cambodia—but it is much less well equipped to do positive things. The UN has evolved into the only forum available to dozens of new, small, and powerless—in the traditional sense—states, but it is also a political arena where words and resolution *can* have consequences.

The agencies that pretend to concern themselves meaningfully with transnational enterprise are the International Monetary Fund (IMF), the UN Conference on Trade and Development (UNCTAD), and the International Labor Organization (ILO). Managers of multinational corporations have no quarrel with the IMF. If anything, they recognize that it is only under an international hat like the Fund's that a team can go into a country and nose out economic truths. There is a touch of madness, as *The Economist* has underlined, in the fact that polyglot banks will only loan to LDCs under IMF surveillance, since it means that to get commercial loans a country has to be in such dire payments trouble that it accepts the Fund's yoke: "The regulatory authorities upbraid the multinational banks for overexposure in the LDCs, yet make no enlightened proposals for rescue."[1] Jacques de Larosière, the former French Treasury official who became managing director of the IMF in 1977, has repeatedly pleaded with world leaders to recognize the "new realities" and to "act with political courage," a tall order for today's weak governments. De Larosière, whose job makes him something akin to a global economic adviser, wants industrialized countries to curb domestic inflation and to adjust to the lower availability of energy, so as to establish the basis for sustained growth.

The first world has an automatic majority in the 130-nation IMF, which is why the LDCs use their own majority in UNCTAD. As UNCTAD's tentacles spread more and more powerlessly, irritating the rich and frustrating the poor, the mountain of the 156-member "conference" regularly brings forth its mouse. The UNCTAD secretariat arranges agendas almost tailor-made for failure—too demanding of the rich countries and overestimating the strength of unity among the LDCs—and the results are usually not even the confrontations that some LDC strategist believes can prove productive, but merely confusion. Rich countries have used UNCTAD as a forum to cancel the official debt of the poorest countries, but there has been little meeting of minds on compensatory finance to try and stabilize LDCs' export earnings, and even less agreement on international monetary reform. When the United States proposes something, the proposal is suspicious because it is American.

In 1976, Secretary of State Henry Kissinger delivered a 10,000 word speech to an UNCTAD gathering in Nairobi, sketching a brand-new idea. To the perennial complaint that the rich don't pay enough for the raw materials they buy from the LDCs, Kissinger suggested the creation of a $1 billion International Resources Bank—not to shore up prices, but to supply development money to the LDCs. The man behind the idea was Charles Robinson, a former mining executive who knew a lot about doing business with developing countries. A year before he was appointed Kissinger's second-in-command, the Peruvian government nationalized a $255 million iron-ore facility of Robinson's old employer, San Francisco-based Marcona Corp., and promptly saw output drop 80 percent. "What's advocated is a means of eliminating the noncommercial risk of doing business in unstable countries," said Assistant Treasury Secretary Gerard Parsky about the Kissinger-

[1] "The IMF Tries Again," *The Economist*, March 26, 1977, p. 88.

Robinson proposal. "It sounds better to them if you call it a bank, and better to multinational companies if you call it an insurance company." The Nairobi meeting ended two days late, and the closing session dragged on until 4 A.M., even though many interpreters had left for another UN meeting in Vancouver. In the wee hours when most third world delegates had either gone home or were in no condition to vote, the International Resources Bank idea was voted down, 33–31.

Even though only 25 percent of the multinationals' total investments are in developing countries, the fact that 30 percent of *all* world trade passes through the hands of the globals makes the LDCs assert that these firms are the modern equivalents of the old colonial trading companies. One function, intended or not, of UNCTAD sessions is that by stressing rich-poor rhetoric, they divert attention from the complicated issues of trade. The NICs want steadfast fourth world support to roll back trade protection in rich nations. South Korea, Taiwan, Hongkong, and Singapore —with a combined population equaling that of Italy and a combined GNP equaling that of Switzerland—want the very poorest to back them, although their TV sets, pocket calculators, and textiles threaten not only the older, less efficient industries in Europe and North America, but their fledgling counterparts in the poorest countries. Thus, while parroting antiprotectionism, many of the very poorest have put up barriers to keep out products from the better-off third world. Likewise, the reluctance of the oil producers and their newly industrializing allies to accept a continuing forum on energy has brought more than one conference to the brink of total breakdown. The OPEC *nouveaux riches* fear that a world energy forum, lumping them together with the rich, will destroy their freedom to decide oil prices. They have gone to great lengths to maintain solidarity with the have-nots by distributing roughly 3 percent of their GNP in aid. But their high oil prices have crippled the development efforts of the thirty-odd fourth world nations and left them profoundly impoverished. The very poorest want much more aid, but they also want debt relief for billions of dollars in past borrowings. They would like simply not to pay the debt back, but faster developing countries fear that large-scale debt forgiveness could hurt their creditworthiness and drive up interest rates. When in 1977 the United States and other developed countries committed themselves to a "more determined basic human needs-oriented approach"—sending more money directly to the very poorest—

many NICs feared that this new philosophy, which downplays the developing of export industries, would lead to lower economic growth and smaller foreign exchange earnings for them.

A raging, if schizoid, UNCTAD debate concerns flags-of-convenience shipping. A third of the world's 670 million deadweight tons is of "open registry," allowing operation under flags foreign to the owner and manning with foreign crews. American companies own and operate one-third of the flags-of-convenience tonnage; the rest is in the hands of Japan, Hongkong, Britain, China, and West Germany. UNCTAD wants open-registry shipping phased out because it allows, in the words of its shipping director Adib al-Jadir, "one country to maintain domination of shipping operations while using the labor of another." But the developing countries are far from united. Some are resentful because Liberia and Panama have carved out a profitable niche for themselves. Others admit that if flags-of-convenience ships are phased out, it is unlikely that they will fly the flags of the poorer LDCs. Rather, there might be a concentration in the lower-cost first world countries.

President Carter dropped the United States's membership in the ILO in 1977, marking the first U. S. withdrawal from a UN agency since the world organization was founded in 1945. The decision was made reluctantly, but the oldest and most venerable of the UN agencies had become too politicized for American tastes. The ILO was no longer committed to its original purpose —to improve the lot of workers around the world—Carter said, and it has increasingly fallen under third world and Soviet domination. It no longer applied labor standards equally among all nations; it frequently issued condemnations "without adequate investigation"; and countries were condemned for extraneous political reasons. As originally established, ILO delegations contained representatives of labor, management, and government, each speaking for his own constituency. Now, Carter charged, "too many delegations represent governments almost exclusively."

Even before the United States actually went through with its withdrawal, measures had been taken to strengthen ILO tripartism, the weakening of which through national bloc voting by government-controlled unions had particularly distressed American labor. The State Department urged the Carter Administration to stay in, but the AFL-CIO leadership and, to a lesser degree, the U. S. Chamber of Commerce were determined that the United States should go through with its announced intention to disaffiliate. Three years later, the United States quietly joined the ILO again.

UNCTAD, ILO, and the Organization of American States have tried their hands in writing codes of conduct for multinational corporations. In self-defense, the Organization for Economic Cooperation and Development (OECD), representing twenty-four developed countries, has agreed on a business code of its own. The OECD action of 1976 marked the first time Western government expressed an opinion about corporate behavior. It followed a series of scandals of bribery and other illicit practices by some companies that brought political ramifications, and the voluntary code was negotiated against a background of demands for new legal restraints upon the corporations.

In April 1974, the UN General Assembly adopted a text calling for a "new international economic order." The proposal demanded "regulation and supervision of the activities of transnational corporations" and asserted all governments' rights to nationalize economic activities without mentioning any reciprocal duty of governments to pay compensation. Nine months later the General Assembly adopted, 120–6, a Charter of Economic Rights and Duties of States. Article Two said that if a country expropriated a foreign-owned company, any disagreement about compensation had to be settled "under domestic law of the nationalizing country." The UN draft, which was still being revised in 1980, echoed the Latin American declaration of January 10, 1975—sovereignty of countries over their resources, wealth, and economic activities; observance by multinationals of the laws and practices of different countries; etc. The UN draft went further and stipulated the global corporations' need to respect national sociocultural identities and human rights and freedoms (meaning they would be forbidden to set up in countries governed by racist minorities). In contrast to the Latin American declaration, however, the UN text could foresee cases of nationalization where international arbitration might be invoked.

The OECD guidelines—"the capitalist way out," according to the UN Development Forum—were limited to direct investment in the twenty-four OECD countries, but, of course, this encompassed 80 percent of all multinationals. The guidelines exhorted governments to treat foreign companies as they would national firms and to reform protectionist incentives and disincentives. They urged global corporations to be competitive, to hire without discrimination, to avoid bribes, to heed host countries' economic policies, and to disclose sales, profits, and employment data by geographical areas. "Motherhood and apple pie," *Forbes* said in reporting the guidelines.[2] It took the rich countries two years to agree on the code. One American victory was to bring state-owned multinationals in the market sector (Renault, ENI) under the disclosure guidelines. The "socialist" Swedish and Dutch negotiators wanted very tough disclosure, largely to find out more about their own multinationals. European companies can be' notoriously tight-lipped. The Michelin family, for example, has never told anyone anything about their company. When the Nazis occupied France in 1940, they never got inside the Michelin factory, and when De Gaulle marched back into France, the family wouldn't let him inside, either. Nobody seems to know much about Nestlé, Hoffman-La Roche, and Brown, Boveri & Cie, and the Swiss globals make few waves in the world.

Nestlé, Exxon, and Du Pont have perhaps gone furthest in drawing up their own codes and toughening up ethics. Conflicts of interest, reciprocity, antitrust violations, insider-trading practices, and corporate political contributions top the list of "don'ts" at Nestlé, Exxon, Du Pont, and Bendix Corp., and often the language minces few words. "We don't want liars for managers," Exxon's statement says under Clifton Garvin's signature. In many cases, the corporation insists that executives sign affidavits attesting to their compliance—and some codes give supervisors the responsibility for making employees live up to the rules. Outside directors are also taking a tougher stand with management. Lawrence Fouraker of Harvard Business School sat on six boards during the post-Watergate corporate bribery scandal and "strenuously" demanded—and got—an assurance from each chief executive that the company had not engaged in any illegal practice. Gulf's directors fired chairman Bob Dorsey because of the political contributions the company had made (both Gulf and its chief lobbyist Claude C. Wild pleaded guilty to special Watergate prosecutor charges), and other boards began vigorous cleanup campaigns.

On the global scale, little has changed since the heady days of code-of-conduct writing. Treating foreign and domestic companies on the same footing in rich countries may sound simple, but IBM, ICI, and Honeywell-Bull can tell stories about very unequal treatment in India, the United States, and France, and

---

[2] "The Multinationals' New Clothes," *Forbes,* August 1, 1976, p. 48.

OECD has even published a large study which, despite extensive national whitewash, proves it. The firms that suffer have more sense of self-protection than to complain out loud against the network of national rules that get translated and distorted in administrative practice. The ILO's multinational labor relations code writers want the companies to talk multinationally with unions. In the UN, the Group of 77 wants a firmly implemented code, not voluntary guidelines, while refusing any corresponding restraint on the action of governments. Prudently, the companies are less than talkative.

What undermines the UN, its agencies, and other government-to-government international organizations is their vulnerability to political pressure. The days are long since gone when the UN's staff was an idealistic and high-caliber civil service insulated from national politics. Most governments seem to regard the UN as a dumping ground for officials unwanted at home, and staff members with grievances or ambitions have made it a practice to turn for help to their governments' delegations. Repeatedly, comparisons are made to the administration under the late Dag Hammarskjöld, who was felt to have championed the independence and integrity of the UN staff against pressures by member governments. However, because he resisted interference in his direction of the peacekeeping operation in the Congo after it became independent as Zaire in 1960, he drew the wrath of the Soviet Union. The lesson has not been lost on his successors, and both the late U Thant and Kurt Waldheim have been chary of offending Moscow. The willingness to accept Moscow's choices for high positions is said to be one measure of the response to Soviet pressure. Moscow doesn't permit direct recruitment in the Soviet Union for the staff but insists on offering screened applicants, and it insists that a number of key positions are reserved for its choices as "Russian" posts. Orlando Marville, UN representative from Barbados who closely follows personnel developments, blames the big powers in particular for the erosion of the Secretariat's independence. The staff member who gets his job through political channels often feels his loyalty is to his government, not to the Secretariat. Journalists covering the ILO in Geneva say openly that international bureaucrats know they have sold out, that they are twiddling their thumbs. Women at the UN's New York staff are particularly bitter about the discrimination they insist is practiced.

If multinational corporations were run as the UN and its

agencies, they would have atrophied long ago. It is ironic that while international civil servants lecture global companies on the virtues of one-world justice, they are locked into their own nationalistic vicious circle; it is organizations like Shell, IBM, Nestlé, and BAT that stand out as having learned to integrate their work forces and hierarchies and to make a staffer's nationality subservient to his or her abilities.

"There is no dialogue at international gatherings, only political confrontations," says Club of Rome's Maurice Guernier. "Each defends his government's position, often without regard to fact or economic reality." The Club of Rome, whose *Limits to Growth* study in 1972 said humanity was courting catastrophe by the way it managed the world's resources, is itself an attempt at a coming together of one hundred policymakers from twenty-five countries, all concerned with global problems but none representing governments. The Club of Rome tries to go beyond the explicit formulations as well as the unexpressed, covert motivations that find expression in national or individual behavior, to the unconscious goals of individuals and societies. "All societies in the world today are in a process of transformation," says the Club's Ervin Laszlo. "Technologies and institutions, as well as values, beliefs, and goals are changing, signs of deep-seated trends and tensions that pose major threats to the future of the human community."

The Club can imagine a scenario for the future where science and business represent the best chances. Both science and business are global in outreach, and their members have little difficulty in communicating with one another. Contacts are highly evolved and frequent; travel for meetings and consultations is worldwide. "Businessmen and scientists are in contact with other strata of their society, including the political leadership and the public at large," says the 1977 study, *Goals for Mankind*. "With the aid of modern communication channels, the revolution of world solidarity can spread at least as quickly as the present revolution of rising expectations. Indeed, unless this revolution does spread wide and fast, the new expectations are slated for early disappointment." [3]

To get beyond the dead end of the UN's nationalism multiplied by 152, the Club of Rome can foresee the kind of "horizontal" integration that Shell, IBM, and the other polyglot companies

[3] *Goals for Mankind, A Report to the Club of Rome on the New Horizons of Global Community* (New York: E. P. Dutton, 1977), p. 420ff.

have already achieved. The UN and its agencies are "vertically" oriented, and they must be reformed and adapted, says *Goals for Mankind*. More important, new horizontal institutions must be set up, institutions that would be consultative and advisory and attached to national governments, regional organizations, and multinational corporations to work with the EEC, the Andean and ASEAN pacts, and the Organization of African Union, seeking to orchestrate global goals better. "The world could change from an arena of marginal security and economic and political conflict to a global society of undiminished diversity but firm collective self-reliance, greater security, and more equity."

The Willy Brandt commission, another international gathering independent of any government based in Geneva, wants both oil-producing and oil-consuming nations to reach an accord to assure mutual economic stability. Made up of twenty members representing a broad political spectrum and headed by the former Chancellor of West Germany, the commission wants OPEC to steady the rate of supply and the advanced economies to agree to some sort of medium-term linking of oil prices to the cost of goods bought by the producing countries, which, in turn, would protect the agreed-upon oil price against inflation. Mutual global dependence and the need to recognize the global impact of almost everything are the underlying concerns. The commission, which Robert McNamara helped to found, recognizes that any consensus between rich and poor is very fragile but that a more equitable relationship must be established in the North-South dialogue that often results in sour exchanges of complaints and demands by poor and wealthy countries.

The Brandt commission, whose twenty members come from the North, the oil producers, and the South, thinks the IMF and the World Bank are outdated institutions. Most of the LDCs were still colonies when the IMF and the World Bank were set up, and the poor countries have never achieved the standing in either, which their numbers or importance as clients deserve. Also, virtually no Communist countries are represented in the two monetary institutions, a fact that allows Marxists to sit on the sidelines and use warnings of "capitalist plots" as a pretext for not getting involved in the South's development. What is needed, says the commission, is a new institution—the World Development Fund, which should have universal membership and allow lenders and borrowers to share decisions less unequally than they do in either the IMF or the World Bank. The World

Development Fund would concentrate on program lending—that is, money not tied to particular projects, as World Bank loans are.

As for East-West consensus, the Club of Rome says that where liberal democracy and Marxism overlap is in their shared humanitarian concerns. Both want the greatest good for the greatest number. Where they diverge is in liberal democrats' deep faith in human nature and corresponding deep skepticism about the possibility of humane social orders and in the Communists' deep-seated mistrust of individuals left to their own devices.

"The 'childhood sicknesses' of these modes of thought have now been largely cured," *Goals for Mankind* says. "Liberal democracy's respect for social rights needs to evolve further, so as to curb the excesses of individuals bent on maximizing their own wealth and power. And Marxist communism's appreciation of individual human rights needs to develop further so as to preserve and enhance the freedom and creativity of persons. There are many progressive elements among the champions of both world views, but many others are lagging behind present realities."

The third world could be their meeting ground, says the Club of Rome. The West could come to realize that international collaboration as a means to assure the greatest good for the greatest number should be the next step. Communists could come to understand that collaboration with societies of different social and economic orders would be a means to liberate people from the oppression of poverty, hunger, and disease and open the way to the all-around development of all human beings.

"Freedom itself liberates immense human energies," says Nestlé's president Arthur Fuerer.

15

North-South

"We can't all go on turning everybody else into our servants forever," *Le Monde* wrote in a survey of the global struggle between the rich and the poor.[1] To illustrate the peculiar perverse domino theory whereby everybody "develops" on the backs of those below, the Paris newspaper recalled the early sociologists who looked for solutions to the appalling costs of Europe's industrial revolution. Full of sympathy and charity toward the proletariat, these sensitive people realized that the only solution would be to advance the least favored, but they never understood that Victorian society relied on a pool of domestic labor so vast as to make the trickling down of bourgeois values impossible. Inequalities are still with us, but development has been achieved, not by dipping deeper into the pool of the dispossessed or making everybody move up one rung, but by the radical changes of industrialization itself. The solution for the great-granddaughters of John Stuart Mill, Karl Marx, and Auguste Comte hasn't been to replace domestic help from rural Europe with servants from rural Africa, but with washing machines and microwave ovens. "Transposed to the contemporary world," *Le Monde* said, "development implies a transformation not only of the standards of living of proletarian nations, but of bourgeois states as well, and not only because the planet's natural resources are finite." *The Economist* has calculated that if everything else remains equal—that is, if the first world, the Newly Industrialized Countries, and the poor keep growing at their 1970s average rates—it will be the year 2220 before the NICs will match .he mature economies, while the less developed will simply slip farther and farther behind.[2] Happily, history has a way of making mockery of such 200-year forecasts.

[1] *Le Monde*, October 26, 1974, p. 1.
[2] *The Economist*, February 3, 1979, p. 50.

Like the contemporaries of the Reverend Thomas Malthus, we seem to feel that it is not so much the rich who are getting too rich as the poor who are too many. Underdevelopment is defined in relation to the style of growth and power of the 750 million citizens of the forty-odd mature, non-Communist economies, but it is nevertheless very real. Of the two billion people in the one hundred underdeveloped countries, a quarter are living in the shadow of death by starvation and disease. And the Malthusian idea that the poor are always too many *is* mathematically correct, according to the UN World Food Council. In many poor countries, population growth outstrips increases in food production, while the land available for growing food is actually diminishing. In raw statistics, the population in LDCs will double in 32 years; in advance countries, the doubling will take 98 years. The birthrate per 1,000 population is 37 in LDCs; 19 in industrialized nations.

The old economic order has not been replaced by a new order, but by new disorder. The phrase "third world" was coined in 1955 to identify the countries containing the impoverished majority of humanity. The Group of 77 was just that—77 countries in 1974 when it was formed to demand nothing less than the total redistribution of the world's wealth and economic power. Today, the Group of 77 includes 120 countries, but high energy costs, worldwide inflation, and recession have provoked cracks in the have-not unity. In fact, the old third world solidarity looks more and more like a constraint of political rhetoric than a bond of mutual economic interests.

When the poor seek aid from the first world, they too often look like beggars. When oil and coffee become exorbitant, they look like crude blackmailers, and when they start developing their own industries they look like sneaky rug sellers, undercutting prices and deepening unemployment. The world's rich minority and its poor majority have radically different ideas about how to close the gross disparity. The LDCs press for reforms—increased aid, lower trade barriers, and a swifter transfer of high technology skills and equipment. The rich react with caution and, quite often, with a sense of futility. In one breath, John Kenneth Galbraith can suggest that, as a small contribution, the rich could liberalize their immigration laws and can also admit that this solution will drain away the best brains that the developing countries so sorely need.

Seen from the other end of the looking glass, the rich nations rig the marketplace to keep prices for raw materials low and the cost of technology high so that poor nations are condemned to remain commodity producers, eternal hewers of wood and carriers of water. In the prevailing cartoon symbolism of the have-nots, a few corporate managers in New York or London determine the world price of sugar, bauxite, and tin; the same men dole out or withhold the means of development, and the fat chairman of the board is always American. Anticolonialism and antiracism are mixed with Spenglerian visions of a West finally punished by the gods and crumbling in its sins. An Idi Amin could still be cheered by university students throughout Africa, not because of his ideas but because he extracted some small and largely symbolic retribution when he had white Englishmen carry him on a sedan chair. Iran's seizure of American hostages had some of the same turn-of-the-tables appeal.

The poor have a hard time shaking the conviction that the industrialized West actually owes them both moral support and cold cash. Since the 1973 oil crunch, they have repeatedly backed away from applying equal pressure to the OPEC nations for help. In 1979 when oil prices shot up 60 percent, the Group of 77 quietly scuttled a plan to demand at least stabilized prices and supplies. It is hard to understand why. As a whole, the third world must find $10 billion or more to cover increased oil bills; OPEC aid to the very poorest oil consumers is at most one-tenth of that amount. The advanced countries had hoped the LDCs could be looked upon as allies of sorts in the struggle with OPEC. A Mexican proposal to the Group of 77 to make energy the subject of urgent UN concern looked as if it would win enough support to induce at least restraint among the oil rich. But the Mexicans dropped the project at UN meetings of the Group of 77. Brajesh Chandra Mishra, the Indian chairman of the Group, said the 120 members never seriously discussed the matter and that he could only hope the OPEC nations could be shamed into assuring oil to the poor, giving cash relief, and inventing some sort of "plowback" whereby third world payments for oil would be reinvested in the less fortunate economies.

The best explanation for the Group of 77's fear of OPEC is, as we have seen, that members imagine they can form "other OPECs." The commodity producers still hope someday to do for sisal, copper, coffee, and bauxite what OPEC did for oil. The great difference, of course, is that these commodities don't have

Seven Sisters to discover, produce, transport, refine, and market them.

Years of UN debate and third world politicking, in and out of nonaligned pacts and the Group of 77, have narrowed the dilemma to What Can Be Done for Us and What Must We Do for Ourselves. Economists recommend that the industrialized world channel a greater portion of financial assistance through international agencies such as the World Bank and the IMF, which allow for both fiscal supervision of projects and defused criticism; that it underwrite the cost of bringing new lands under the plow; help stabilize the export earnings of the very poorest; eliminate remaining barriers to imports of LDC goods; transfer technology; and pursue research specifically suited to the least developed. What the third and fourth world nations must do themselves is to concentrate on developing farming and limit population growth —the two real *musts* for the have-nots—reform education to stress vocational training and encourage entrepreneurs and foreign investment.

Private enterprise figures in the last two categories. The LDCs' quickest route to first world capital, technology, research, and marketing skills is through the local branch of a multinational. Leaders of poor countries increasingly recognize that by choosing the social mode of "equitable" distribution they may be delaying or even preventing development. In rhetoric, they are hostile to business and take a dim view of profits, but the more their countries develop, the more they realize that they need not only their own skilled workers and innovators, but also their own successful businessmen, and that these people must be rewarded with higher earnings, even if it means that their living standards rise faster than the rest of society's.

After years of expropriations and gunpoint nationalization, after years of general multinational bashing and misunderstanding, global corporations show some reluctance when it comes to investing in developing countries. Between 1967 and 1975, the LDCs' share of total direct foreign investment *dwindled* from 31 to 26 percent. This pullback may cause the globals to miss a great opportunity, however. "If you're looking for continued expansion, this is the real underdeveloped business area of the world," says Columbia University's multinational expert Stefan Robock. "It comprises the bulk of the world's population, so these areas should be attractive to the multinationals, and yet the marriage is not taking place. One reason is an exaggerated perception of political risk. Another is a reluctance to go into joint ventures." [3]

The multinationals follow the herd instinct and usually set up their regional headquarters—as opposed to plants or branch offices—in the same places. They establish themselves after looking at the fine print of tax laws, office rents, telephone links, airline timetables, and bilingual staff. The semisecret checklist they use to determine whether to go into a country isn't very long, but it is significant. Before moving in, corporate decision makers want to know 1) the size of the GNP, 2) the stability and convertibility of the currency, 3) local rules on repatriation of capital and tariff restrictions, 4) what kind of tax concessions, if any, the country offers, 5) the freedom to hire and fire, and such political questions as 6) the government's stability, 7) threats of nationalization, and 8) the personal safety of foreigners.

If a company were to check off Kenya and Tanzania, neighboring countries divided by opposite strategies for development, Kenya would be a candidate; Tanzania would not. Pragmatic Kenya recognizes that the road to economic independence requires at least a period of dependence on and cooperation with foreign companies. As a result, the government of Daniel Arap Moi has continued the beneficial climate created by the late founding president Jomo Kenyatta. Foreign companies can repatriate their profits, and Nairobi is a city where foreign managers and their families can live in comfort and security.

Following the egalitarian visions of Tanzania's founding father Julius K. Nyerere, Tanzania is seeking to transform itself into a self-sufficient and essentially agrarian state. To prevent outside economic participation from leading to foreign influence, Tanzania has set stringent conditions for foreign investment. It is even ambivalent about tourism, although it has some of Africa's finest game parks, because it fears that a flood of foreigners demanding attention may debase a population clinging to a fragile sovereignty. The country is proud of the advances made in expanding literacy and education. The collectivization of rural villages has not strengthened the economy in ways that show up in economic tables, and some of the agricultural programs are not working well. The nation's once efficient sisal industry is run down, the nationalized sector is inefficient, and West Germany, Tanzania's

[3] James Cook, "A Game Any Number Can Play," *Forbes*, June 25, 1979, p. 55.

chief benefactor, continues to give hundreds of millions of dollars every year in the form of nonrepayable grants. But Tanzania believes it has some of the "hard choices" behind it, while Kenya admits it has perhaps concentrated on the easy problems first. Kenya is tough with restrictions on foreign companies in its commitment to "Kenyanization," under which top managers of multinational firms are expected to be replaced by Kenyans by the end of the 1980s. This kind of forward plunge by government decree is widespread in new countries emphasizing national pride and dignity, but it is also one of the darker ironies of racism that its victims have been delivered to a crass nationalism that forces them to play out nineteenth- and early twentieth-century Europe's ideological rifts and deceptions.

Kenyanization, Nigerianization. The least secure governments demand percentages of local equity, while those with open arms forge ahead—Hongkong, Singapore, Taiwan, Sri Lanka. Certain principles, however, have been adopted by nearly all. Weapons and explosives are out of bounds for multinationals everywhere, although much of the manufacturing is done under licensing. So are public utilities and, to some extent, communications. Foreign investment is forbidden in the Philippine press and television, but the Indonesian Satellite Corp., which built and manages the country's international telephone, telex, and TV system, is a wholly owned ITT subsidiary. The area which everywhere raises big questions—and high emotions—is natural resources. All oil-producing nations have set up national monopolies à la Pemex, making Exxon, Shell, and the other Sisters general contractors for the exploration, development, and pumping of oil. The companies are paid by results.

The electronics industry and textiles have become almost synonymous with fast-developing Asia. Sanyo has moved its citizens' band transceiver and microwave oven assemblies from Japan to Singapore, Taiwan, and South Korea. Hitachi ships 10,000 television sets a month from its Taiwan factory to the United States; Aiwa makes tape recorders in Singapore; Sharp makes them in Malaysia and Taiwan. Standard Oil of Indiana makes intermediate materials for polyester fiber in Taiwan, and Yves Saint Laurent has his menswear made in Hongkong. The ASEAN countries are ambitious, however, and don't like the fact that this is nearly all assembly work ("screwdriver stuff") on components made in the United States and Japan. In a bold move, Singapore raised minimum wages in 1979 in an attempt at moving itself upstream toward the Silicon Valley, and Hewlett-Packard is indeed planning to do some R and D in Singapore.

But, as the ASEAN countries say, it doesn't take much hindsight to see that American companies were bound to catch up with the British who dominated Southeast Asia during the first half of the century, and in turn that the U. S. investment would be matched by the Japanese. It is much harder to point to the *next* wave of investment. Kaiser Aluminum & Chemical of Oakland, California, is the heaviest investor in Africa; Union Carbide put $5 million in an expansion of its Ivory Coast dry-cell battery plant in 1980; Volkswagen and BL assemble cars in Nigeria; Ericsson makes telephones in Egypt; but it is indeed hard to imagine vast semiconductor booms in the Caribbean or the Sahel belt of Africa. The problem for the poorest is that they are largely outside the recycling process. The first world and the NICs may lose money to the OPEC nations through ever higher prices, but they gain *some* of it back in the form of investment or the higher prices they themselves charge for the goods they export. But the poorest countries have little to sell to OPEC nations and little to attract OPEC or recycled Eurocurrency investments.

Some do try. "Let the robber barons come," was the way J. R. Jayewardene, president of Sri Lanka, expressed it when his government decided in 1977 to scrap import quotas, lower tariffs, devalue the rupee by 55 percent, and allow multinationals or any other investor to use some expatriate staff. These moves won Sri Lanka the IMF seal of good housekeeping, large hunks of World Bank and bilateral aid, and kudos from multinational executive suites. The government set up export-processing zones (EPZs), minifree ports which allow imported raw materials and components to be processed and exported again without being subject to tariffs or quotas. Situated on the edge of Colombo's airport, the biggest EPZ features international direct dialing (not available elsewhere on the island) and Swiss-style secret bank accounts (in the hope, apparently, of attracting the world's less honestly acquired money for investments) and will eventually employ 35,000 Sri Lankans. The first companies attracted were textile and garment manufacturers—mostly from Hongkong in another trickle-down effect—followed more recently by semiconductor assemblers. "The new climate is putting some zip back into domestic industry," *The Economist* reported on the Jayewardene Administration's effort. "Most of the smaller projects in the EPZ are joint ventures between local and foreign investors, and four wholly owned companies plan to establish themselves there." [4]

Everybody is going for growth, and the world's poor are all making strides. Rich countries have gotten richer at different speeds and times. Steady demands for goods and services have caused increases in supplies; resources have shifted from farming to industry to services; productivity, especially in manufacturing, has increased also, so that it can be said that countries which maintained and increased their industries' relative importance usually achieved the best overall growth. Catching up is a long-term endeavor. (*The Economist* thought that if Sri Lanka went full steam ahead for the next twenty years, it would not be another Singapore by 2000, only another Malaysia.) It would take the NICs, growing at their 1970s average, seventy years to match the first world's GNP per capita.

To demythologize the idea that all a poor country needs to be off is a blueprint and a fair price, multinationals have had to explain that their investments are not necessarily all for the best. Daimler-Benz has told several Group of 77 nations that small-scale automobile plants are a rather inefficient way of using a country's resources. High, beggar-thy-neighbor tariffs in surrounding lands can cause difficulties, even if economies of scale don't represent a barrier to efficient use of resources. BAT Industries can tell stories of being considered such a formidable competitor that local tobacco manufacturers have decided not even to try but have moved their money abroad. "We have in fact been accused of driving capital out of Pakistan," says Peter MacAdam, "and in Uganda of the loss of the productivity that some entrepreneur *might* have created if we hadn't come in."

Host countries' perceptions of foreign-owned projects tend to change with time and, in a perverse way, to confirm the globals' worst fears about entropy. A project which is viewed favorably at the outset may be criticized a few years later. The costs, in terms of interest and royalties, were seen to be worthwhile in the beginning. A few years later, however, local firms may have mastered the multinational's know-how and, typically, the cost of obtaining the technology from abroad has gone down. Brazil staged a ver-

[4] "There Are Two Sides to Every Bargain: Foreign Investment in Asia," *The Economist*, June 23, 1979, p. 10.

itable trial of Siemens, Hitachi, Toshiba, Telefunken, General
Electric, Westinghouse's Belgian subsidiary ACEC Charleroi,
Brown, Boveri & Cie, Sweden's Asea, AEG of Germany, and Italy's
Ercole Marelli in 1974 after its state company had become its own
major heavy electric machinery supplier. The Conselho Administrative de Defensa Economica (CADE) zeroed in on Brown, Boveri & Cie and accused the Swiss multinational of being the
mastermind of a ruthless nine-company cartel that destroyed a
half dozen Brazilian firms. CADE investigators even came up with
Kurt Rudolf Mirow, the thirty-eight-year-old German-Brazilian
businessman and owner of a 400-employee transformer factory.
Mirow said he had become the cartel's "enemy Number 1" because he had tried to sell transformers at below cartel prices. He
testified that cartel hirelings had invited him to a party where
The Godfather was shown. When he didn't get the point, a Brazilian lawyer placed a pistol on the table in front of Mirow.

Many developing countries have ambivalent attitudes toward
"screwdriver stuff," but even India has export-processing zones
(in Kandla and near Bombay). There may be grounds for criticism of the effects of such projects in the political and social areas,
but EPZs certainly don't harm a country's economy. EPZs are
efficient export machines. Because nearly all their nonlabor in-
puts are imported, not all the output is foreign exchange gravy.
What matters is the value-added. An electronic EPZ typically
achieves a value-added ratio of about one-third, but this can rise
to two-thirds or more, once the zone is well established.

One of the thorniest issues is the size of royalty payments in
partly owned multinationals. Local shareholders tend to resent
paying royalties to the parent company, saying they are paying for
all the technology while getting only part of the benefits. Western
countries are only mildly sympathetic to this complaint. They will
not easily forget how Japan bought their technology at what now
seem rip-off prices, then used it to slice through their own markets
with always cheaper and usually better products. BAT Industries
has the highest ratio of third world ownership and has learned to
live with it. Most of Mitsubishi's subsidiaries are joint-venture enterprises with local partners. IBM and Unilever, on the other
hand, prefer 100 percent ownership as it makes for a more effective
conduct of business as a whole, and Daimler-Benz, which originally
only owned 25 percent of Mercedes-Benz do Brasil, has bought
control of the subsidiary. "The problem was to escape minority

holding," says Joachim Zahn. "Acquiring control was a ticklish job because our so-called partner was in reality an adversary."

Most multinationals will "dilute to taste," and most Asian governments have successfully obtained the foreign investment they need on terms that they like. "It is much harder to find examples of multinationals ripping off poor countries (with the connivance of their rich elite) in Asia than it is in Latin America," *The Economist* has written.[5] The worst of the bad projects probably come about because of the policies of the host countries themselves. It is government policies—import protection, subsidized prices—that lead private decisions to differ from socially desirable ones. The foreign investor is not at fault. That, however, doesn't make the effects any more bearable to the host countries. Ironically, it is developing countries' own import barriers that have forced many companies to set up behind them, but if rich nations began matching the LDCs' tariff barriers, there would be no more reason to set up EPZs. Trade unions in rich countries will tolerate the "sweatshops" of the developing world as long as there is full employment at home. But when the advancing economies slow down, it is hard for labor leaders to adapt to fast-growing imports from the LDCs—especially when the imports are actually produced by subsidiaries of large domestic corporations. So far, governments in North America, Europe, and Japan have remained unmoved by such arguments, although some companies have been persuaded by their unions (notably in the Netherlands, Sweden, and France) not to expand overseas. Said *The Economist*, "If trade unionism ever goes genuinely multinational, foreign investment in LDCs will probably fall; or rather it will fall in those countries where there is genuine trade unionism and rise where the boss of the local trade union federation just happens to be the president's brother." [6]

The third world remains difficult for the $10 billion plus and the Next Ten, but they *are* trying. Since the mid-1950s, Shell has been engaged in a specialized form of rural technical assistance, which began in Italy and has been followed up in Venezuela, Portugal, Trinidad, Nigeria, Thailand, and Ethiopia. Nestlé, blackballed in radical circles for pushing condensed milk on third world mothers and making them abandon breast feeding, takes

[5] Ibid.
[6] Ibid.

considerable pride in its activities in LDCs: "By creating a source of permanent wealth for milk producers in regions far from industrial centers, Nestlé has furthered industrialization with effects on regional economy which are now established facts." The John Deere Co. has studied the technical and economic feasibility of building a two-wheel walking tractor for small farmers in LDCs. Philips runs a pilot plant in Utrecht for the special purpose of converting manufacturing processes to techniques better adapted to the production of smaller series. Here, Philips employees from LDCs are trained to become plant managers. It is not only machines and tools that are adapted, but also paperwork and methods of inventory control. IBM has operated at a loss for fifteen years in several LDCs, and Nestlé, Unilever, BAT Industries, Philips, ICI, Bayer, and Saint-Gobain now employ expatriates as less than one percent of their total overseas manpower.

By and large, they have all made their peace with governments in both the first and second worlds. Nationhood is more important to the elite of underdeveloped countries than it is in industrialized states. Still, as Eastman Kodak's Wylie Robson says, "The economic interdependence of the world's nations rises year by year. The great question is whether enough politicians and rulers will recognize the mutual benefits of cooperation before the increasingly global economy suffers serious damage."

Who's Making It?

Regional average annual growth per capita, 1970–1980

	percentage of growth
East Asia, Pacific	6.2
Centrally planned economies	4.6
Southern Europe	3.4
Middle East, North Africa	2.9
North America, Western Europe	2.7
Latin America, Caribbean	2.6
Capital surplus oil exporters	1.8
Sub-Saharan Africa	1.4

Source: World Bank.

To the Hilt

Less Developed Countries' outstanding debt is, typically: 39 percent commercial borrowing, 25 percent export credits from first world countries, 13 percent World Bank and IMF debt, 11 percent official aid, and 10 percent "other."

	Loans outstanding to Top Ten commercial banks mid-1979 $ billion	external public debt	total foreign reserves
Brazil	35.7	27.2	9.8
Mexico	25.8	24.8	2.7
Venezuela	16.6	6.9	9.9
Argentina	10.6	6.2	10.8
South Korea	9.4	12.0	3.2
Algeria	8.3	12.6	4.5
Iran	7.7	8.3	15.0
Indonesia	5.8	12.8	3.9
Philippines	5.5	4.1	2.7

Source: World Bank, IMF.

16

The Long March

President Carter's economic assault on the Soviet Union for its invasion of Afghanistan might, at first sight, look like a powerful reaffirmation of government power over corporate power, a challenge to the notion of global economic interdependence and a setback for multinationalism. The scope of the measures that the Carter Administration imposed against Moscow in early 1980, on top of those mounted against revolutionary Iran, was unrivaled in the postwar era and recalled the economic sanctions imposed on the East bloc during the Korean War and even the League of Nations' sanctions against Benito Mussolini for his invasion of Ethiopia in 1935. As the U. S. government explained its actions against the Soviet Union, the Russian military incursion into Afghanistan had to be met with a sharp response. Moscow had to be signaled that aggression would be met with countermeasures and would not be cost-free.

But global corporations, as we have seen, tend to regard war as transitory, business as permanent. Less than a week after President Carter announced the cancellation of the sale of 14.5 million metric tons of grain ordered by the Soviet Union and the suspension of all exports of sophisticated technology, the Japanese government let it be known that the Mitsui Group had no intention of walking away from $3.9 billion worth of natural resources projects in Siberia, and the French government that it would not stop the export of the sophisticated CII Honeywell-Bull computers.

Since the government of William Pitt tried sanctions during the Napoleonic Wars, embargoes have never worked. To be effective, historians agree, sanctions must be universally applied and really hurt a sore spot in the target nation's economy, since they tend to produce a rally-round-the-flag mentality among the target country's citizens while increasing the divisiveness among the imposing power and its allies. The invasion by North Korean troops of South Korea in 1950 produced a swift and tough re-action. An existing embargo on strategic exports to Eastern Europe was tightened, and an even more restrictive embargo was placed on trade with China. Western governments set up per-manent committees to coordinate the sanctions, and the Battle Act of 1951 even authorized President Harry Truman to cut aid to any Marshall Plan recipient that declined to cooperate. But the economic war was a bust. It was a constant source of friction in the West and was only marginally disruptive of the Communist bloc, which probably became even more self-sufficient as a result of it. "It was inefficient, counterproductive and more costly to the West than to the Soviets or the Chinese," said Robert Gilpin, an expert on political economy at Princeton University, the week President Carter announced his 1980 sanctions. "If we couldn't succeed then, when we were stronger and they were weaker, how can we succeed today?" "All in all, economic sanctions are not an effective weapon of political warfare," wrote Milton Fried-man. "They are likely to do us as much harm as they do their intended target . . . by weakening the system of free markets that is our greatest source of strength. The resort to economic sanctions is a confession of impotence, crafted primarily for domestic consumption, to reassure the public. It will have little or no influence on the Russians." [1]

Although they cannot really fit the virtues of business into their ideological framework, Communists, like everybody else, want to prosper. They, too, are willing to sell a hunk of their soul for upward mobility. For the multinationals, a beckoning mass market of 400 million undersupplied consumers stretching from Berlin to Vladivostok—not to talk about China's 800 million Communists—can be positively hypnotic. The difference between them and the Communist states is that for the globals, this "transideological" business is still only marginal. For the Com-munists, it is becoming vital.

The geopolitical image that the Soviet Union and the United States maintain is one of a pair of superpowers staring down each other's nuclear muzzles and, through détente, entente, and pe-riodic cold wars, an image of a Europe riven down the middle, if not of a planet divided into "them" and "us," with the third world spinning in uneasy orbit somewhere between the mutually exclusive polarities. The economic reality is quite different. With

[1] Milton Friedman, "Economic Sanctions," *Newsweek,* January 21, 1980, p. 76.

an annual GNP of $1.5 trillion, the United States outproduces—and outconsumes—the Soviet Union, two to one; by 1990, the Soviet empire may suffer a falling real GNP because the system may simply be too rigid for a modern economy. In the meantime, the Soviet leadership, mindful of the need for technology, speaks repeatedly of its desire for still more East-West trade. Western business and bureaucrats, mindful of vast new markets and of keeping up employment at home, speak of safeguarding their interests. Rhetoric apart, the interpenetration is already so complex that, in Jean-François Revel's eloquent metaphor, it is hard to see "how the ideological quarrels can be anything more than a punch-and-judy show, behind which the real play is being acted out and a mixed bureaucratic-capitalist economy is being erected." [2]

Led by Fiat, and Thyssen-Hutte and Mannesmann—the two West German steel and machinery giants—a global choice selection of *Fortune* 500 corporations has gone East to set up transideological firms—profit-making forty-nine to fifty-one, even fifty-fifty, deals with Soviet state enterprises. About 1,500 such arrangements exist between capitalist companies and socialist states. Production remains state-owned, and if dividends and profit sharing are out, capital partners can earn royalty payments for patents and know-how, engineering fees, and interest on capital.

"Early in the 1970s, East bloc leaders believed they had found an original solution to making their economies perform better," says Saint-Gobain-Pont-à-Mousson vice president Patrick Bonazza. "Instead of trying to better the economy from within, they decided to try a blood transfusion: buy heavy industrial equipment from the West and increase home-made consumer goods. The strategy was a kind of double détente—first you import Western cutting-edge technology and then you pay for it by selling back the product of this new technology. A thousand contracts were signed, everything from rechargeable cigarette lighters and apricot juice factories to whole chemical complexes and natural gas pipelines." Western exports to the Comecon countries boomed, going from $7.3 billion in 1971 to $30 billion in 1978, marginal for the West (4 percent of its trade), vital for the East (30 percent).

Virtually all the $10 billion plus and Next Ten are there.

[2] Jean-François Revel, "Detente: l'occident baillonné?" *L'Express,* August 15, 1977, p. 51.

Hoechst, IBM, Siemens, and ICI have cooperation agreements with all eight Comecon countries—Bulgaria, Czechoslovakia, the German Democratic Republic, Hungary, Poland, Rumania, the USSR, and Yugoslavia. BASF, Philips, Unilever, and ITT are in most of them; Exxon, Shell, Daimler-Benz, Mobil Oil, and BP are in the Soviet Union and at least four other countries; Volkswagen in three; Dow Chemicals and Gulf Oil are in two; and Hitachi and Nestlé in one each only. GM has deals in four countries, Ford in three, and PepsiCo is all over (its fast-food Pizza Hut chain is in Bulgaria). Volkswagen is introducing the Dasher in the USSR and licensing its Rabbit engine to Czechoslovakia's Skoda works. Rhône-Poulenc has $2 billion worth of chemical contracts in the USSR alone; Renault makes 100,000 cars in Yugoslavia a year, second only to Fiat's implantation in all eight Comecon countries. Caterpillar has been selling the Russians tractors since 1970; FMC of Chicago has an ongoing contract for food-processing systems in the Soviet Union; and Armco Steel shares a $353 million Russian steel-plant-construction contract with Nippon Steel.

The petrochemical giants have all built plants in Eastern Europe, all in so-called compensation deals, whereby the East bloc nations pay for each factory with its product (the amount to be bought back by the multinationals often exceeds the value of the plant itself). In retrenching European markets, Hoechst, BASF, ICI, and Bayer have come to see the technology they peddle to the East as a Trojan horse. As long as the chemicals were intermediate products wanted by the companies themselves, they had no trouble absorbing them. But compensation deals are becoming indigestible when they involve more sophisticated plastics, fibers, and industrial chemicals. When Hoechst, BASF, ICI, and Bayer cannot absorb the Comecon production, Eastern traders aren't afraid of placing the chemicals on the spot market in Rotterdam, thereby making the companies lose control of the market.

The buy-back arrangements with Western suppliers of technology has worked marvelously for the Comecon countries. In the West, the provisions were first considered harmless, but as recession began to bite in the late 1970s, compensation deals became a cause for apprehension. The EEC nations, especially, began to worry about the threat to jobs and income standards from an onslaught of manufactured Comecon goods, even if Soviet exports of manufactured goods have some real limits imposed by the Russian way of running its economy.

Communist leaders like to deal with captains of industry. They may hold talks with bourgeois politicians, but they know how short-lived the professional lives of politicians are. Nikita Khrushchev summed it up in his brutally frank manner in 1958 when he met a delegation of Italian politicians and industrialists. The Soviet premier abruptly left the two Italian ministers he was chatting with and advanced, pointing his finger, toward Giovanni Agnelli, the head of Fiat. "It is *you* I want to talk to. In ten years these clowns will be gone, but you will always be there. You're the real power, the only man I want to negotiate with."

Pirelli Rubber was in the Soviet Union along with Fiat in the 1950s, while Olivetti was one of the first capitalist advisers to the Soviets on office-system automation. Olivetti computerized Pirelli's six Russian rubber plants, using General Electric equipment and processes. ENI and its overseas engineering subsidiary built refineries in the USSR, Poland, and Rumania and put up Czechoslovakia's first ethylene glycol plant, followed by similar factories in Poland and East Germany. But even more than Fiat and Pirelli, it was Montedison which pioneered the compensation deal formula. In 1977, Montedison had seven chemical plants under construction in Russia, based on the buy-back principle.

Experience shows it is not easy to stop Western governments from bidding against each other when it comes to providing cheap credits to Communist regimes. When the emigration of Soviet Jewry to Israel became an issue in the U. S. Congress in 1975 and the Senate considered delaying Import-Export Bank credits, a subsidiary of Groupe Vallourec in France and Occidental Petroleum sold $900 million worth of engineering and know-how to Techmashinimport for a 2,400-kilometer ammonia pipeline to be built between Togliattigrad and the port of Odessa. Vallourec supplied $100 million worth of steel pipeline, with the French government granting $250 million in financial aid. Today, Western Europe receives 1.4 million barrels of Soviet oil a day and 16 billion cubic meters of natural gas a year through the pipelines Vallourec, Thyssen-Hutte, and Mannesmann sold to the Russians in a variety of complicated joint ventures. The East bloc is now in a curious halfway house in its economic relationship with the West. "If you give someone a small loan, you have a debtor; if you give a big sum, you've got yourself a partner," says Parisian lawyer and East-West trade authority

Samuel Pisar. Squeezed by this debt and strapped for hard currencies, East bloc state enterprises have had no choice but to
resort to barter, or the variety of trade agreements that pass for
its modern-day equivalent. Already, 10 to 30 percent of the $1.2
trillion annual stream of world trade takes place in the form of
"countertrade," that umbrella term that covers everything from
the straight payment-in-kind swaps, commonly thought of as
barter, to intricate three- or four-way deals that link the sale of
U. S.-made forklifts to Peru, to, say, the purchase of telephones
by ITT's Egyptian subsidiary through a Zurich bank.

Such deals can be profitable, as the globals have discovered;
among American firms, Control Data and PepsiCo have become
masters in countertrade. One of the more imaginative swaps involved Minneapolis-based Control Data selling a $3 million com-
puter to Leningrad's renowned Hermitage Museum for the
cataloging of its priceless collection. Control Data agreed to sell
the computer and the Hermitage to lend some of its masterpieces
for a two-year tour of the United States, with Control Data
getting exclusive rights to sell reproductions and art books during
the tour. One of the most widely publicized of the U. S-Soviet
barters is PepsiCo's exchange of soft-drink syrup and aid in
building eight Pepsi Cola bottling plants in the Soviet Union
in return for exclusive marketing rights in the United States for
Stolichnaya vodka—a deal that is understood to have become very
profitable for both parties.

Gorenje is the first socialist multinational. Headquartered in
Valenje in northern Yugoslavia, the company makes home appliances in thirteen plants at home and ten abroad, in Austria,
Greece, Denmark, France, and Nigeria, among other countries.
Its biggest coup was its 1978 acquisition of Koerting Radio AG in
southern Germany. The Bavarian company had been losing
money and was up for sale. Gorenje's $15 million bid was ac-
cepted. Avtoexport, the Soviet car and automotive accessory
agency, has subsidiaries in Scandinavia, France, England, Canada,
Nigeria, and Cameroon; the five Soviet companies doing business
in the United States include Balarus Machinery, which assembles
tractors in Milwaukee and has a plant in New Orleans. The Budapest firm Tungsram has set up a joint venture in New Jersey to
make seven million light bulbs a year, produced with Hungarian
machinery and technology. Poles supply electronic components
in Illinois via Unitronex Corp., and Hungarians of Babolna Ag-

ricultural Enterprise have built complete poultry farms in Russia and the Middle East with American technology and management methods.

Stranger hybrid corporate creatures include joint British and Belgian subsidiaries of Soyuzneftexport and Belgian Bunkering Co., and Marine Resources Ltd., jointly owned by Sovrybflot and Bellingham Cold Storage Co. of Bellingham, Washington, for processing American catches aboard Soviet factory ships for export to EEC countries. Leasing, which is widespread in electronics, has given birth to such companies as City Leasing, jointly owned by Morgan Guaranty and Moscow's Narodny Bank, and Promalease, owned by Crédit Lyonnais and Banque Commercial pour l'Europe du Nord, itself an East-West joint venture.

Gorenje apart, says Samuel Pisar, these companies are not really multinationals. "These firms neither invest worldwide nor are their strategies globally organized," he says. A natural extension of bilateral economics has been East-West cooperation in third world countries. Saint-Gobain and the Yugoslav enterprise Pragues Invest have created a joint venture in chemical plants in a number of LDCs. Bulgaria exports cars to LDCs under a Renault license. "Hungarian and Czech enterprises joined an Austrian utility in building power plants in Lebanon, French and Czech textile companies built a mill in Iraq, Germans and Hungarians cooperated in Morocco," says Pisar. The UNCTAD secretariat puts the number of such tripartite projects between 100 and 200 and the price tag at $50 million. The Western partners bring capital and know-how, the East bloc raw materials and engineers, and, says Pisar, such cooperation can be profitable if the partner who has diplomatic or economic advantages in one market is willing to let the other benefit also.

The Soviets love to do business with multinationals. Invariably, they stress the convergence of interests between themselves and the holders of real power in the West. In the case of Italy, the relations with Agnelli have always been more cordial than the relations with Italian Communist Party leader Enrico Berlinguer. "While politicians or militarists may conduct their affairs on short-term operational considerations, long-term billion-dollar economic programs are not formulated and implemented without ensuring the maximum degree of very long-term guarantees and safeguards," says Charles Levinson in *Vodka Cola*. "The critical and essential safeguard of the financier is stability—that there should be no serious confrontation capable of stopping the grand design." [3]

The Soviets can guarantee that stability. Moscow is proud of its nearly sixty-year record of never defaulting on a debt, and there are no such things as strikes in Comecon factories. In return, they expect the multinational seeking a deal to invest time and effort in a project. "They want the latest and the greatest, but they do their homework," says James Blow of the U. S. Department of Commerce. "They expect to negotiate on the top level and want the chairman of the multinational to show up either for the opening of talks or for the signing of the contracts."

Quality control is a raw nerve. PepsiCo must content itself with selling its soft-drink concentrate to its Russian plants without any continuous quality control. Bendix Corp. almost made it one step further when it agreed to build a $40 million spark-plug factory in Russia in 1977. Since 25 percent of the 75 million spark plugs the plant would turn out every year were to be exported and bear the Bendix name, the Southfield, Michigan, company insisted on having its own people checking the output. The project became unraveled over financing, however, and capitalist overseers in Soviet plants are not yet in place. More common are the experiences of Fiat, Mitsubishi, Pullman, and a hundred other companies that have built "turnkey" projects (facilities delivered completely finished with the host country ready to turn the key). "It's very hard to get downstream," says Pullman's Clark P. Lattin. "You have million-dollar machinery for a project that isn't needed immediately. Can it be stored? Sure, they say, but the warehouse turns out to be an open shed. It's very hard to have access to the actual site, to talk to the engineer."

In the secretive world of East-West trade, the clue to success is to talk to the right person. Dzherman Gvishiani, deputy chairman of the State Committee for Science and Technology to the Supreme Soviet, is the right person to see. Gvishiani is an expert on American management techniques, has a powerful voice in all contracts signed with U. S. firms, and also happens to be Premier Alexei Kosygin's son-in-law. Vladimir Alkhimov, chairman of the State Bank, Yuri Ivanov, chairman of the Foreign Trade Bank, and Ignaty Novikov, chairman of the State Committee for Construction Affairs, are other people to know.

"Person-to-person contacts are very important," the late David Karr used to say. "If someone powerful knows you, things begin to happen." Karr, who died in suspicious circumstances in Paris in 1979, arranged numerous deals, from the Lazard Freres syndicate that raised $250 million on the Euromarkets to build four luxury hotels, including Moscow's Kosmos Hotel, to Occidental Petroleum's oil and mineral deals (he had Gvishiani obtain landing rights at Moscow for Oxy president Armand Hammer's Gulfstream jet). "Karr had a tendency to be involved with two sides of every equation," says Pisar.

Until his death at ninety-five, Cyrus Eaton was the Soviets' favorite capitalist. In recent years, Cyrus Eaton, Jr., has followed his father's footsteps and even leapfrogged into China, with a $110 million paperboard mill in Peking. With C. B. Sung, erstwhile Bendix executive, Eaton, Jr., has formed ES Pacific Corp. to invest $200 million in Russia and China. "In ten to fifteen years, most of what comes from Japan will come from China," says Eaton, Jr. "What is needed is an understanding of how their system works, how to deal with it, and make money out of it."

Multinational managers and pragmatic technocrats from Stockholm to San Francisco are convinced East bloc leaders will, within a few years, sign any deal that will bring them Western technology. The planned economy is not working, and Russia especially needs a second industrial revolution of the kind Western Europe, North America, and Japan have undertaken since 1945. Although official policy in the Soviet Union favors innovation, in practice the system protects the status quo. It has always been the proud claim that socialism helps modernization, while capitalism represses it. Experience suggests otherwise.

After decades of less rapid growth, Soviet industry is running into serious difficulties. Poland is borrowing in the Euromarkets, two out of three Hungarians moonlight in the "black economy," and Russia's leaders are worried that any real change might fuel demands for yet more extensive reforms. GNP, it is claimed, rose by 3.7 percent in 1979, 2 percent less than planned and the lowest peacetime growth since the 1930s. Industrial production is not expanding on schedule; steel, engineering, and petrochemicals are falling far behind. After years of assurances that their country has plenty of energy, Russians are being told to brace for oil shortages. Inflation is the talk of Moscow. Tourists are pestered by touts offering to change rubles for hard currencies at three to four times the official exchange rate, and the official press feels repeatedly obliged to deny rumors that the Soviet currency has become so debased that it will soon be replaced or devalued. The battering of the ruble is partly the result of a paradox. Thanks to state subsidies, prices have not risen for most of the necessities of life. But there are so few luxuries around that prices for those the state has tried to make available have skyrocketed, making people feel their money isn't worth much if it "can't buy anything." The needs people want to satisfy are still huge, and the Comecon economy is still one of penury.

The drift toward economic pessimism started in the early 1970s. Economic shortages are no longer regarded as exceptions but as the norm, and the Soviet middle classes are disenchanted. Endemic shortages of consumer goods, poor quality, and limited choice are nothing new, but the slowdown in overall growth has been a recent trend. Middle-class Russians conclude that the Soviet economy is being mismanaged, and, says *Survey*, the international quarterly on East-West relations published in London, the leadership is increasingly held responsible. In middle-class eyes, "Economic nonsuccess will erode the regime's political legitimacy. Because of the crucial position occupied by the middle class in Soviet society since Stalin, the middle-class disenchantment could in time become politically significant." [4]

Meanwhile, the impressive new marriage brokers at Peking's International Trust and Investment Corp. (CITIC) are trying to find multinational grooms for state-enterprise brides, and in joint ventures CITIC has dared to step into the delicate areas of quality control and capitalist discipline. CITIC has assured several U. S., Swedish, and French firms that it isn't afraid of any of these foreign partners exercising veto powers. It can even foresee the day when a foreign partner decides he wants to fire an activist "troublemaker" in a Chinese plant. Says vice premier Gu Mu, responsible for investment, imports, and capital investment, "State enterprises have the right to reward—and punish—individual workers according to their performances." An awkward point, however, is how to calculate labor cost. At Shumchun Town, China's first EPZ, workers on piece rates in factories involved in compensation deals are earning as much as three times the average Chinese wages. But Hongkong-based companies calculate labor cost in Chinese projects to be only 10 to 15 percent lower than labor costs in the Colony.

[4] *Survey*, Winter, 1979–80, p. 39.

Soviet Quasimultinationals

Name	Business	Subsidiaries
Avtoexport	cars, automobile accessories	Konela, Finland; Konela Norge Bil, Norway; Matreco Bil, Sweden; Scandia-Volga, Belgium; Actif-Auto, France; United Machinery Org., England; Belarus Equipment, Ltd., Canada; WAATEGO, Nigeria; CATECO, Cameroon.
Machinoexport	heavy machinery	Marinexport, Morocco; Stankofrance, France; Stankoitaliana, Italy; Coram South America, Argentina.
Soviet Bank	banking	Moscow Narodny Bank, U.K., Lebanon, Singapore; Banque Commerciale pour L'Europe du Nord, France; Ost-West Handelsbank, Germany; Wozchod Handelsbank, Switzerland; Danube Bank, Austria; Banque Unie Est-Ouest, Luxembourg.
Soyuzkhimexport	chemical products	Ferchimex, Belgium; Sogo Cie, France; Sobren Chemie Handel, Germany.
Soyuzneftexport	petroleum products	Nafta GB, U.K.; Nafta B, Belgium.
Traktorexport	farm equipment	Konela, Finland; Actif-Auto, France; Belarus Equipment, U. S., Canada.
Exportles	wood	Russe Bois, France; Russian Wood Agency, U.K.

Source: Die Weltwoche.

17

Future Tech

A classic marketing case taught in business schools deals with the cake mix that bombed with consumers. The mix required homemakers to do no more than add water, but the company found in a study that housewives wanted to "add value" as well. The company reformulated the mix so that the cook had to add one egg—and sales took off. The world's mammoth corporations are learning to allow governments to add that one egg to the mix, and multinational bashing seems to be a thing of the past. It never got very far in the rich countries (except, perhaps, in Italy and Canada). Many thoughtful people in Newly Industrialized Countries think the adversarial relationship of government and business is a bankrupt idea anyway, and leaders in countries with centrally planned economies and in LDCs have few choices when it comes to moving up-market.

To avoid the dinosaur's fate, big corporations have learned to roll over; they are now learning to become socially responsible citizens. "At first, they undoubtedly did it with their tongues in their cheeks," *The Economist* says. "Later, they began to believe what they were saying, and to believe that it should indeed be true, not just for public relations reasons but for reasons of—well, social responsibility. The 1960s were perhaps the last decade in which any sizable company could act merely as its own interests, as profits or growth, demanded. After the traditional 1970s, the 1980s may prove to be the last decade in which any serious company would want to." [1] Corporations of the future may function more and more as public trusts toward both society and their employees. "Government's role will increase as an intermediary in social interactions, but the government will take on only what business

[1] *The Economist,* December 29, 1979, p. 57.

doesn't accept," predicts Martin L. Ernst, vice president of management sciences at Arthur D. Little Inc.

With even conservative projections putting the sales of the top twenty multinationals in double-digit billions, the clamor for government restrictions on their operations will continue. Soon, says Harry Levinson, head of The Levinson Institute and an acknowledged behavioral science guru, corporations "will no longer be able to leave psychological pollution in their wake." Freedom to hire and fire is already restricted by age- sex- and race-discrimination laws in many countries. Environmental safety, health, and consumer protection legislation force companies to be good citizens. Michelin is Europe's most secretive company, but laws requiring companies to disclose their total economic profile are being enacted everywhere, further enhancing the move to what the Wharton School's Howard Perlmutter calls "a glass-walled corporation."

Ambivalence persists. We will not allow the corporations to become too big, yet we must allow them to become big enough to fulfill the social goals we demand of them. "There is a belief that with our technology we could lick almost any problem we put our minds to," says Du Pont chairman Irving S. Shapiro. "It is assumed that, being big, our companies are insulated against risk and have a deep pocket, so it follows that if we're not living up to public expectations in every way, it's because we don't want to."

Governments always say they are forward-looking when they are, at best, for the existing state of things. Power seeks to control events, to insure its own continuity, and it generally equates a stable world order with the status quo. Regimes may "modernize" at a frenetic pace, but they are usually making sure that together with building roads and factories goes a really efficient secret police. Imperial powers are counterrevolutionary almost by definition, including the Soviet Union and the United States. What saves the latter is its relative economic freedom. Philosophically, business is also for the status quo, but its saving grace—sometimes despite itself—is also economic dynamics. At the worst of times when corporate managers are facing recession, energy crises, capital shrinkage, and inflation and are forced to tighten budgets and concentrate investments on a few narrow markets, they rely on research to spur growth. However trite and banal it may sound, innovation is not a constant in modern statecraft; it is a constant in the modern market economy.

Milton Friedman and his wife Rose think that the rise in government, beginning with the Depression, stems from an antibusiness climate, plus a combination of a romantic socialist notion of "fairness"—that it was unjust when some won success and wealth while others lost and suffered failure and poverty—and envy. Envy came from intellectuals. Unlike medieval and socialist societies, industrial capitalism granted little status, power, honor, or wealth to mandarins, who therefore, the Friedmans claim, grew to hate free enterprise.[2]

Most economists regard psychology as irrelevant. They formulate microeconomics as a theory of rational behavior which, almost by sleight of hand, becomes a theory of actual behavior. Tibor Scitovsky is an exception, saying that, while all external circumstances remain constant, the same collection of consumer goods and services will not be continually chosen (which is the economists' test of rationality), that novelty is pursued for its own sake. Sociobiology, a new and controversial theory of human behavior, has joined the debate and come up with "bioeconomics," variously claimed as a genetic defense of the free market and reviled as master-race theorizing and glorified neo-Nazism. Bioeconomists say that government programs that force us to be less competitive and selfish than we are genetically programmed to be are preordained to fail. And a socialist society, predicated on self-lessness and devotion to a collective ideal, simply will never work.

Sociobiologists admit that cultural factors can influence behavior and even at times offset genetic influence. Even so, they contend, most aspects of human culture, such as law and religion, ultimately serve the drive for what they call "genetic fitness." What appears to be altruistic behavior is really genetic selfishness. We are unselfish toward blood relatives, who share common genes. And the degree of altruism depends on how many genes we share. Parents, for example, will be more generous toward their children than the offspring will be toward one another, because parents and children have more genes in common than do brothers and sisters. A fearless economist like John Kenneth Galbraith has dared to explore "genetic" ideas which rarely get mentioned in the copious literature on development. In *The Nature of Mass Poverty*, he says that the Asian evidence "suggests that it makes far less difference as regards the causes or conquests of poverty whether a country is capitalist or communist than whether it is Chinese or not." On colonialism: "There is also the problem as to how the English-

[2] Milton and Rose Friedman, *Free to Choose* (New York: Harcourt, Brace, Jovanovich, 1980), p. 134.

speaking colonies of the British Empire emerged so successfully from this blight and why a centuries-old tradition of independence did little for Ethiopia and not much for Thailand." [3]

Managing glass-walled giant corporations has also come in for a dose of genetic analogy. Man, say some much-criticized sociobiologists, is an animal who has a genetic urge to hunt in packs, but also to make those packs less than one hundred strong. Most governments and established religions have tried to make us feel that we want to belong to packs larger than one hundred, for the greater good of either society or the ruling classes. "Big business corporations now face the difficulty that they are too large to inspire people to hunt together as a pack, so, behind many of their facades, the employees from just below the managing director to those around the shop steward are forming separate packs to hunt each other," says Norman Macrea. "The top forty or so executives in a really big corporation do hunt together as a pack for the good of the dear old firm, even when stock options, etc., do not tie their personal fortunes to its prosperity. The reason is that forty or so (with good management more) probably is a natural size of pack to make cooperating with into fun, even cooperating with unsympathetic people." [4]

Jay W. Forrester, a computer specialist at MIT who thinks complex social systems are too wildly interactive for us ever to untangle, says big corporations are so cumbersome and noninnovative that they will topple under their own weight, to be replaced by a host of technologically energetic and organizationally lean entrepreneurs. Many managers of giant businesses agree that smaller organizations can inspire more dynamic motivation but say that economies of scale will continue to tilt the balance toward the increased returns and, as we have seen with the oil giants, toward making more industries into quasi-public utilities. And the advantages that come with size also include covering more bets in Research and Development.

The ongoing information revolution promises to allow any pack of forty executives to run mammoth enterprises, even to create subsystems that we can all comprehend and within which we can function. The electronic technology permits interrelatedness, says René Dubos of Rockefeller University, while at the same time

[3] John Kenneth Galbraith, *The Nature of Mass Poverty* (Cambridge: Harvard University Press, 1979), p. 115.

[4] Norman Macrea, "The Coming Entrepreneurial Revolution: A Survey," *The Economist,* December 25, 1976, p. 60.

allowing us to "turn away from the notion of a world's evolving into one system with one government." The electronic data network puts the relevant information at the fingertips of whoever has the foresight to ask for it. As corporate planners are beginning to say, "The ruling scepter is passing from those with the answers to those who ask the questions. The best questioners will run the most successful corporations." [5]

Taking the monotony out of information flows opens up new avenues for participatory management among peers, across departments, and up and down the hierarchy. The personal satisfaction that comes from this participation can be heightened even further by the ease with which the microprocessor can track down the factual information needed to apply individual ideas and exercise judgment.

The information, or "smart machine," age will soon change the way people work, play, travel, and even think. By 1985, the world market for microelectronics will top $20 billion a year and will expand by 50 percent each year, even though the chips themselves and the computing power they represent are falling in price. The transformation will not be easy because smart machines bring with them widespread economic dislocation and perhaps even social unrest, displacing millions of blue-collar workers and even making office workers feel the crunch. Economists peering into the near-term future think that the smart machines are on the verge of repealing the labor theory of value, that is, that full automation of many factories will make labor cost irrelevant. As microelectronics experts are fond of saying, if the carmakers had improved their technology at the same rate computer science has, they would now be turning out Mercedes-Benzes that cost $70 apiece. The implication of this is that we can not maintain for very much longer the idea that we can be paid in terms of our labor. Smart machines may also put an end to world trade patterns based on comparative advantages. Microprocessors and satellite communications mean, essentially, that it doesn't matter where you are on the globe. The new information age is fired by a seemingly limitless resource—the inexhaustible supply of knowledge itself.

Forecasting the future is always hazardous. In 1874, the American Scientific Association could predict both that rapid urbanization would make the horse obsolete, leading breeders to breed a minihorse with low oat consumption, and that a hundred years

[5] Rene Dubos, interview, *Omni*, December 1979, p. 126.

later the work week might be as low as fifty hours. Master strategist and futurologist Herman Kahn is not afraid of foretelling increasing scientific and technical knowledge as our most basic resource in a "world city—not global village" with institutionalized scientific and technical change. Increasingly sensate, secular, and humanistic people will conduct impersonal and businesslike interactions as opposed to the close human ties implied in the words "community," "village," and "marketplace," while at the same time pursuing a sense of "world public opinion" and of shared responsibility. Global goals will be espoused and actively pursued in security, in food production, in population trends, and in socioeconomic growth and development.

To implement such goals, existing institutions will have to be reformed and adapted, and new institutions set up. Governments are vertically oriented, whereas global issues are horizontal. We are beginning to see regional institutions emerge, not only in the EEC, the Andean, and the ASEAN pacts, but in international bodies established to meet specific emerging problems and needs —communications, the oceans, space, the environment. The next set of institutions, the Club of Rome believes, will be designed to monitor and assess the setting of goals at various societal levels by consultative and advisory organs attached to national governments, regional bodies, and multinational corporations. "The world would change from an arena of marginal security and economic and political conflict, to the global society of undiminished diversity but firm collective self-reliance, greater security, and more equity." [6]

Multinational corporations are already there.

Of the one hundred wealthiest entities on the international scene, well over half are corporations. Growth and profitability are the primary objectives. Multinationals frequently balance growth and profits as relatively equal goals and even place the prime emphasis on growth. The corporate search for growth, which is continuous, is both selective and conditional. At any given time, most global enterprises find themselves with more options than resources—something that rarely happens for governments. Our $10 billion plus and Next Ten routinely include public policy considerations and social expectations in their decision making. Many of them, as we have seen, are opting for longer-term and globally conscious strategies. Big oil and the

[6] *Goals for Mankind,* op. cit., p. 422.

chemical giants are rolling over into next century's energy and molecular building blocks, the automotives into world cars. The pharmaceuticals are literally developing drugs for the world. The electronics are living permanently on the cutting edge of invention, while consumer companies like Unilever and BAT Industries are "diluting" into entirely new and quasi-experimental entities. The industrialists' ability to obtain their natural resources worldwide, and particularly among their own affiliates, creates new possibilities for Less Developed Countries. The carmakers' product complementation allows countries with too small markets to justify the investment required to achieve mass production and begin to industrialize by manufacturing and exporting one or more components in high volume.

The source of friction remains the gap between the companies' priorities and the criteria and goals that the political process sets up. The corporations plan their future by assessing such factors as competitive strength, relative market growth, availability and cost of resources—including capital—and efficiency. It is entirely possible for these corporate criteria to be in harmony with national objectives, but, says UN Secretary General Kurt Waldheim, we must look for such overlapping, not just assume it. Few things in this world are in perfect harmony, of course—or in a state of universal conflict—but the harmony of interest that does exist among nation-states and global corporations is rarely underlined. If anything, the grossness of the charges against the multinationals heard in international forums and the companies' insistence on their dependence on a hospitable environment and their assurance of close collaboration with governments tend to produce an impression of stalemate, of a dialogue among the deaf. Yet each investment *is* made with the explicit or implicit consent of the country for which the investment is intended. To be acceptable, says Shell's Frank McFadzean, such decisions must offer mutual advantages.

Profits are the golden standard of efficiency, but all of the $10 billion plus and the Next Ten are adopting forms of planning that allow each company's leaders to take a holistic view of their business and its environment. This view relates specific goals to the overall reality, recognizing that the biggest corporate entities have an existence other than the mere sum of their parts. The emphasis on defining the "mission" of the corporation as the first step of planning motivates an explicit consideration of its basic *purpose*. The information revolution will heighten this "Delphic-type" system by allowing management to retain the ultimate role of oracle while decentralizing decision making. Many corporations are hamstrung by chief executives who are sequestered at headquarters but who insist on overseeing divisional decisions. Once financial, sales, and product data are accessible to all managerial levels, headquarters can delegate decisions more comfortably and can eliminate the reams of reports that strangle most managers. Regional offices could disappear altogether.

What is right about global enterprise is that it works. If the world is not an easy place to govern, it is increasingly a better— if more confusing—place to live in. The multinationals' principal contribution is unquestionably commercial, but they are also a growing counterforce to the extremes of nationalism. More and more, they take on local nationals as leaders, work well with a stupefying variety of governments. Some of them share ownership and go easily into joint ventures. "Wherever you go with Mobil, for example—to 42nd Street in New York, the Steinstrasse in Hamburg, or to a cluster of small buildings in Medan, Sumatra—you will find a multiplicity of accents: people of many nationalities mingling, making friends, and learning from each other," *Fortune*'s Gurney Breckenfeld has written. "You find English geophysicists working with Indonesians, French, and German scientists cooperating on a research project; a Japanese planner working with his American counterpart." [7] In the course of their business contacts, these employees are bridging cultural barriers and establishing personal relationships. None loses his or her nationality, but all gain from "multinationality." This sense of mutual solidarity doesn't follow the pattern in which one culture or ideology imposes itself on another; fellowship here is commonplace, workaday, and routine. Every country possesses religion, heritage, and culture that stress uniqueness, and to assemble world-car components or punch a terminal keyboard shouldn't threaten anyone's selfhood. It should merely make formerly isolated people recognize the interdependent global community by making them compare their lot with that of others.

It is clear, however, that not even a realistic image of the multinationals and their powerful capacity for economic growth will silence their critics as long as nationalism is increasing, but

[7] *Saturday Review*, January 24, 1976, p. 12.

both science and business are global in outreach. Contacts among scientists and business people are highly evolved and frequent; their travel for meetings and consultations is worldwide, and their example cannot help but sensitize public opinion to global issues. They are more adaptable than government leaders to changing policies and geography. Their impact on the modern mind is great and they may be crucial in solving the negative side of interdependence—the opportunity of being held hostage and the likelihood of sharing bad fortune.

Ideally, commitment and solidarity need to grow both within and among the nations. Private power's foremost virtue is its efficiency, and in grappling with the ramifications of interdependence in a smaller world, governments may learn something from the multinationals about flexibility, resilience, warding off entropy, and even a degree of "disconnectedness." If a subsidiary goes under, corporate strategy is to help save it, not to go down with it.

Those who look forward to a world in which national boundaries lose their importance, those who are impatient with the aching slowness with which humanity seems to converge, those for whom geography still matters but in new ways can only welcome the rise of forms of enterprise whose potential for efficient technology on a global scale already exists. All societies are in a process of transformation, and whether aspirations and dreams of nations and people falter or succeed, networks of banal trade crisscross the globe, and the big companies exert a prosaic, but increasing, influence on the economic and political processes of nation-states.

Technology and its potentials may be growing faster than our emotional or institutional ability to absorb them, but within the advanced nations, technology has already succeeded to an amazing degree in surmounting the cleavage between rich and poor, not by making the rich poorer, but by making the poor richer. The revolution of rising expectations has now embraced the developing world. Our hope must be that our ingenuity stays ahead of it.

Selected Readings

Aron, Raymond. *In Defense of Decadent Europe*. South Bend: Regnery/Gateway, 1979.

Barnet, Richard, and Muller, Ronald. *Global Reach*. New York: Simon & Schuster, 1975.

Cole, H. S. D. et al. *Models of Doom: A Critique of the Limits to Growth*. New York: Universe Books, 1973.

Considine, Bob. *The Remarkable Life of Dr. Armand Hammer*. New York: Harper & Row, 1975.

Coyne, John R. *The Big Breakup: Energy in Crisis*. Kansas City: Sheed Andrews & McNeel, 1977.

de Closets, François. *La France et ses Mensonges*. Paris: Denoel, 1977.

Drucker, Peter. *The Age of Discontinuity*. New York: Harper & Row, 1969.

Edmonds, I. G. *Allah's Oil: Mideast Petroleum*. Nashville: Thomas Nelson, 1977.

Fatemi, Nasrollah; Williams, Gail; and Saint-Phalle, Thibaut. *Multinational Corporations*. New York: A. S. Barnes, 1976.

Friedman, Milton and Rose. *Free to Choose*. New York: Harcourt Brace Jovanovich, 1980.

Galbraith, John Kenneth. *The Age of Uncertainty*. Boston: Houghton Mifflin, 1977.

Galbraith, John Kenneth. *The Nature of Mass Poverty*. Cambridge: Harvard University Press, 1979.

Galbraith, John Kenneth and Salinger, Nicole. *Almost Everyone's Guide to Economics*. Boston: Houghton Mifflin, 1978.

Hayek, Friedrich. *New Studies in Philosophy, Politics, Economics and the History of Ideas*. Chicago: Chicago University Press, 1978.

Kahn, Herman; Brown, William; and Martel, Leon. *The Next 200 Years*. New York: William Morrow, 1976.

Laszlo, Ervin, et al. *Goals for Mankind, A Report to the Club of Rome on the New Horizons of Global Community*. New York: E. P. Dutton, 1977.

Levinson, Charles. *Capital, Inflation and the Multinationals*. New York: Macmillan, 1971.

Levinson, Charles. *Vodka Cola*. London: Gordon & Cremonesi, 1978.

Myrdal, Gunnar. *Asian Drama*. New York: Pantheon, 1968.

Nader, Ralph; Green, Mark; and Sigelman, Joel. *Taming the Giant Corporation*. New York: W. W. Norton, 1976.

Realities, Multinational Enterprises Respond on Basic Issues. Paris: International Chamber of Commerce, 1974.

Sampson, Anthony. *The Seven Sisters*. New York: Viking Press, 1975.

Stocking, George W. and Watkins, Myron. *Cartels in Action*. New York: Twentieth Century Fund, 1946.

Toffler, Alvin. *The Third Wave*. New York: William Morrow, 1980.

Tugendhat, Christopher. *The Multinationals*. New York: Random House, 1972.

Vernon, Raymond. *Storm Over the Multinationals*. Cambridge: Harvard University Press, 1977.

Wright, J. Patrick. *On a Clear Day You Can See General Motors*. Grosse Pointe, Mich.: Wright Enterprises, 1979.

Index